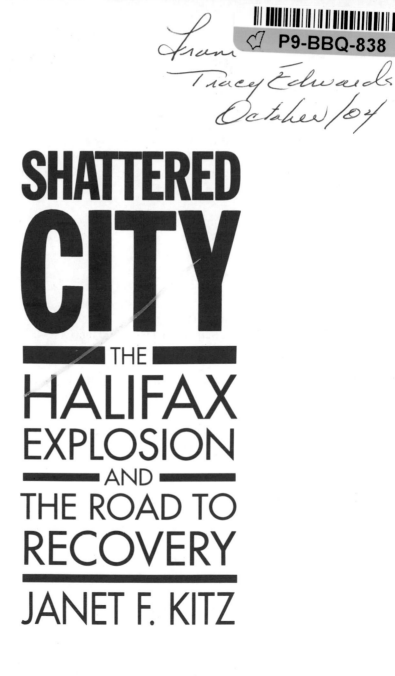

SHATTERED CITY

THE HALIFAX EXPLOSION AND THE ROAD TO RECOVERY

JANET F. KITZ

NIMBUS PUBLISHING LIMITED

Nimbus Publishing Limited
PO Box 9166
Halifax, NS   B3K 5M8
(902) 455-4286

Printed and bound in Canada
Design: Steven Slipp, Semaphor Design, Halifax

National Library of Canada Cataloguing in Publication

Kitz, Janet F., 1930-
Shattered city : the Halifax explosion and the road to recovery / Janet F. Kitz.

Includes index.
ISBN 1-55109-490-8

1. Halifax (N.S.)—History—Explosion, 1917. I. Title.

FC2346.4.K58 2004   971.6'225   C2004-901813-2

Canada

The Canada Council | Le Conseil des Arts
for the Arts | du Canada

We acknowledge the financial support of the Government of Canada through the Book Publishing Industry Development Program (BPIDP) and the Canada Council for our publishing activities.

*To the survivors, to those who suffered loss and deprivation,
and to those who dropped everything to rush to their aid.
To my husband, Leonard, for his understanding.*

CONTENTS

IT MUST HAVE BEEN THE GERMANS

THE RETURN TO NORMAL

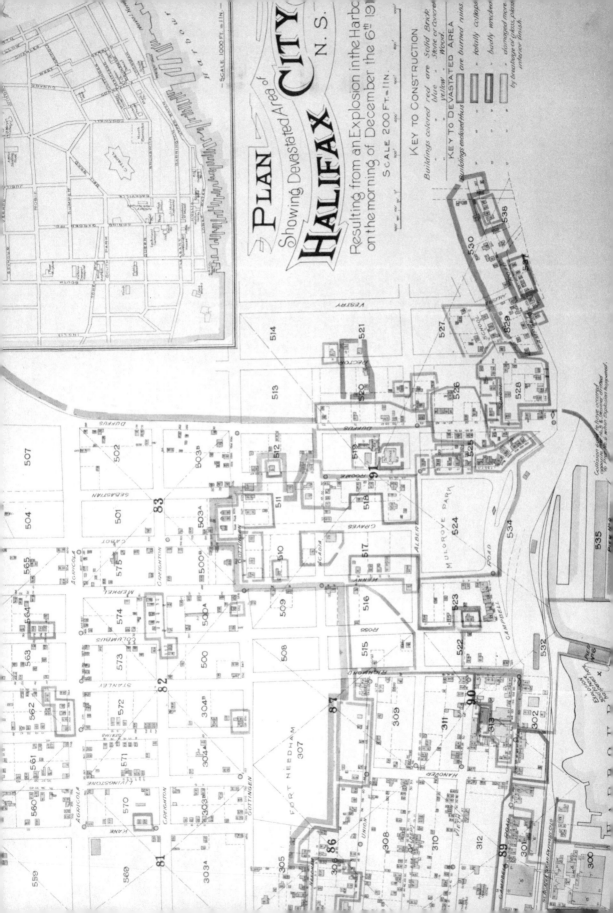

PLAN
Showing Devastated Area of
CITY of
HALIFAX N. S.
Resulting from an Explosion in the Harbor
on the morning of December the 6th 1917

SCALE 200 Ft.=1In.

KEY TO CONSTRUCTION

Buildings colored red are Solid Brick
blue - Stone or Covered
yellow - Wood.

KEY TO DEVASTATED AREA

Buildings colored red are burned ruins.

Buildings endorsed thus - totally collapsed
- badly wrecked
- damaged more
by breakage of glass, Plaster,
interior finish.

- SCALE 1000 Ft.=1In.

PREFACE

MY INTEREST in the Halifax Explosion began in 1980, sparked by research for an anthropology paper at Saint Mary's University. I started interviewing survivors, collecting materials, spending long hours at the Public Archives of Nova Scotia (PANS), and poring over old newspapers. My husband's sister and mother were among the first survivors I spoke with. Their home on Brunswick Street was wrecked during the explosion, and they had to leave the city and live in the country for some time before their house was repaired and fit to live in. Harry Kitz, the father, stayed behind and did emergency relief work for several days. Family friends also told me how the explosion had touched their lives, even though they had not been in the most seriously affected area. David Macnab, for example, might have grown up without a mother. The morning of December 6, 1917, his mother and uncle went to North Street Station to meet his father, due to arrive from Sydney. The train was delayed, so Mrs Macnab and her brother went into the concrete telephone booth to call home to see whether David, an infant, was all right. Then the *Mont Blanc* blew up. The station was badly damaged, and many people were killed. But the thick concrete saved the lives of David's uncle and mother.

On November 27, 1981, Marie Elwood, curator of history at the Nova Scotia Museum, invited me to examine some boxes of cloth bags containing unclaimed effects from the Chebucto Road mortuary. There were three large boxes of jumbled bags and loose objects that had been lying in the basement of Province House since 1918. In minutes we were grimy from sixty-four-year-old soot and dust, but we were convinced that something had to be done with the bags. It had been assumed that these were possessions of unidentified victims of the explosion, but that was not the case. There were names and even some documents. I said I would try to catalogue them. The materials were consigned to the Nova Scotia Museum, and I went home with the boxes, not really knowing what was in store.

The task became completely absorbing. To begin with, I tried to use the museum system of cataloguing, which concentrates on the individual artefact. As I began to make connections between possessions and people, however, I found my interest in the human side increasing. Most bags had labels with numbers and information on them. Some labels were broken or torn, the numbers faded; sometimes the effects were listed. If victims had been positively identified, their name and, in some cases, their address had been written down. I checked the numbers on the labels without names against those on the descriptions of the unidentified dead and found that they and the effects in the bags corresponded. One label, for example, said, "138. Unidentified. Female, about 30." The description on the list read, "Long dark hair. Medium light complexion. Good teeth. Plaid coat. White blouse. Light underwear. Black stockings. On third finger of right hand one 10K gold set ring with sides chased. Six stones of which three are missing, the remaining are red. Pince nez glasses. One patriotic brooch (British and French flags with maple leaf on shield in centre) and seven morning car tickets." The effects in the bag matched the description exactly.

Some of the objects in the bags were of interest for their own sake, but I was beginning to find out more about the people connected with the bags: where they had lived, their appearance, their age, and how many other members of the family were listed among the identified dead. Instead of making a catalogue of the objects and their functions, which I had intended, I ended up making a catalogue of the people who had owned the effects.

The reports, lists, and descriptions of the mortuary committee, part of the relief structure, then occupied my time. The more I learned, the greater my admiration grew for the meticulous work done by this committee under incredibly trying conditions. After going through the bags, I had a list of names with no numbers and one of numbers with no names. With these in front of me, I scanned the manuscripts or microfilm containing mortuary reports at PANS. Other details gradually emerged: the place of work, where the body had been found, who had identified it, and the date of burial. As I recognized a name that was repeated over and over again in different places on the numerical lists, I realized why no one had come forward to claim the effects.

Another problem concerned the addresses. On a label it might state, for example, "Julia Carroll, 192 Campbell Road." The possessions of Julia Carroll, including letters with her name on them, were in the bag of a child whose address was given as "Flynn's Block." The address, 1410 Barrington Street, appeared on a bill with Julia Carroll's name on it. Using the 1917 Halifax City Directory, I discovered that all three addresses referred to the

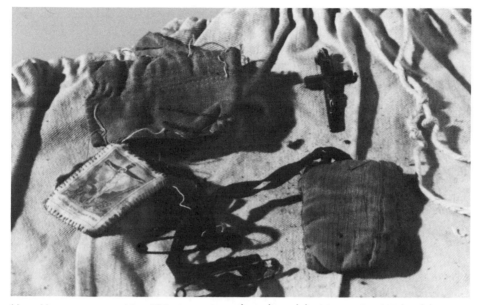

Hans Hermanson was No. 603. A crew member aboard the Norwegian *Hovland,* he wore these scapulars and this crucifix. (MARITIME MUSEUM)

same place. In 1917 Campbell Road had become part of Barrington Street, and the numbering had changed. It takes time to become used to a new system, and most people still used the old name. The directory also told me who had lived at the different numbers. The variously written "Flynn Block" or "Flinn Block" or "Building" became one of my categories. So many of its residents were victims of the explosion, the survivors as well as the dead.

After I had the address puzzle straightened away, I tried to find out what had happened to the various places—the stores, industries, docks, railway yards, ships—where people had worked. One set of effects, scapulars and a crucifix, had belonged to a young Norwegian sailor from the *Hovland,* a ship that had been in dry dock on December 6. I have a photograph of it after the explosion and also know a survivor who was working nearby at the time. Later, while perusing pensions material, I learned more about the young man, as problems had arisen over claims for crews of foreign ships.

The belongings of children led to research on what had happened to schools in the area. There were two notebooks from Richmond School. They were crammed with long-division problems that ten-year-olds are, happily, no longer subjected to. The first spelling list sent shivers through me: *thou, eternity, away, forever.* Fortunately the girl who owned the notebooks did not die for many years. I later learned she had been injured. Probably her books had been scattered and picked up. Perhaps they had been near a dead child and brought to the mortuary with the body.

With information from city directories, Halifax Relief Commission documents, and personal interviews, I gradually found out more. By now the people connected with those bags were no longer statistics. They had acquired identities.

Other effects depicted wartime Halifax. Bills from a well-known grocery store gave an idea of living costs. Insurance books with weekly premiums of ten or twenty-five cents, a soldier's paybook, letters from the front, all testified to a way of life in 1917. Descriptions of clothing, a pipe, cigarettes, keys, jokebooks, bitten pencils and military insignia collected in a little boy's pockets, gave a picture of ordinary people hit by an extraordinary catastrophe.

In all, there were 187 bags, some empty, and more than a thousand objects. Some lay loose, but it was often possible to connect them with a bag, either from the information on the label or from the descriptions of the unidentified. The condition of the effects varied: several were covered in soot and partly burned, sandy, torn, or bent. Ranging in number from 1 to 1878, the bags and their contents are now in the Maritime Museum of the Atlantic, in Halifax. Some are on display in the explosion exhibit *A Moment in Time,* which opened on December 6, 1987, seventy years after the blast.

In the autumn of 1982 a vault in the basement of the former relief commission offices on Young Street was opened. It contained appraisal board records, as well as some objects found by workmen clearing out ruined properties prior to reconstruction. The contents were taken to PANS. By this time I had become a research associate at the Maritime Museum. As archives specialize in documentary material and museums in artefacts, I was asked whether I would catalogue the articles from the vault before they were transferred. Of course I said yes.

Most were metal, naturally, as fire had swept through the houses and little else remained; many had burn marks. Some were in envelopes that also contained details of where they had been found. A few of the envelopes were labelled "Halifax Hotel," headquarters of the reconstruction committee. One envelope bore the name Cavicchi & Pagano, the firm that had had the contract to clear the devastated area. There was also some information that showed how the work had been carried out. Finally there was a letter asking people to come and claim their belongings.

Although there were far fewer objects this time, their cataloguing led to my learning about other aspects of the explosion. Once more I consulted the 1917 city directory to find out who had lived at each address named on the envelopes. Next I tried to trace, through documents at PANS, what had happened to those families. I then understood why they had not retrieved their possessions. These articles are also in the Maritime Museum.

My fascination with the explosion continued. I interviewed more survivors, one of whom was Barbara (Orr) Thompson, and her story moved me deeply. My talks with survivors have coloured the way I now read news of sudden, unexpected disasters. In 1917 the economic situation in Halifax was better than it had been for years, and people were able to afford a higher standard of living, a few luxuries, and many planned a better education for their children. In an instant it all changed. Homes were gone, families fragmented, hopes for the future, even the expectation of a normal life, shattered. Listening to the memories of people who had experienced this, I wanted to find out how they had rebuilt their broken lives and how they had been helped to do so.

In 1983 I became a member of the Halifax Explosion Memorial Bells Committee, established to build a new tower to house the carillon of bells from the United Memorial Church. The church was the result of the union of Kaye Street Methodist and Grove Presbyterian, both levelled in the explosion, and its tower had originally contained a chime of bells donated by Barbara (Orr) Thompson. The spirit of companionship is still prevalent in this church, and members, especially those who have connections with the explosion, travel some distance to attend services there.

Through the bells committee and members of the church's congregation, I gathered more documentation and met more survivors, such as the families of the ministers of Kaye Street Methodist and Grove Presbyterian churches. I received extremely interesting material from both families. I am especially grateful to Jean (Crowdis) Murray for photographs and booklets, including *A Common Sorrow and a Common Concern,* by her father, the Reverend Charles J. Crowdis. Written partly to raise funds for the new church, this work described the destruction of Kaye Street Methodist and Grove Presbyterian and the plight of their congregations. Judge Robert Inglis, a member of both United Memorial and the committee, was another source of information. He had already helped write, along with others, Mr Crowdis in particular, two histories—*Historical Sketch of the United Memorial Church* and *United Memorial Church, 1918–1975*—and I was given copies of these booklets. The minister, the Reverend Lawrence Bone, allowed me to copy church photographs. William Orr, Barbara's cousin, took the chairman of the bells committee, Reg Prest, and me on a flight over all the explosion-related sites in Halifax. The late Charles Vaughan was also a member of the committee. A survivor himself, he had acquired a remarkable collection of explosion photographs, all documented. Copies of these are now in the Maritime Museum, and they make an invaluable record. His personal knowledge was helpful as well.

Second-hand shops were a source of maps, postcards, newspapers, and booklets, many contemporary with the explosion. In one store, for example, I found a 1917 map of Halifax Harbour; in another, the Royal Print & Litho's *40 Views of the Halifax Disaster*. Gradually I managed to accumulate most of the books of photographs that were published after the explosion. All my purchases yielded good first-hand evidence.

Another resource was the work of Archibald MacMechan, a Dalhousie University professor who had opened the Halifax Disaster Record Office on December 17, 1917, in order to prepare an official history of the explosion. His report, which he did not complete, was ably edited by Graham Metson and published in *The Halifax Explosion: December 6, 1917* (McGraw–Hill Ryerson) in 1978. The original work is in the Killam Library at Dalhousie University, and I have gone back to it, particularly for the chronology of events, but have also referred to Metson's book. MacMechan's report and Metson's book both supplied descriptive material on Richmond, as well as information concerning Dr W. B. Moore, the panic at Wellington Barracks, Colonel Ralph B. Simmonds, the railways after the explosion, the messages sent by their employees, and the No. 10 train.

*   *   *   *   *

Without Marie Elwood, who originally showed me the mortuary bags— which opened a Pandora's box, not of troubles, but of the most enthralling and unusual insights into the Halifax Explosion—I would never have been led down the many unexpected avenues of research. I owe thanks to David Flemming, director of the Maritime Museum of the Atlantic, who has taken a great interest in everything connected with the explosion. He and I worked together on the exhibit *A Moment in Time,* and I have been fortunate in having his help in so many aspects of my research. There has been a lot of feedback from the exhibit. Visitors from as far away as Norway and Sweden have left notes, always followed up by David or me. For example, we have heard from the daughter of an *Imo* crew member and from people who knew one of the Norwegian *Hovland*'s crew. Both sent newspaper clippings of interviews with these men. Another note led to a meeting with survivor Jack Tappen.

Other staff members of the museum have been supportive. Ron Merrick, of Education Media Services, took numerous present-day survivor photo-graphs, and many appear in this book. Christine Callaghan, though not with the museum, took many photographs for me as well, mostly of Halifax Harbour and explosion sites.

Members of the staff of PANS were a constant source of assistance, especially Wendy Thorpe, to whom I am particularly grateful. Without her help, I would never have been able to put many pieces together. Allan Dunlop, too, uncovered hard-to-find sources, such as a 1982 paper by University of King's College professor Henry Roper, the only information I have seen on the Halifax Board of Control. Margaret Campbell and Gary Shutlak provided maps and photographs; Brian Cuthbertson, while still at PANS, suggested informative material.

At PANS a wealth of explosion-related documents are catalogued in detail under MG 36 and MG 27 and, to a lesser extent, under MG 20. These contributed greatly to my understanding of the effects of the explosion and the relief work that followed, including the committee activities and the relief commission's undertakings. The commission's minute books from its fifty-eight-year existence, as well as those of the Massachusetts–Halifax relief committee and of the initial meetings to organize relief, are available. Reports from the various committees involved in early relief work are included, and I have used them in appropriate sections of the book, as well as snippets from pamphlets, letters, and booklets.

Reading relief commission documents and corresponding newspaper reports from *The Halifax Herald, The Morning Chronicle, The Evening Mail, The Evening Echo,* and *The Daily Echo,* all on microfilm at PANS, I obtained varying views of explosion-related events. A phrase in a report or an unexplained organization or reference often added hours of research, but most of it was fruitful. I also collected information from newspapers from outside Halifax and Canada, some brought by friends or collected abroad: *The Amherst Daily News* and *The Truro Daily News* (both available at PANS), *The Times, The Scotsman, Die Neue Preussische Zeitung,* and the *Kölnische Zeitung.*

Donald J. Morrison, QC, of Halifax, gave me a book that I have used continuously, as well as some fine photographs. One thousand pages long, the book contains the entire proceedings of the inquiry and the subsequent court case and appeals resulting from the collision of the *Imo* and the *Mont Blanc.* The witnesses' accounts were revealing, and their evidence, though at times contradictory, appears throughout the book, especially in the chapters that discuss the movement of the ships through the harbour and the accounts of the collision. If I had used all the notes I made while reading this tome, I would have produced several more chapters. In fact, that was one of my main problems when I was writing. So many survivors told interesting stories, so much relief commission material unveiled important information, and so many photographs were evocative that another book could hardly do them justice.

Numerous people have taken the trouble to send copies, or even originals, of letters and photographs from 1917 and 1918, and I am very grateful. They include Mildred (Bishop) Moir, for the letters of her aunt Josephine Bishop, the young teacher in Truro; Margaret J. Wournell, of Edmonton, daughter of Bertha (Bond) and Sandy Wournell, who sent me her mother's letters, photographs, and telegram; Thelma (Brannen) Dasburg, daughter of Captain Horatio Brannen, and Gordon Brannen, his grandson, for photographs and material relating to the *Stella Maris*.

I would like to thank Bishop Leonard Hatfield, who sent me a copy of Dr Samuel Prince's paper "The Halifax Explosion, Fourteen Years After" (1931). Dr Prince also wrote a book entitled *Catastrophe and Social Change* (Columbia University, 1921), which provided some useful information for Chapter 6. Another book I found helpful was *Heart Throbs of the Halifax Horror*, by Stanley K. Smith, which offered some insights into temporary housing. Both books were among my finds in second-hand shops.

Lawrence Hines supplied me with 1917 and 1918 Maritime Telegraph and Telephone bulletins that proved valuable when discussing the state of communications systems after the disaster. Marilyn Peers, of the Nova Scotia Children's Aid Society, gave me copies of the letters offering to adopt explosion orphans. These are now in PANS. Helen (Crowdis) Fawcett, Nita Graham, Margaret Grant, Sister Mary Martin, Helen (Upham) Matheson, Anne (Swindells) Ihasz, Doris (Driscoll) Dunsworth, Mary Alma Dillman, Mr and Mrs William Orr, Dr G. Meyerhof, Margaret Martin, Mrs G. Van Beek, Mrs Charles Hubley, Douglas How, Muriel Swetnam, Dagny (Astrom) Nillson, Ports Canada, Greg Mackenzie, Rita Griffin, Alan Ruffman, Francine Gaudet, of the Isaak Walton Killam Hospital, have all added to my knowledge, with a letter, a booklet, a story, a photograph, a newspaper, a piece of information, or an introduction to a survivor, and I thank them all. I wish to express special gratitude to Margaret Fader, who lent me her copy of the 1917 city directory. It has yielded many small but necessary facts: names, jobs, addresses. I have used it so often while checking last-minute details, and it has saved me a great deal of time. Many others not mentioned here have sent material not used in the book, but it has all been valuable. If I have accidentally omitted anyone, I apologize.

Descendants of some of the people who figured in explosion relief work have been helpful. Margaret Millard, of Hunts Point, sent me a box of documents and newspaper cuttings collected by her great aunt Suzanne Haliburton. Later I discovered that Miss Haliburton had been a public health nurse from New York, and at PANS I found correspondence between her and Howard Falk, of the rehabilitation department of the relief commission. He offered her a temporary position as superintendent of medical–social work for four months, and she arrived at the end of March 1918. The information contained in the documents, including general medical and Canadian and American medical–social reports, added enormously to my understanding of the medical–social service. These papers also covered the Massachusetts relief expedition.

Nellie Adams lent me an interesting collection of photographs. Her father was a professional photographer, best known for his school groups and individual portraits. The explosion shots were not taken by him, but he did the processing.

I am grateful to my editor, Nancy Robb; Dorothy Blythe, also of Nimbus, encouraged me to write the book and suggested the title.

Most of all I am indebted to the numerous survivors who granted interviews. Some searched their attics and basements, their old photograph albums, and found treasures to lend or give me. One particularly rewarding and moving experience was meeting some forty people who had gone to Richmond School in 1917. They formed a special group at the Richmond School Reunion in 1984. Jean Hunter and Merita Dobson showed me class photographs and told me the names of most of the children. I also met James Pattison for the first time and saw his explosion mementos. (Survivors often have one or two precious keepsakes.)

I am frequently asked how many people died in the explosion, but I am reluctant to give a definite answer. I have come across so many different figures; for example, 1,635 or 1,963. The names and addresses on most of the labels in the mortuary bags did appear in the list of the dead in the 1918 city directory, the most comprehensive list I have found. It is not, however, complete. It was stated that a full list would be printed in the 1919 directory, but it did not materialize. No list I have seen has included all the people I know to have died. I believe the figure was higher than 2,000. The death rate over the following years, even during 1918, from explosion-related illnesses and injuries, for instance, was never taken into account.

I have been truly inspired by the survivors who surmounted the terrible tragedies of their youth. Many seem to have become much more appreciative of life and to have achieved a wide degree of tolerance—perhaps because of the bizarre segment of history they accidentally experienced.

Edith Hartnett used to help care for her aunt Rita, blinded in the explosion.
(RON E. MERRICK)

They, along with others who suffered from the blast, are the kind of ordinary people always affected by history but so rarely depicted as part of it. Too often we know of historical events only as they happened to kings and queens, political leaders, generals and revolutionaries.

Consider the Hinch family, which lost more than forty close relatives. Arthur, born after the explosion, grew up in an unusual household. His older brother had been killed, and after his mother died in 1926, he and his father moved in with an uncle and aunt, where the remnants of four families lived together. Arthur's grandmother, Margaret Stokes, widowed by the explosion, was blinded and badly scarred. His uncle, eight years old at the time, was also blinded. So was his cousin Tommy, at the age of six. His aunt Agnes, age twenty-two, lost an eye, and her sister Kathleen, five years younger, had a leg amputated. All carried marks and scars, physical and emotional. Visitors to the house were rare and had to be especially understanding. When he first met his future wife, Arthur prepared her carefully before taking her home.

The achievements of this family are a tribute to their determination. Both blind boys earned university degrees, Kathleen went on to get a doctorate, and Arthur became a dentist.

The Griswolds also suffered greatly. Alfred and Frederick were both killed at Hillis & Sons Foundry. Alfred's wife and five-year-old son were killed at home, and their six-year-old daughter, at St Joseph's School. The only survivor of that family was Mary, age eight. Frederick left a wife and four children, ranging in age from seven months to eleven years.

Amelia Mary Griswold, mother of the two men, owned two houses on Needham Street. Her three daughters, one with two children, lived with her. Mrs Griswold received a bad facial injury when her home collapsed and caught fire. She managed to pull her daughter Edna out of the house and lay her on the ground but could not find her two-year-old granddaughter,

Sadie. Vera, Edna's other child, was saved, but for a long time did not have the power of speech and was extremely nervous. Edna's body disappeared, and no trace of it was ever found. Mrs Griswold's oldest daughter, at school, was unhurt, but her youngest child, Rita, age fifteen, was blinded and burned.

Mrs Griswold brought up Mary (Alfred's daughter), Vera (Edna's child), and Rita and, despite the terrible losses, tried to make sure it was not a gloomy household. All three girls settled in the United States. Edith Hartnett used to stay with her aunt Rita, who married the son of an explosion widow, to help her, but she adapted very well to her sightless condition.

Survivors or their descendants who helped me greatly do not necessarily figure later in this book. Edith Hartnett went out of her way to seek out information for me. Walter Murphy took me for a walk all around the area that had been Richmond, describing it as it had been in 1917 and pointing out post-explosion rebuilding.

Although I have read many survivors' accounts, I have used almost entirely those of which I have personal knowledge. (There is one informant I have not met, Ruth Poole Poirier, interviewed by Greg Mackenzie as part of a summer works program I organized.) It was difficult for me to make a selection from all the interesting experiences I have heard, and unfortunately it was not possible to include every one. The following are the survivors and relief workers whose stories I have used in whole or in part. I extend my utmost admiration and gratitude to them all: Max Barnes, Frank Burford, Leo Campbell, Dorothy Chisholm, Pearl (Moore) Clattenburg, Linda and Garnet Colwell, Don Crowdis, Eric Davidson, Leighton Dillman, Al, Cliff, and Noble Driscoll, Joe Glube, Jim Gowen, Dorothy (Swetnam) Hare, Edith Hartnett, Dr Arthur Hinch, Jean Hunter, Margaret (Wallace) Jarvis, Yetta Kitz, Evelyn (Johnson) Lawrence, Dr Percy McGrath, Frances MacLennan, George Mitchell, Ethel (Mitchell) Morash, Jean (Crowdis) Murray, James Pattison, Ruth (Poole) Poirier, Marjorie (Drysdale) Quinn, Reg Rasley, Sister Eileen Ryan, Hildred (Kitz) Silver, Millicent (Upham) and Wilbert Swindells, Jack Tappen, Barbara (Orr) Thompson, Archie Upham, Annie (Liggins) Welsh, Helena (Duggan) Wheeler.

Janet Kitz
Halifax, N.S.

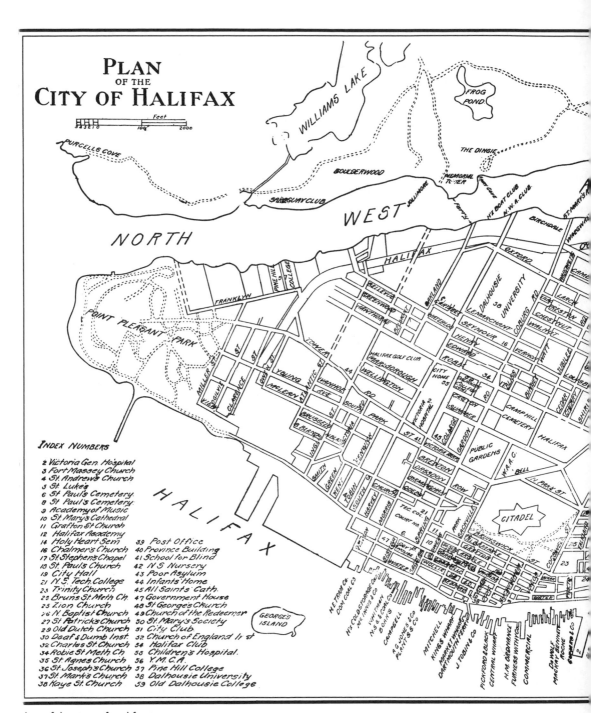

PLAN
OF THE
CITY OF HALIFAX

Feet

INDEX NUMBERS

2 Victoria Gen. Hospital
3 Fort Massey Church
4 St. Andrews Church
5 St. Luke's
6 St. Paul's Cemetery
8 St. Paul's Cemetery
9 Academy of Music
10 St. Mary's Cathedral
11 Grafton St. Church
12 Halifax Academy
14 Holy Heart Sem.
16 Chalmer's Church
17 St. Stephen's Chapel
18 St. Pauls Church
19 City Hall
21 N.S. Tech. College
23 Trinity Church
22 Bruns St. Meth Ch.
23 Zion Church
26 N. Baptist Church
27 St. Patricks Church
29 Old Dutch Church
30 Deaf & Dumb Inst.
32 Charles St. Church
34 Robie St. Meth Ch.
35 St. Agnes Church
36 St. Joseph's Church
37 St. Mark's Church
38 Kaye St. Church

39 Post Office
40 Province Building
41 School for Blind
42 N.S. Nursery
43 Poor Asylum
44 Infants Home
45 All Saints Cath.
47 Government House
48 St. George's Church
49 Church of the Redeemer
50 St. Mary's Society
51 City Club
52 Church of England Inst
54 Halifax Club
55 Children's Hospital.
56 Y.M.C.A.
57 Pine Hill College
58 Dalhousie University
59 Old Dalhousie College

Plan of the City of Halifax" (PANS, V6/240 c.[1910])

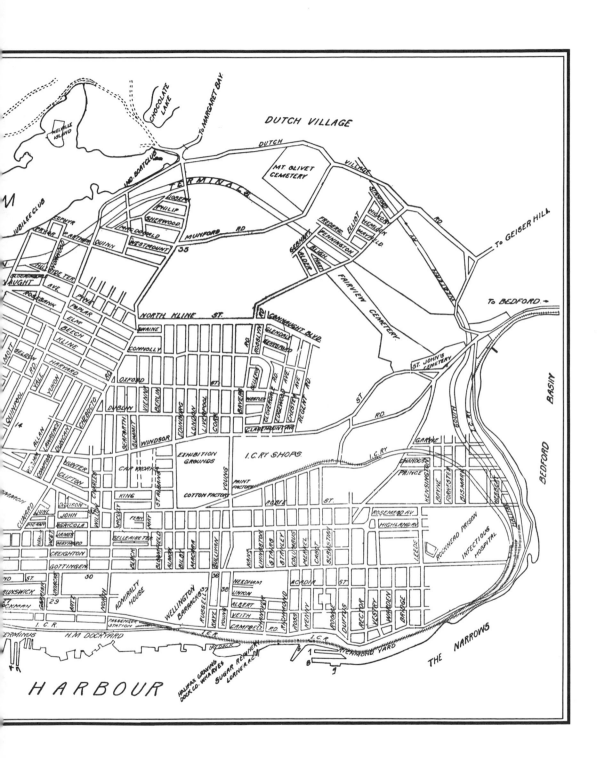

SHATTERED CITY
SHATTERED LIVES

PRELUDE

ON SATURDAY, DECEMBER 1, 1917, at 11:00 p.m., the *Mont Blanc*, under cover of darkness, slipped out of Gravesend Bay in New York Harbour. Owned by the Compagnie Générale Transatlantique, commonly known as the French Line, the steamer was 330 feet long and 40 feet wide. She carried a dangerous cargo of volatile explosives for the French government: 2,300 tons of wet and dry picric acid, 200 tons of TNT, 10 tons of gun cotton, and 35 tons of benzol. For her defence, there was a 90-millimetre gun forward and a 95-millimetre one astern; some practice shells had been fired, but more than 300 live rounds still remained on board, some on deck and some in the lower compartments. Considering the cargo, the forty-one-man crew must have uttered a prayer for calm seas, undisturbed by patrolling German U-boats. The men had expected to be in a convoy with the comforting presence of heavily armed destroyers, but British naval authorities in New York, the organizers of Atlantic convoys, had rejected the *Mont Blanc* because she was too slow.

World War I had lasted more than three years by this time, three years of bitter fighting and heavy losses. France had been invaded in 1914, and since then warfare on French soil had been a series of advances and retreats, costly to both sides in men and materials. The French government's agent in New York bought munitions in quantities that required the use of forty to fifty ships every two weeks. Only under such desperate circumstances could French authorities have even considered using the *Mont Blanc* for munitions or allowed such a mixture to be carried on one ship.

British losses during the war had been heavy, too. In 1917, for example, 1,134 British ships had been sunk, mostly by enemy submarine action. The widely read Nova Scotia newspaper *The Halifax Herald* reported that in the last week of November alone, 16 British merchantmen of more than 1,600 tons each, 1 smaller ship, and 4 fishing boats had been lost. Every Allied vessel was vital to the war effort, but no place could be made in a convoy for a member that might endanger the others.

The captain of the *Mont Blanc* had received orders to proceed north to Halifax, where another convoy was gathering for an Atlantic crossing. He had been told, however, that it was unlikely that the steamer would be accepted there, either. Convoys from Halifax generally tried to maintain a speed of eight and a half knots, travelling two hundred miles a day. The *Mont Blanc* could attain that speed in fine weather, unusual in the stormy North Atlantic in winter. In Halifax, if the ship did leave with the convoy, the captain would be given special sealed instructions before sailing, not to be opened unless the *Mont Blanc* dropped behind. The instructions would show how to get to Bordeaux, France, the final destination, alone.

At age thirty-nine, Aimé Le Medec, master of the *Mont Blanc,* had been a captain for two years. This was his first voyage on the *Mont Blanc*—he was not even completely familiar with her workings—and his first experience with munitions. He had previously commanded two other vessels, but both had been a different tonnage and had been used for more conventional commercial shipping. French merchant marine captains had been mobilized for the war effort and had been given special certificates as lieutenants of the naval reserve.

The rest of the crew belonged to the merchant navy. The men spoke little English, but they did not need to know much to understand the devastating potential of the *Mont Blanc*'s cargo. Precautions had been taken in New York. The TNT, picric acid, and gun cotton had been stored in the holds, in specially constructed wooden magazines that had no iron features— copper nails had been used to prevent sparks when hammering—and each type of explosive was separated by wooden partitions. As a further safeguard, the stevedores who had stocked the holds and the magazines had worn linen cloths over their boots to avoid sparks when they walked on the metal decks. Even the bars closing the holds had been covered with tarred cloth, and the holds then hermetically sealed to close off access altogether. The benzol, a high-octane gasoline, had been stored in iron drums and placed on the open deck. As a result, smoking was prohibited in nearly all areas of the ship, and vivid posters proclaimed that matches, even hidden in a pocket, were banned on deck; as an alternative, the crew chewed tobacco. No safeguard, it seemed to the men, had been overlooked.

Luckily the voyage to Halifax was uneventful, with no sightings of German U-boats. A northwest gale blew for two days, however, and delayed the *Mont Blanc*'s arrival. On December 4 a crew member finally spotted the coast of Nova Scotia and spread the welcome news throughout the ship.

In December 1917 the *Mont Blanc,* a dangerous cargo of explosives on board, steamed north to Halifax to join a convoy in Bedford Basin. (MARITIME MUSEUM)

On Wednesday, December 5, at 4:00 p.m., at the mouth of Halifax Harbour, Pilot Francis Mackey boarded the *Mont Blanc* directly from a departing ship. Halifax was a compulsory port, meaning that ocean-going ships had to use the services of a pilot. Mackey, with twenty-four years' experience in the Port of Halifax, had never been at fault in a shipping accident. He directed the *Mont Blanc* to the examination boat nearby, as every ship entering the harbour was, since the outbreak of war, required to report for inspection. The examining officer, Terence Freeman, a mate in the Royal Canadian Navy, boarded to interview Le Medec and to inspect the manifest before allowing the *Mont Blanc* to proceed through the harbour, to Bedford Basin. The manifest listed the explosives carried, and Mackey learned the nature of the cargo.

Four years earlier the *Mont Blanc* would not have been permitted to go into the inner harbour. The harbour master, Captain Francis Rudolf, having read a pamphlet on the dangers of explosives, had ordered that all ships carrying such cargo had to anchor at Georges Island. The cargo was then unloaded onto lighters, and all work was carried out in daytime only. Both ship and lighter had to fly red flags to warn that explosives were being handled on board. Only under adverse weather conditions could a munitions vessel proceed as far as the basin. After World War I broke out, control of Halifax Harbour was transferred to the British admiralty, with Rudolf overseeing only local craft, and munitions ships regularly joined convoys in the basin.

The *Mont Blanc* passed Freeman's inspection. At last, with this part of the voyage over, the ship's crew could prepare to relax. But the men received disappointing news. The *Mont Blanc* was not permitted to enter the harbour, not because she carried dangerous cargo, but because the submarine nets were closed for the night. Booms held up by steel buoys blocked the entrance to prevent enemy submarines from getting within torpedo range of valuable shipping. A gate wide enough for a large ship to pass through was opened or closed at different times, which frequently varied in case of watching spies. This gate was opened only during the day, never after dark.

At 4:30 p.m., just off the lighthouse on McNabs Island, Pilot Mackey remaining on board, the *Mont Blanc* anchored to await morning.

*   *   *   *   *

On Monday, December 3, 1917, the *Imo,* en route from Rotterdam, Holland, to New York to pick up relief supplies, dropped anchor by the western shore of Bedford Basin. Owned by the Norwegian Southern Pacific Whaling Company, she was under charter to the Belgian Relief Commission. Of single screw, 5,041 tons gross register, she measured 430 feet by 44 feet. As a neutral vessel handling no war materials and with the words BELGIAN RELIEF painted in huge letters on her sides, she sailed unescorted at her normal speed of eleven to twelve knots. She carried a crew of thirty-nine, including Norwegians, Swedes, Danes, a Dutchman, and a French Canadian. The captain, Haakon From, was Norwegian but spoke fluent English. He had been in and out of Halifax twice the previous summer.

Neutral ships had to be examined by naval and customs authorities in Halifax after crossing the Atlantic; before 1916 they had been checked at a British port prior to sailing, forcing many to travel the mine-infested North Sea. In Halifax no communication was allowed between the crews of neutral ships and the shore, and every precaution was taken to prevent contraband or subversive papers from landing. Before leaving port, captains had to obtain both naval and customs clearance. Although local agents for shipping companies made arrangements, ships could sometimes be detained for weeks, causing considerable frustration among confined sailors.

On the afternoon of December 5 the *Imo* speedily received clearance. Arthur Lovett, customs officer, arrived at 2:30 with the necessary papers.

On the way, he had reported to the guard ship, in the basin, that the *Imo* had permission to leave. William Hayes, another of Halifax Harbour's most experienced pilots, was already on board.

But all was not well. The coal tender ordered by Pickford & Black, the agent for the owners of the *Imo,* pulled alongside later than expected, at the same time as Lovett, and needed a further two or three hours to fill the ship's bunkers. The submarine nets would then be closed.

Lovett returned to shore without informing the guard ship that the *Imo* had been delayed. His only responsibility, as he saw it, was to relay information that the ship had been cleared.

Hayes, with too little time off duty since the war began, went home for the night. On the way, he stopped at the pilotage office and reported that the *Imo* was still at anchor in the basin.

* * * * *

On either side of the harbour lay the cities of Dartmouth and Halifax. Dartmouth, on the eastern side, was the smaller settlement, less than one-tenth the size of Halifax, with its fifty thousand people. Chosen by the British government to offset the French stronghold at Louisbourg, Nova Scotia, Halifax was first settled in 1749 and planned as an instant fortress. It was an obvious choice, offering one of the finest natural harbours in the world, sheltered and ice free, with a clear deep passage to an inner harbour where a whole naval fleet could lie in safety. The harbour stretched eighteen miles, from Chebucto Head, at its southern entrance, to the far end of Bedford Basin. Ten miles farther the inner harbour began, at Georges Island. Ships steamed past the island, then by the city centre, on past the northern industrialized part of the city, through the Narrows (today spanned by the A. Murray MacKay Bridge), and into the basin. Over the centuries defences were built to guard the harbour and the city: York Redoubt and Chebucto Head, at the entrance, four forts on McNabs Island, Fort Ogilvie and other defences in Point Pleasant Park, Fort Charlotte on Georges Island, Citadel Hill, and Fort Needham, above the Narrows. From the time of its founding, the city's fortunes surged like the Fundy tides, rising during wartime and falling with the advent of peace.

During World War I, Halifax was the war base of the Dominion of Canada, becoming one of the busiest ports in the British Empire. It was the embarkation point for Canadian, West Indian, and most American troops headed for Europe. Enormous quantities of supplies and munitions passed through its harbour: trainloads of grain arrived from the Prairies; lumber from the West filled waiting ships. The dry dock was in constant use, the piers always busy. So were the barges and the freighters. Much of the activity could be watched from Fort Needham and Citadel Hill, above the clusters of piers, the dry dock, and the dockyard.

The evening of December 5 was typical. Among the many ships in the harbour were the British *Calonne,* at Pier 9, and the American *Curaca,* at Pier 8, both loading horses for Europe; tons of valuable wheat were already in their holds. The *Olympic,* in the basin, had on board five thousand Chinese labourers bound for France. The hospital ship the USS *Old Colony* was in port. The Norwegian *Hovland,* suffering some minor damage, lay in dry dock. Also in for repair was the British *Picton,* which carried a load of ammunition beneath her cargo of foodstuffs. British ships usually transported mixed loads of this kind, rather than a full cargo of explosives like the *Mont Blanc*'s.

The HMCS *Niobe,* a Canadian cruiser purchased from Britain, now lay permanently moored at the dockyard for use as a training and depot ship. She no longer looked like a trim fighting craft, as oddly shaped wooden structures had been added to her decks to provide extra accommodation. The offices of the chief commanding officer (CXO), naval control, and naval intelligence were on the *Niobe.*

Commander Frederick Wyatt, of the British Royal Navy, CXO since September 1915, was notified of the comings and goings of ships. The afternoon of December 5, for example, the examining officer informed him by telephone of the arrival of the *Mont Blanc*—earlier he had received news of her cargo, in a telegram from New York—and he was told that the *Imo* was ready to leave. (Telephonic communication among the various ships and offices had not increased along with the volume of shipping during the war. Wyatt had a public telephone outside his office, and the lines to the guard and examination ships were in the nearby naval control office. The headquarters of the Halifax Pilotage Commission, responsible for hiring and scheduling pilots, was located on Bedford Row, near the city centre.)

Blackout regulations prevailed during the war. At night streetlights were darkened, and curtains or blinds were drawn to cover all lighted windows. A German naval bombardment, it was believed, was always a possibility. In addition, York Redoubt and Chebucto Head, the forts on McNabs Island and on Georges Island, the batteries in Point Pleasant, and the Citadel all had full complements of soldiers. Throngs of troops filled the barracks— troops stationed permanently in Halifax, troops in training, or troops waiting to leave for Europe to replenish depleted forces.

Casualties had been heavy. On December 4 newspapers praised the bravery the Nova Scotia Highland Regiment had shown at Passchendaele,

Halifax offered one of the finest natural harbours in the world. A channel called the Narrows led into Bedford Basin, where whole fleets could lie in safety. (PANS/NOTMAN)

The docks were always busy, and factories such as the Acadia Sugar Refinery (in the background) dominated the seascape. (PANS/NOTMAN)

Belgium. Several hundred men, however, had been killed or wounded. Each day brought newspaper lists headed "KILLED IN ACTION," and hospital ships carrying wounded men arrived regularly. Their solemn reception was a far cry from the bands and the cheering crowds that had seen them off to the war. Black armbands and black patches were visible reminders of the losses suffered by families. Black-edged writing paper, black-bordered handkerchiefs, and black clothing sold well. Military-hospital beds contained numbers of returned veterans, and rehabilitation programs had been established for those who had been blinded or who had suffered other permanent disabilities. Damaged ships seeking shelter and repair also disgorged their wounded.

The night before the explosion Ethel Mitchell attended an impromptu party aboard the HMS *Highflyer*. When she arrived home, she dropped into bed, her cat, Buttons, nestled at her feet.
(COURTESY ETHEL MITCHELL MORASH)

Nonetheless, Halifax was alive with excitement. The city was crowded with civilians from other parts of Canada and from Allied countries who were attracted by the plentiful employment and with soldiers and sailors who were eager to spend their pay. Places of entertainment prospered, and stores thrived, as more liberal wages than had been seen during the lean prewar years encouraged freer spending. Along with the influx of transients, however, came an increase in social ills. The sale of alcohol, though prohibited in 1916, continued with illicit drinking in "blind tigers" and "blind pigs," or speakeasies, and with supplies from bootleggers. The number of illegitimate births had increased, and prostitution and venereal disease were on the rise.

Activities connected with the war were not limited to those directly concerned with profiting from it. In schools girls knitted socks and Balaclava helmets, comforts for the troops, and many an encouraging note was sent with the parcels. They learned first aid, became junior Red Cross members, and rolled bandages. It was useful work, and it kept up morale. Many women who had never done their own housework did not object to carrying out menial tasks such as serving tea or even cooking in voluntary canteens so long as their efforts were enhancing the well being of the servicemen far from home. Organizations such as the Red Cross or the Imperial Order Daughters of the Empire (IODE), founded in 1900, had no lack of volunteers.

Servicemen were often invited to local homes, and sometimes the hostess was kind enough to provide young company for them. One such party took place on the evening of December 5. Nineteen-year-old Ethel Mitchell was among five young ladies invited to a dinner party to meet five officers from the British cruiser the HMS *Highflyer,* which had arrived in port on December 1, ready to escort the next convoy leaving the basin. The *Highflyer's* sinking of a large German cruiser had been well reported in the press, and her sailors were welcome everywhere in the city. The evening was a great success, and the girls, to their great joy, were invited on board the ship, where an impromptu dance took place in the captain's quarters. They even had cookies and wine. But this had to be kept a deep secret, as civilians were forbidden on battleships during wartime. Ethel had a wonderful time. It was after midnight when the *Highflyer's* launch took her to the north ferry terminal in Dartmouth and Lieutenant Commander Percy Ingram escorted her home to Hester Street. She was so tired that she did not, as she had been taught, put away her clothes, a rose-pink evening dress and matching satin slippers. She dropped into bed, and her fluffy white cat, Buttons, settled, as usual, at her feet.

* * * * *

Many soldiers and their families who came to Halifax chose to live in Richmond, a settlement in the North End. On the slopes of Fort Needham and along the shoreline, it had developed after the railway had been completed in 1858. So called for the wharves where flour had been unloaded from Richmond, Virginia, the community, with its proximity to the railway, had become the industrial section of the city.

Almost all the homes in Richmond were wooden, and many were privately owned single-family dwellings. Often, though, houses contained three or four apartments. Some were occupied by relatives, but many were occupied by soldiers or by workers drawn to Richmond industries. Renting flats and rooms and running boarding houses were good sources of extra income.

Kaye Street Methodist Church was situated on the southern slope of Fort Needham, in Richmond. (COURTESY MARGARET WOURNELL)

House lots were fairly large, so it was not unusual for residents to keep a cow, a hen, or even a pig; farms and market gardens on the outskirts of the community supplied produce. In 1917 a fair amount of the land in Richmond was still undeveloped, and most of the streets remained unpaved; some, sloping upwards from the harbour, were very steep. Automobiles were on the increase, but the hills were hard on clutches and were impassable in icy or snowy conditions. Horses and wagons, or sleighs during winter, were much more common.

As in the rest of Halifax, jobs were easy to come by, though only a small minority of residents, mostly owners of local businesses, were actually well to do. Few were really poor, largely those who suffered ill health and were unable to work. This was just as well, because social services were scarce. Generally, churches or charitable societies provided the greatest assistance.

Railways and dockyards employed the most people, in shifts night and day, with sons often following in their father's footsteps. The Acadia Sugar Refinery, Hillis & Sons Foundry, the Richmond Printing Company, and other manufacturers, mills, and stores added to Richmond's vitality and prosperity.

Richmond was also a close-knit community, with its churches and schools acting as centres of social life. There were three schools. Roman Catholic girls attended St Joseph's, on Gottingen Street. In December 1917 boys were also going to St Joseph's because their school on Young Street had burned down the previous year. They were waiting for the completion of a new one, the Alexander McKay, on Russell Street, early in the New Year. In the meantime girls had classes in the morning; boys, in the afternoon. Protestant children and the few of other faiths attended Richmond School, on Roome Street, and Bloomfield, on Agricola. Richmond School had inaugurated its winter timetable only a few days earlier, so classes began half an hour later, at 9:30.

There were four churches: St Joseph's Roman Catholic, St Mark's

Anglican, Kaye Street Methodist, and Grove Presbyterian. St Joseph's, with Father Charles E. McManus as priest, included two other buildings, the school and a convent. St Mark's, on Russell Street, its clergyman the Reverend N. Lemoine, had been consecrated in 1866 but had been enlarged twice to provide seating for the naval and the military personnel who had attended service there. St Mark's had a military history. Fine parades of earlier soldiers in their red coats, led by smartly uniformed bands, had marched to St Mark's over the years. At one time a regimental mascot, a goat, stayed in the Sunday-school room during service. Kaye Street Methodist, completed in 1869, occupied a prominent site on the southerly slope of Fort Needham, its parsonage across the road on Young Street; the Reverend William J. W. Swetnam was minister. Grove Presbyterian, built in 1872, stood on the northerly slope of Fort Needham, on Duffus Street, the manse a short distance away, on Gottingen; its minister was the Reverend Charles J. Crowdis. Since 1915 both churches had undergone extensive renovations, a sign of their flourishing congregations.

Samuel Orr, Jr, his wife, Annie, and their six children—Barbara, Ian, Isabel, Mary, Archie, and James—attended Grove Presbyterian. Samuel was part owner of the Richmond Printing Company, on northern Barrington Street, along with his two brothers, William and David, and his father, Samuel Orr, Sr. In December 1917 he, his family, and his father had recently moved into a newly built house at the corner of Kenny and Albert streets, in the heart of Richmond and within easy walking distance of the printing company.

The family was delighted with the spacious modern house. It offered a panoramic view of the harbour, and it seemed to the children that all the world's ships passed right by their dining-room window. Watching ships was a favourite pastime of Richmond children, and many boys had become experts, able to identify a vessel with the ease of connoisseurs. On December 5 the Orr children were home from school, quarantined because one of them had measles. No matter, they spent much of their time gazing out of the window, looking at the boats in the harbour. For them, in the comfort and warmth of their brand-new home, the future promised well.

A NEW DAY

DECEMBER 6 DAWNED, the kind of bright, clear, windless day common in Halifax in early winter. The air was crisp and cold, and the ground was clear of snow. A light haze hung here and there over the harbour, but visibility was generally good.

At 7:30 the ships at the mouth of the harbour prepared to proceed to Bedford Basin. The first ship through the gate in the submarine net was a newly arrived American freighter piloted by Edward Renner, who had seen the *Mont Blanc* ready to follow. Renner was making for an anchorage near the western shore of the basin. After rounding Pier 9 and while proceeding through the Narrows, he sighted the *Imo* heading towards him, on her way from the guard ship, where signal flags had been hoisted, giving the vessel permission to depart. On the guard ship nothing was known of incoming traffic, and there had been no communication with Commander Frederick Wyatt, on the HMCS *Niobe*.

Normal practice held that ships pass port side to port side. The *Imo* gave one whistle blast, signalling her intention to veer to the right, to her correct channel, nearer the Halifax shore. Renner decided that, though not strictly proper, it would be simpler and quicker for his vessel not to change course but to pass starboard to starboard. He gave two blasts, indicating he proposed to keep to the left, the Halifax side. The *Imo* replied with two blasts, signifying her agreement, and maintained a course to her port side. So they passed each other, the *Imo* continuing down the wrong channel, farther from the Halifax shore than she should have been. Through a megaphone, Renner hailed Pilot William Hayes, who had returned to the *Imo* early that morning, telling him that another ship was close behind. Hayes acknowledged the information: Renner recognized his voice.

At 8:15 the tug *Stella Maris,* a former British gunboat in the China Sea now under the command of Captain Horatio Brannen, steamed out from

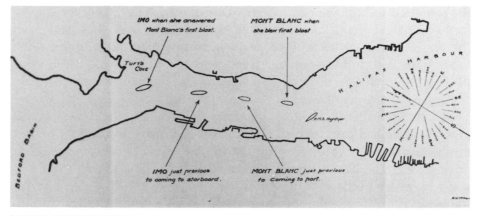

(RECORD OF PROCEEDINGS)

the dry dock. Bound for the basin, it was towing two scows loaded with ashes from the dockyard. The tug, scows, and tow ropes stretched about 320 feet. When Brannen sighted the *Imo*, which he thought was going pretty fast, he hauled the *Stella Maris* around closer to the Halifax shore to get out of the way. To avert a collision, the *Imo* was forced to stay on the Dartmouth side of the channel, still off her correct course.

The *Mont Blanc* had also left her anchorage at 7:30. Pilot Francis Mackey stood on the bridge, Captain Aimé Le Medec beside him, ready to relay directions. The ship steamed past Georges Island, following the Dartmouth shore, on the eastern side of the harbour, its proper route. The *Mont Blanc* exchanged flag salutes with the HMS *Highflyer*, anchored in the upper harbour. Suddenly Mackey spotted masts above the land ahead. Immediately the *Imo* appeared, emerging from the Narrows, about three quarters of a mile away, approaching at what Mackey considered an unreasonable speed and heading southeast, directly cutting across the *Mont Blanc*'s course.

On the bridge of the *Imo* Captain Haakon From and Pilot Hayes, having just avoided the *Stella Maris* and her scows, now sighted the *Mont Blanc* bearing down on them. The *Imo* was a big ship and needed room to manoeuvre.

On the *Mont Blanc* Mackey was astonished to see the *Imo* advancing quickly and in his ship's waters. He tugged at the cord of the signal whistle and gave one short, sharp blast to establish that the *Mont Blanc* was in her proper channel and that she had the right to be there. (Normally the ship giving the first signal is considered to be in command of the operation.) To his amazement two short, sharp blasts were issued from the *Imo*, meaning she intended to bear to port, towards Dartmouth. This brought her even farther into the *Mont Blanc*'s channel. (It also took her farther away from the *Stella Maris* and her tow.) Mackey blew one blast again, signifying a move starboard, and brought the ship as close to the Dartmouth shore as he dared; she was now at "dead slow." But two short blasts came again from the *Imo*, and she maintained her course.

Mackey could hardly believe it. Had the *Imo* swung to the right, towards Halifax, as he had expected, all would have been well. He and Le Medec now shouted orders almost in unison. Both saw only one solution as the *Imo* drew closer. Simultaneously they grabbed the whistle cord, sent out two short blasts, and yelled for the *Mont Blanc* to be swung to the left, across the bow of the *Imo*—now between the *Mont Blanc* and the Dartmouth shore—to bring the two ships parallel. This gave them plenty of room to pass on the opposite side, starboard to starboard.

"The Frenchman has blown a cross signal. A collision cannot be averted," remarked Captain Daniel Maclaine of the *Douglas H. Thomas,* a tug moored outside the dry dock, as he stood watching the two ships. Before the *Mont Blanc*'s last change of course he had not thought that there was any real danger.

For the brief time the two ships were parallel, Mackey thought the same thing. The *Mont Blanc*'s engines were now stopped, but the *Imo* issued three blasts, meaning "full speed astern!" Le Medec bellowed to the crew to put the *Mont Blanc*'s engines at full speed astern as well. A collision was now certain, and Le Medec's first thought was to prevent the impact from taking place at Hold 2, where the TNT was stored. But the engineer had no time to carry out the order. As the *Imo*'s crew reversed the ship's engines, her bow swung to the right, and her stem struck the starboard bow of the *Mont Blanc*, missing the TNT but striking Hold 1, where barrels of picric acid were stowed directly under the deck and its drums of benzol. The ships were now in mid-stream, right opposite the busiest wharves in the North End.

The Imo had turned slowly, and the *Mont Blanc* was practically at a standstill, but the impact was enough to cut a wedge in the forehold of the munitions ship and to create sparks. The two ships met briefly and parted. The bow of the *Mont Blanc* slewed around and headed towards Pier 6, on the Halifax side, just off the community of Richmond.

* * * * *

Soon after eight o'clock, at her home in Dartmouth, Ethel Mitchell got up to have her usual hour's piano practice before breakfast. She was studying for examinations at the Halifax Conservatory of Music. Her mother came into her room and said that as she had been out so late the night before, it might be better to stay in bed a bit longer and miss her practice that morning. Happy with the idea and not quite awake, anyway, Ethel snuggled back under the blankets. Her mother sat down, and Ethel told her all about her exciting experiences of the night before. "Now I shall leave you to have a rest," Mrs Mitchell said and went out, closing the door behind her. Buttons and Ethel settled down again.

About half past eight that morning Barbara Orr stood in the dining room of her parents' new home, looking out of the large bay window. She was not going to school because her brother Archie was not completely over the measles. Her father, Samuel, delayed for some reason, had just left for the printing com-

Barbara Orr, a schoolgirl in 1917, watched the strange behaviour of two ships in the harbour.

(COURTESY T. W. THOMPSON)

pany, near the dry dock. The fairly new two-storey building, which housed the presses, was well constructed of granite blocks. Behind it lay the warehouse, right beside the railway tracks.

The strange behaviour of two ships caught Barbara's attention, and she called her younger brother Ian, age eleven, to come and take a look. Their excited comments drew their mother and six-year-old Isabel to the window. They all observed the scene on the harbour with astonishment. The ships looked as if they were actually trying to run into each other, even though they had plenty of room to get by. Then they saw them collide and smoke curl up from a big hole in one of them.

"That's an ammunition boat," Ian, the expert, said.

"What do you mean, an ammunition boat?" Barbara asked.

"It has barrels on it, and it looks like the kind that might be carrying ammunition and things for the war," he replied.

"Will it explode?" Barbara asked, more out of curiosity than out of apprehension.

"Oh, I don't think so," their mother said calmly. She could see other

George Mitchell, a cadet at the Royal Naval College of Canada, was going about his regular routine until someone shouted that there was a fire to the north. (COURTESY GEORGE MITCHELL)

vessels nearby and many dock workers and sailors looking on with interest and talking; some were pointing and even laughing. Soon the fire was spectacular, and Barbara, Ian, and Isabel asked whether they could go down to the harbour for a closer look. Their mother, seeing no sign of any danger, gave permission so long as they put on their coats and boots. They rushed out. Ian and Isabel headed straight down Kenny Street towards the waterfront; Barbara decided to go and see whether a friend would like to come with her. She turned left and cut across Mulgrave Park.

In the dockyard, not far from the Acadia Sugar Refinery, stood the former naval hospital, in temporary use as the Royal Naval College of Canada. George Mitchell was a cadet there. So far it had been a day like all others: up at 6:30, then a quick cup of hot chocolate, followed by an hour's exercise in the gymnasium. After that it was back to the college for a cold bath before breakfast at 8:05. Now came a little free time.

Someone shouted that there was a fire to the north and that the flames could be seen, even over the high sugar refinery. The cadets rushed to the north end of the building, where the view was best. Then the bell rang for cleaning up. That meant brushing uniforms and making themselves spic and span for inspection. George was one of twenty cadets in the junior gun room. Two were standing on a table, while two others were brushing their dark trousers.

*　　*　　*　　*　　*

After the collision the men on the bridge of the *Mont Blanc* stared at the hole in their ship. In no time black smoke enveloped the deck. It was so thick that it was impossible to tell whether the fire had begun in the benzol or in the picric acid. Soon flames from the benzol were shooting upwards through the smoke. Captain Le Medec, speaking in French, and Pilot Mackey, speaking in English, shouted together, "Look to your boats!"

The command was speedily obeyed, and the two lifeboats hurriedly made ready. Le Medec and the first officer collected the men, who quickly scrambled down the ropes. The only one missing was the chief engineer, who had remained at his post in the engine room. He lifted the safety valve in the starboard boiler to let off steam as a precaution, and then he and Le Medec ran to the lifeboats, the last to leave the *Mont Blanc*. The crew expected the steamer to explode immediately. They wasted no time and rowed as fast as they could away from the burning ship. Then one of the live shells on the forward deck blew up with a report that lent strength to their arms. They rowed to the closest shore, Dartmouth, at that time only sparsely inhabited to the north. As the lifeboats sped through the water, some of the crew shouted warnings to crafts in the vicinity, but they either went unheard or were not understood. When the boats landed, the captain took a roll call. All present. They told the people on the shore to get away and then ran into the woods to take cover.

The *Imo* had suffered little damage in the collision. Many of the crew had seen the lifeboats leave the *Mont Blanc* but had heard no warnings and assumed that the fire alone had been the reason for abandoning ship. Because of the ferocity of the flames, someone mentioned that gasoline or kerosene could be on board. Captain From and Pilot Hayes decided to turn the *Imo* around and go back to Bedford Basin. After trying for some time to turn at right angles, they changed their minds and agreed to head towards the mouth of the harbour, where the open ocean would give the large *Imo* more space to wheel around. Now the crew had work to do.

*   *   *   *   *

Herbert Whitehead had seen the crew of the *Imo* leaning over the side of the ship to assess the damage. A mate in the Canadian Naval Service, he commanded a drifter that supplied provisions to other boats in his branch. "A lot of whistling" had caught his attention, and that meant trouble, so he had stayed close by. After the collision he moved alongside the *Mont Blanc* to see whether he could help. The lifeboats were already lowered and almost ready to leave. Shouting through a megaphone, he offered to take the men on board his ship and then to Bedford Basin, but they did not respond. They just took off for the Dartmouth shore. He heard talking and yelling from the boats but no clear warnings. His lookout was a French

Canadian sailor, but he, too, heard nothing that gave him cause for alarm. Whitehead remained near the burning *Mont Blanc* for a few minutes. Then, noticing three small explosions, he decided that the *Mont Blanc* was probably loaded with oil and that it would be safer to get his boat out of the way. He headed back to the *Niobe,* at the dockyard.

Other ships approached the *Mont Blanc.* A workboat had been heading for the basin when the *Mont Blanc* and the *Imo* collided about 350 yards away. Ralph Smith, a marine engineer with Burns & Kelleher, was on the boat. It had moved down the harbour, come back, and stopped beside the *Mont Blanc* just as the men took to the lifeboats. One of them stood on a seat waving his arms in the air and yelling towards Halifax. The word he shouted was foreign, but Smith thought it sounded like *explosion.* Like so many others, he assumed that the ship was loaded with oil when he saw the black smoke. Seeing that the crew of the *Mont Blanc* did not need help, Smith and the men took the workboat to the basin, and Smith reported what he had heard to an officer on a naval boat.

When Captain Brannen of the *Stella Maris* realized the extent of the fire on the *Mont Blanc,* just after he entered the Narrows, he gave orders to anchor the scows and get the hose ready. The tug, now near the Dartmouth shore, raced over, but by the time it reached the *Mont Blanc,* she was almost touching Pier 6. When the hose was in position, the crew played it on the fire, but it had absolutely no effect. They backed off a short distance, and then the commander and six crew members of the *Highflyer* pulled alongside in a rowboat. The commander boarded the *Stella Maris* to talk with Brannen, and they were soon joined by an officer and some sailors from the *Niobe* who had arrived in a steam launch. The *Niobe* officer asked Brannen to get out a cable to try to tow the *Mont Blanc* away from Pier 6, as the pier itself was beginning to burn. A crew member produced the five-inch hawser, but the *Niobe* officer said that it was too weak. Then Second Mate William Nickerson went below with a deck hand to fetch the ten-inch cable. Brannen's son Walter, first mate of the *Stella Maris,* stood at the entrance to the hold.

Commander Wyatt, meanwhile, was walking towards the dockyard. On the way, he was told about the collision. He ran to the coaling wharf for a boat and waited anxiously while one was brought from the other side of the slip. Wyatt, after all, knew full well what was on the *Mont Blanc.*

*   *   *   *   *

The harbour was becoming a stage with hundreds of people watching the show. Mothers and children stopped school preparations and housework to rush to their windows. On every ship nearby, sailors and stevedores forgot their work and found the best vantage point; on shore, flat roofs of tall buildings were in great demand, and factories were at a standstill, with employees vying for a good view.

The drama was spectacular. Edward McCrossan, a Scottish sailor from the American *Curaca*, at Pier 8, counted at least six or seven occasions when "a pounder would go off in the holds, and after, you would hear a sound like a gun. Then smoke would go up and burst in the air." While watching the burning *Mont Blanc*, he became desperate for a cigarette and went below to roll one. The rest of the crew was at the stern watching and commenting. The shells on board the *Mont Blanc* continued to explode when the fire reached them.

Jack Tappen was a nineteen-year-old apprentice aboard the *Middleham Castle*, anchored off the Halifax Graving Dock Co. wharf. (RON E. MERRICK)

At the Halifax Graving Dock Co. wharf, outside the dry dock, practically every man on board the *Middleham Castle* stood on the seaward side of the ship's deck. Nineteen-year-old Jack Tappen was employed by Burns & Kelleher, Marine Engineers, which held the contract for all the pipe work at the graving dock. He had been helping carry a large cast-iron pipe to the engine room when someone yelled, "Two ships just collided off us!" He and the others abandoned the pipe and hurried onto the deck. He saw the *Imo* and the *Mont Blanc* drifting apart, flames rising at water level from one of them, and its crew rowing away, the cook still in his white apron. One engineer casually observed, "I saw a coal ship burn like that once." When he saw puffs of flames, he added, "If she has explosives aboard, this is no place for us." But no one paid any attention.

Soon some of the crew put bumpers out for protection in case the *Mont Blanc* drifted alongside. At that point the foreman yelled at Jack and his mates to move the pipe, which they had left hanging. They moved it as fast as they could and returned to their grandstand places. By that time the *Mont Blanc* had drifted into Pier 6 as straight as if someone had piloted her. Jack saw a huge column of smoke and a burst of flames, but he heard no roar.

The men on board the *Picton,* the British ship that contained a mixed cargo of ammunition and food, were far more apprehensive than those on the *Middleham Castle.* The boat was at the Acadia Sugar Refinery wharf, and its explosives had not yet been unloaded. If fire reached the ammunition, it would be serious. Francis Carew, the foreman, ordered the longshoremen to put on the hatch covers and to make the cargo as secure as possible.

A few others realized the gravity of the collision and took precautions. The terminal agent of the Canadian Government Railways, Henry Dustan, whose office was at the foot of Cornwallis Street, received a telephone call from William Lovett, chief clerk of Richmond railway yards, behind Pier 9. "There is a steamer coming into the wharf on fire, loaded with explosives," Lovett told Dustan. "There is likely to be an explosion." The men at the yards had been warned by a sailor, and they were leaving work. Vince Coleman, the train dispatcher, was about to leave with Lovett, but he realized that trains were due shortly. He stayed and sent one last message down the line: "Munitions ship on fire. Making for Pier 6. Goodbye."

The warning was not spread—probably because there was no time—and crowds continued to gather. Work had nearly come to a halt at Hillis & Sons Foundry, located just below Veith Street on the slope overlooking the harbour. Frank Burford, at age fifteen, was the youngest and newest employee, there only temporarily until accepted for a plumbing apprentice-ship. His father operated the engine room and had been with the firm for several years, ever since the family's emigration from England. The men crowded around the windows, and Frank managed to squeeze into a pretty good place. He noticed that the words BELGIAN RELIEF stood out clearly on the side of one ship and that the other had a deckload of barrels. Flames were licking up the sides of them, and the ship had begun to drift towards Richmond Station, very near the home the Burfords rented in the Flynn Block, on Barrington Street near Kenny. The fire was growing ever more furious when the telephone rang. The boss answered, and Frank heard him say, "Frank's not here to run errands. He's not going … Oh, well, in that case. Just this once then." He told Frank to go to the office and get a parcel and deliver it to the dry dock, a few blocks away. "You won't need your coat," he said. "It's not cold, and you'll run faster without it. When you come back, we'll find a good place for you again."

Frank fetched the parcel and ran as fast as he could along northern Barrington Street. He was passing Constant Upham's big general store when a fire engine raced by. Mr Upham had called the fire department and reported the blaze in the harbour. The firetruck was brand new and motorized. In fact, the firemen were so proud of the machine that they had even named it. They called the fire engine "Patricia."

The Patricia also caught the attention of some children on their way to Richmond School. The three Pattison boys had just left their mother and sister at home. The Pattisons lived on the east side of Barrington, near Young, in one of the houses owned by the sugar refinery, where their father was mechanical superintendent. The boys noticed the *Imo* aslant the harbour and ran single file across the road in front of the Protestant Orphanage, at Veith Street. Gordon, the oldest, age fourteen, went first, then James, a year younger, and, finally, Alan, who was eight. They wanted to see what all the commotion was about. Noble Driscoll, another pupil, had followed

This photograph of the Pattison children was taken about five years before the explosion. Alan and Gordon are in back; James and Catherine, in front. (COURTESY JAMES PATTISON)

The Patricia, the new, motorized fire engine, and her crew raced to the scene of the burning *Mont Blanc*. (PANS)

the fire engine, too, but Cam Creighton, standing outside Creighton's store, had advised him not to go any closer to the harbour, because it sounded as if there were bullets down there—he might get one in the leg.

Barbara Orr knew the Pattison children and Noble Driscoll, as she also attended Richmond School. Noble sat at the desk behind her and had once dipped one of her pigtails into an inkwell. Red hair flying, high laced boots crushing the crisp winter grass, Barbara ran across Mulgrave Park on her way down the hill towards her friend's house. Suddenly she stopped, spellbound, and stared as the column of smoke from the *Mont Blanc* rose higher, balls of flames rolling up through it and bursting. Loud shouts and the noise of the fire filled the streets. Then there was no sound at all.

THE NIGHTMARE
BEGINS

SECONDS BEFORE 9:05 A.M. the *Mont Blanc* blew up with a force that shattered her 3,000 tons of steel. Fragments erupted like rocks from a volcano, and a rushing torrent fanned outwards, sweeping a swath of destruction in its wake. The barrel of one of the ship's guns landed 3-1/2 miles away, at Albro Lake, in Dartmouth. Part of her anchor shank, weighing 1,140 pounds, flew more than 2 miles and embedded itself deep in the ground at Armdale, near the North West Arm. Chunks of metal crashed through roofs, damaged ships, killed and maimed people. Windows were broken more than 50 miles away. The shock was even felt in Sydney, Cape Breton, more than 270 miles northeast. The *Mont Blanc* 'the white mountain' disintegrated completely, leaving a huge black cloud.

In the immediate vicinity it was as if night had suddenly fallen. But the darkness was thick and oily, filled with a rain of soot and shrapnel. It stung, cut into flesh, and blackened whatever it touched. When the cloud that shrouded Richmond slowly cleared, it revealed nightmarish scenes. Trees and telegraph poles were snapped in half as if they had been hit by a tornado. Pier 6 was gone; piers 7, 8, and 9 were a mass of jumbled debris. The large buildings and the works behind and alongside Pier 6 were piles of rubble, with bits of broken machinery the only clue to their former function. In an apron around three sides of Fort Needham, on its lower slopes, houses had been smashed. They had been split open, splintered, or had collapsed like cards, showing pieces of broken furniture, stoves, bathtubs, and unrecognizable remains of household goods. Trickles of smoke and darts of flame licked the wreckage. Behind the mound of the fort, which had provided some protection, walls had moved, and houses had strange gaping wounds. Doors were missing; roofs were full of holes.

Total destruction spread for 325 acres, killing more than sixteen hundred

When the cloud from the exploding *Mont Blanc* slowly cleared, it revealed nightmarish scenes.

people instantly and wounding more than nine thousand others. Among the ruins were corpses, many lying in unnatural positions, headless or with limbs missing. Sometimes their clothing had been ripped off. Survivors staggered aimlessly, bleeding and confused, not knowing what had happened or where to go. Flying shards of glass, sharp as daggers, had pierced vulnerable watching faces and eyes. For some the blackness that had fallen so suddenly never lifted.

*   *   *   *   *

Nearly every ship in the harbour was tossed around relentlessly, first by the explosion and then by a tidal wave. The *Imo*, riddled with holes from flying metal, was hurled aground on the Dartmouth shore. Captain Haakon From, Pilot William Hayes, and five crew members were killed; others were seriously wounded. John Johansen, the helmsman, was knocked unconscious, but he came to and found himself trying to swim. Then the water receded, and before he knew it, he was back on the deck of his ship.

The tidal wave crashed against the Dartmouth side with incredible force. Tufts Cove, on the eastern shore of the Narrows, felt the full impact of the wave: the single-storey houses there were swamped. Several families of Mi'kmaq lived near the cove. Their homes were wrecked, and at least nine people were killed. George Dixon was working at a small shipbuilding plant in the cove. He said that the water was literally boiling with flying pieces of metal. When he and his brother-in-law got to their feet after the explosion, his brother-in-law said, "We might as well have been killed as to find this thing coming at us." Ethel Mitchell's grandfather, walking near the shore, had to cling to a lamp post for safety. Three times a wave washed over him and then receded.

No doubt the sailors on the *Imo* also feared being swept away. Nonetheless, some men did manage to get ashore; a boat from the HMS *Highflyer* later rescued the rest.

This post-explosion photograph, which shows the *Imo* (at left) and British relief vessels HMS *Highflyer* and *Changuinola,* appeared on the front page of the December 22, 1917, issue of the Montreal *Standard.* The ruins of the Acadia Sugar Refinery are visible in the foreground.

In Richmond, homes were smashed, showing only jumbled remains of household belongings. (PANS)

Having rowed to safety, Pilot Francis Mackey, Captain Aimé Le Medec, and the rest of the crew from the *Mont Blanc* were much more fortunate. Only one sailor received serious injuries. He later died from loss of blood. Commander Frederick Wyatt never did get the boat he had ordered. The *Mont Blanc* blew up while he waited.

The tug *Stella Maris,* whose crew had been preparing to tow the *Mont Blanc,* was beached almost where Pier 6 had been. Five of the twenty-four men on board survived, including William Nickerson, who had gone to fetch the ten-inch hawser, and Walter Brannen, who had been standing at the entrance to the hold. Walter was thrown beside William. He escaped with a punctured eardrum and cuts and bruises, but his father, Captain Horatio Brannen, was killed. There was one survivor from the *Highflyer*'s rowboat but none from the *Niobe*'s steam pinnace.

Edward McCrossan, the sailor from the American *Curaca* who had been so anxious for a cigarette, was one of the lucky ones. Thirty-two of that ship's fifty-five-man crew died. With nothing between her and the *Mont Blanc,* the ship bore the full brunt of the explosion, shielding the British *Calonne,* at Pier 9, from severe damage, though seven of her sailors did not survive. McCrossan managed to leap onto the *Calonne* before his ship drifted to her final resting place, in Bedford Basin. He saw houses coming down and women and children covered with blood.

On the British *Picton* Francis Carew (the foreman), sixty-four longshore-men, and many crew members perished. Their brave attempt to ensure that the ship's cargo would not endanger the surrounding area had not been completely in vain. The *Picton* did not blow up, and later in the day, with great difficulty, it was towed away from the shore, where fires were raging. It had to be anchored farther out, for fear its cargo of munitions could still explode.

The *Niobe* lost a funnel, and the decks, with their wooden additions, were in shambles. Fire broke out, but the trained crew quickly had it under control.

The *Highflyer* had been designed to withstand enemy attack. Her hull was damaged, three crew members were killed on board, and fifteen men were injured. Geared for war as she was, however, she was soon ready for duty again.

In the basin and in other parts of the harbour that were far away from Pier 6, ships heaved and pitched, but injuries and damage were minor. On the *Olympic* and the USS *Old Colony,* for example, the sudden shock and the turbulence were alarming, but calm was restored when nothing further happened.

This portrait of Captain Horatio Brannen was taken as a surprise Christmas gift for his wife. She received it after the explosion. (MARITIME MUSEUM/THELMA BRANNEN DASBURG)

The tug *Stella Maris,* under Brannen's command, was beached almost where Pier 6 had been. (MARITIME MUSEUM/VAUGHAN)

The force of the blast hurled the *Imo* aground on the Dartmouth shore. (PANS)

Aboard the *Middleham Castle,* just off the Halifax Graving Dock Co. wharf, young Jack Tappen shot through the open doorway behind him and right down the corridor. He landed safely on a soft pile of bodies. Everything was pitch black, and he could not see a thing. The ship was plunging up and down, up and down, from the turbulence of the water. He pulled himself together and looked around. The blackness was gradually lifting. He seemed unhurt but had lost every button on his vest. Two other apprentices were also in fairly good shape, and the three of them took stock. Huge round boulders weighing tons lay on the deck, blown from goodness knows where, maybe from the bottom of the sea. They found a workmate who had been standing with his hand on Jack's shoulder, but a steel bulkhead had been behind him, not an open doorway, and his head had smashed into it with great violence. Nothing could be done for him or for many others.

The three young men watched for their chance and then jumped from the *Middleham Castle* to the collier *J. C. McKee,* between them and the wharf, now floating like a raft. The lines securing both ships were fastened to anchors mounted in concrete that were holding them fast. The three-some slid down the ropes and landed on the drifting wharf. Men were flailing in the water, some struggling and shouting, "Give us a hand!" Others bobbed up and down lifelessly. In a daze, Jack and his companions hauled up as many of the drowning men as they could.

Then the three youths made it to shore by stepping on debris floating in the water. They went to the shed where they had left their coats, but it had been flattened and was on fire. They met the graving dock manager, who seemed unnaturally calm.

"All right, boys?" he asked.

"I think so," one of them replied uncertainly.

They were trying to get to Barrington Street, but the wreckage of the Acadia Sugar Refinery blocked their way, and they had to go over the bridge by the dry dock. It was still dry. The tidal wave had not swamped it, even though it was close to the explosion. In it lay the Norwegian *Hovland,* damaged but not extensively so, probably because the dock was so deep. Jack Tappen and his friends did not know it then, but 5 of the *Hovland*'s crew had been killed, and some 120 men working at the dry dock had lost their lives.

Suddenly, at the naval college nearby, all routine had ended. There was a fearful noise, and the building collapsed around the cadets, plaster and glass flying. George Mitchell realized that it had to have been an explosion. He had seen the burning ship. The only way out was by the window, ten feet from the ground. Some hesitated, but all took the big drop, except for one of the cadets who had been standing on the table. He had been blown out. Outside, a thick black hailstorm was raining down, and it made a noise as it landed. The cadets stood still until the strange storm stopped. They could not see through it to go anywhere. Finally it cleared, leaving a great mushroom of smoke. Over on the opposite shore George saw a ship beached.

An officer arrived and lined up the uninjured cadets. They were told that as there was nothing they could do to help, they should disperse and find friends or relatives to give them shelter. George's family lived in Halifax, and he headed for home. His face was bleeding from cuts—one was a straight line down his cheek, like a shaving cut; another, deeper one was on his upper lip—but only later was he conscious of them.

A Dartmouth resident, Dorothy Chisholm, worked at the Royal Bank and had taken the 9:00 ferry to Halifax. The boat, about five minutes out from the dock, had almost reached mid-channel. Most of its passengers had been lined up along the rail watching the burning ship to the north when it blew up. People had time to dive for protection, but Dorothy was a bit slow. The blast tossed them all in one direction, and she landed on top of the heap. She thought that the heavens were falling in on her. She had seen the ship blow up but assumed that the Germans were attacking. Everything seemed to be flying around them, into and over the water. She wished she had landed underneath, where she would have been protected from the enemy bullets.

Gradually the passengers got themselves sorted out. Those who had been below deck in the saloon had been cut and more injured than those on the open deck. The ferry continued on its way to Halifax, and Dorothy, considerably shaken, made her way to the bank, near the ferry terminal, but was told to go home again. This time the ferry trip, though less eventful, was made horrendous by the sights to the north.

The ferry service was never interrupted. The superintendent and the other operators stayed at their posts, though they were anxious to find out what had happened to their homes.

*　　*　　*　　*　　*

On shore it seemed as if Halifax had been wiped out. Richmond railway yards were completely destroyed. Vince Coleman, who had stayed behind to send a warning to approaching trains, died instantly. Even if he had left with his co-worker William Lovett, he might not have survived: Lovett later died from his injuries. Constant Upham and his fine big store perished. So did Isaac Creighton and his store. Upham's and Creighton's were the two biggest general stores in Richmond. Both not only sold groceries but also sundry other goods.

Barbara Orr, standing right in the path of the blast, had a miraculous escape. When she overcame her bewilderment, she found herself flying on top of Fort Needham, more than a quarter of a mile away from where she had been standing when the *Mont Blanc* exploded. Never com-

Constant Upham was killed, his big general store destroyed. (MARITIME MUSEUM)

pletely unconscious, she remembered having a sensation of moving violently, of somersaulting into and out of deep holes.

She lay still for a moment. Her leg hurt. When she put her hand down, she found that one tightly laced boot had vanished. She was covered with oil and soot, which would leave permanent marks where they had entered the broken skin. All around her, people were crying, "It's the Germans!" She tried to say that it had been a ship, but her voice would not come out properly. No one would have paid any attention, anyway.

Barbara was unable to walk, because her foot and her leg were crushed. So she crawled to find help. She started off towards home, but she stopped when she saw the devastation, the thick smoke, and the leaping flames. She had relatives on Gottingen Street, not far away, but in the opposite direction. Going by sheer instinct, not reason, she struggled down the slope on hands and knees. She saw other people groping their way along, but she ignored them. She could concentrate on only one thing, on getting down the hill. She did not ask for help, and no one offered it.

Her schoolmate Noble Driscoll had also been thrown to higher ground and almost the same distance. He had been standing near Creighton's store, on Barrington Street, watching the fireballs in the smoke coming up from the ship in the harbour, and the next thing he knew, he came to lying among roof shingles and rubble on Duffus Street not far from Gottingen. He was black, and his cap was gone. So was his coat. It was as if he had carefully taken it off: not a trace of it was left. The darkness was abating, and the sun coming through. Noble thought that it looked like a full moon shining through a haze. For a time he lay there thinking he was the only person left alive in the world. "Where will I get something to eat?" he thought. He got up and started to walk. He met a man he knew, and then he realized that there had to be other people around. The man asked, "Was it the Germans?" Noble said he had no idea what it was, and he set off to find his home. A boy came along, unrecognizable, coated in black grime. Then he opened his mouth and revealed white buck teeth. It just had to be Noble's brother Lou. Nobody else had teeth like that. The two boys did not say much. Like everyone else, they were in shock. They wandered northwards along Barrington to their home, about two blocks away. Three walls of the house were down, and they were about to leave when they heard a sound. Taking shelter behind the fourth wall, seeking some warmth from coals that were still burning, were their mother, father, and eight of their brothers and sisters.

The blast stripped clothing off many victims who remained unhurt. Hildred Kitz, six years old, rushed home. Her mother tried to find out whether she was all right. All the child could say was, "I saw a man—a sailor—and he had no clothes on." Mrs Kitz was a precise and practical woman, even at times like these. "How did you know he was a sailor?" she asked. "Because he still had his hat on," Hildred replied.

There were also many incidents of people being carried uphill. Most did not survive, but some, like Barbara Orr and Noble Driscoll, escaped without serious injury. Two sailors later reported the same phenomenon. Dr W. B. Moore, a Kentville physician who did relief work, subsequently recorded his impressions of an incident described by one of the sailors:

> Standing exactly in the centre of a terrific cyclonic disturbance of the air around him which probably destroyed all outside of that centre within its influence, he was compressed equally on all sides and carried by the whirlwind upwards until its force was exhausted, which, luckily for him, occurred on high ground, by which he escaped the destruction of a fall to a lower level. Many incidents have occurred in western cyclones where people and much heavier bodies have been carried for miles, but the former seldom or never lived to tell the tale because they were not released under such rarely favourable circumstances as in the case of the Halifax man.

Dr Percy McGrath, another physician who did relief work, later attended a sailor recovering in the house of Will Hart, owner of the Green Lantern Restaurant. The sailor remembered being beside his ship, where he had been watching the burning *Mont Blanc* at close range. After the blast Mr Hart picked him up at the top of Fort Needham. Dr McGrath described the man as in shock, lying in bed almost comatose, but conscious and not critically injured. Had he been thrown down onto low ground, the doctor surmised, he probably would have been killed.

James Pattison was not thrown uphill by the explosion, but he was knocked unconscious. He came to his senses lying in the middle of Barrington Street, the power lines for the trolley cars on top of him. Luckily they were not live, and he tried to push them aside. Then he lost consciousness again. Next time he came to, the road seemed to be covered with water. Coated in oily soot, he tried to stand up but fell, striking his face on the road. Finally he managed to sit up. His nose was bleeding, and a shingle nail protruded from his hand. He pulled it out, and blood spurted.

James climbed over a pile of wreck-

Frank Burford, fifteen years old in December 1917, was pinned under a timber. (RON E. MERRICK)

Forty-one people on duty at Hillis & Sons Foundry died, including Frank's father.

age and saw his brother Gordon in a field, probably the playing field of the Protestant Orphanage. The orphanage was gone, flattened completely. Gordon limped over to him but did not seem seriously hurt. The silver face of his watch shone through the filth that covered him. Both boys had lost their jackets, and Gordon one laced boot. But James still wore his schoolbag on his back. The books inside were intact, even though the thick leather bag had a jagged tear in the front. It must have protected James from something sharp. They looked for little Alan but could not find him.

Wandering vaguely in the direction of their home, they came across a house that looked like a beaver dam. On top was a man with a horrible gash on his face. He was tearing at the wooden beams with his hands. Underneath, somebody was screaming. A house nearby had just caught fire. The shivering boys snuggled against one of its walls for a time, trying to get warm, but the fire grew too fierce, and they had to move on. They were being urged by soldiers to go westward, away from the fires—and away from where they had lived.

Frank Burford, also on Barrington, thought he was in the middle of a recurring nightmare that had been troubling him lately. He was boxed in, a heavy timber pinning his legs and plaster choking him. It was dark. He struggled, and the pain wakened him fully. It was no nightmare. Eventually, after what seemed an eternity, he realized that there was an opening, a small hole way back, and beyond it was light. But he could not just get up and run. He had to draw himself out slowly from under the timber so that nothing would move, so that he would not find himself trapped under the entire heap. He had to twist between the timbers, careful not to dislodge anything. He was thin and agile. Gingerly, with many cuts and scrapes and with blood seeping from a painful gash in his leg, Frank squirmed his way to the top of the pile of debris. All around he saw fires and wreckage. He stared in disbelief and sat down on the pile of rubble. He did not recognize this world.

Slowly it came back to him. He had seen a fire ... on a ship. He remembered men clambering over the side. Two sailors came over and looked up at him. "Mister, have you seen our boat?" they asked. Frank just shook his head. He was as lost as they were.

Not far away a smashed wagon and a dead horse lay side by side. Frank stumbled down and wandered off. Then he saw the Patricia, stripped and battered, its glory gone; nearby was a wrecked car. Frank did not know that the fire chief, his deputy, and all but one of the Patricia's six crew had died instantly.

Finally his older sister, Winnie, found him. Frank was one of the few who had escaped with his life from Hillis & Sons Foundry. Forty-one other employees on duty that morning, including his father, had lost their lives. The general manager, Frank D. Hillis, and the assistant manager, James B. Hillis, were among them.

*   *   *   *   *

The cloud that had risen from the exploding *Mont Blanc* was no longer black. After shedding its grime, it became white and shone in the sunlight. It attracted the attention of more distant observers, many of whom were unaware of its significance. "It was like a huge mushroom—pretty, too," said Ruth Poole, a girl who saw the cloud from the far side of Dartmouth.

Seventeen-year-old Jim Gowen, a future journalist, spotted it from St Mary's College, on Windsor Street. The school was damaged, mostly broken windows and upset furniture, but the Christian Brothers in charge of the school quickly had everything under control. When Jim emerged from the building, an elderly gentleman was having a hard time trying to calm his terrified horse, still harnessed to a wagon. The old man managed to get a rein around a fence post to steady the poor beast and then pointed upwards. "There it is," he said, "a Zeppelin."

A huge thermal cloud hovered in the distance. "It was in constant turmoil," Jim recalled. It looked like a cumulus cloud, all curly, giving off sporadic flashes of light. The strange thing was, the cloud seemed to be moving northwest, against the wind.

"THEY'RE ALL GONE"

PEOPLE INSIDE BUILDINGS during the blast endured one horror after another: shooting glass, tumbling ceilings and walls, crashing furniture. With incredible speed, fire also added to the deadly work of the explosion. Burning fragments flew everywhere, and the shattered houses burst into flames as easily as the kindling they had come to resemble. Unsuspecting Richmond families had lighted their stoves and stoked their furnaces early that morning to ward off the winter chill. Before people realized what had struck, their houses were in chaos, the stoves and furnaces smashed or overturned, spewing live logs and coals onto the ruins.

Constant Upham's brother Charles was one of six thousand left homeless on December 6. He lived on Rector Street with his wife and five children. Yardmaster at Richmond railway yards, he had been on night duty, and when he returned home, he filled the furnace with coal and replenished the fire in the stove. Then he had some breakfast and went upstairs to bed. The two older children, Millicent, age nine, and Archie, almost seven, were in a bedroom next door. Millicent was sick, and Archie, almost ready for school, was visiting her; the rest of the family was in the kitchen. Millicent was facing the window, and Archie had his back to it. Then the explosion hit. Millicent had one eye wrenched out and was cut on other parts of her face. Archie received wounds to the back of his head. Their father had a habit of burrowing under the blankets when he slept, so he escaped injury. Jolted awake, he rushed to Millicent and Archie, both screaming in pain and fright.

The whole harbour side of the house had collapsed. The stairs were gone, but the oilcloth that had covered them was, amazingly, still intact. Mr Upham helped his two children, black and bleeding, to slide down the oilcloth. He was barefoot and in his nightshirt, and he cut his feet on broken glass lying all over the ground. Carrying Millicent piggyback and holding

Archie by the hand, he led them to safety, away from the falling timbers and chimneys. He sat them down on an undamaged door that was far from the opening it had covered. "Stay put!" he said firmly and ran back to the house to rescue his wife and three younger children, Charles, Ellen, and Jennie. But he was too late. The house was already blazing. No matter how hard he tried, he was barred by the flames. Later he was slightly comforted by the thought that he had heard no cries from inside.

The family would have gone to the funeral of Mrs Upham's father that afternoon. His body lay in the parlour of the Rasley home on

Millicent and Archie Upham were about five years older when the *Mont Blanc* blew up. Their father, Charles, led them to safety. (COURTESY ANNE SWINDELLS IHASZ)

The Reverend William Swetnam sawed the timbers pinning his daughter, Dorothy, despite her screams of pain.
(COURTESY DOROTHY SWETNAM HARE)

Bertha (left) and Ethel Bond (right), standing with their mother, helped rescue Mr Swetnam and Dorothy.
(COURTESY MARGARET WOURNELL)

Longard Road (now part of Robie Street). A heavy piece of metal, part of a ship, crashed through the roof and smashed a chair beside the coffin. Esther Rasley, cousin of Millicent and Archie, was seriously cut. Annie, age nine, lost an eye. Reg, a little younger, thought that the Germans had landed, and he ran out of the house.

At Kaye Street Methodist Church a mission concert had been arranged for the night of the sixth. In the manse that morning Lizzie Louise Swetnam was playing the piano for her son, Carman, who was going to practise his song for the concert before he left for school. The Reverend William Swetnam stood in the doorway listening, and Dorothy, their daughter, sat in the rocking chair across the room. It was a typical family scene. Then the house fell in, and the floor gave way.

Mr Swetnam was knocked unconscious for a short time and lost all of his outer clothing. But he was not seriously hurt. He pulled himself up and looked around for his family. The piano was on top of his wife and son, and it was obvious they were dead. But Dorothy was still alive, trapped under heavy ceiling beams. Her father searched frantically for his saw. When he found it, he started on one of the timbers. Dorothy screamed in agony, and he stopped. The house was already on fire. Two neighbours arrived, and they urged him to continue. He told Dorothy she would have to put up with the pain and, gritting his teeth, sawed with a strength he did not know he possessed. At last they were able to free the little girl. Although she had been dressed for school, she was now practically naked. One neighbour threw a coat around her, and not a moment too soon they all ran outside.

Bertha Bond and her sister, Ethel, were those neighbours. On December 10 Bertha wrote to her fiancé, Sandy Wournell, serving on the front lines in France. She described the scene at the Methodist manse and in her own home:

> It may be beyond my power of thought to collect enough to put on paper but I want you to see my hand writing first because that may convince you that I am all right. Both Ethel and I had a most miraculous escape and for that we are so thankful, but Sandy when we got out of the house and found our dear dad, it made us, well, I can't describe the sensation I had. He had just gone to the mill to get some sugar which was in a barrel inside the door and there we found his body. Our greatest comfort is that his death was instant and that he was ready to go. You know, Sandy, that neither Ethel nor I are of a collapsing nature, so, as hard as it was, we had to cover the body and leave it.
>
> I wasn't half dressed. We had been up late the night before so that morning Ethel said for me to take another nap and she would get the breakfast so I

didn't wake up till about nine o'clock. Then I hurried into my underclothes and corsets, stockings and an old pair of boots which I didn't button. Then I put on a heavy bath robe and went into the bath room and I was there when the explosion occurred. The first shock didn't stun me but the church fell and I saw it go. Maybe a shell struck it or maybe it was simply the concussion: then in another instant I was knocked into the hall, face down and walls and I don't know what all began to tumble in and I felt the stuff piling up on my back. I was sure that was the end of me and all I was thinking of was you. I remember saying, or rather thinking, your name over and over but when I hit the floor first and for a few seconds I was stunned and if I had never lived I'd never have known what happened to me or felt any pain but as it was I began to move and wiggle out from under the stuff. My face and head was bleeding considerably—I could tell by the look of the floor and also by the way the blood was dripping off my chin but for all that my knees didn't shake a particle. I called Ethel and at the same time she called me and she came scrabbling up what was left of the stairs and met me at the top. She says she never expected to see my face whole again by the look of it then and I felt sure too that it would have to be patched up but I might as well tell you now that I don't expect to have a scar—only two new upper front teeth to replace the ones that were broken off.

The robe I had on went I don't know where—I didn't see it so I picked up a flannel dress and put it over my head as I followed Ethel to go outside.... [We] finally landed at the parsonage.

I didn't expect to find a soul there, but I did. Little Dorothy was unhurt, but so completely hemmed in that her father was doing his best to saw her out. The other two were gone.... By now the fires were blazing in pretty good shape.... I'll never forget Mr Swetnam's look when he saw us and if we hadn't gone she'd never in this world have been saved. Then it was time to run so we ran to our place and grabbed what clothes we could. We got upstairs and I thought of my ring. It had been in my jewel box on the bureau. I found it among the plaster but the tray had gone. In a minute I located it, but no ring. I just had to get it, and I did, also my watch which was in the mess. We had no time to hunt for anything more or any way of gathering or carrying it so as we went we picked up a few clothes. I picked up enough odd pieces to finish dressing later and all the old coats in the coat room we took.

We rigged out the two Swetnams and were ready to leave when I dropped my load and went to see if the safe was anywhere. It flashed through my mind that if it had been a shell from sea another might come and so I opened it up first try—ripped open a couple of little cushions and dumped everything in the safe into these rude bags—shut the door and when we got out Ethel didn't know what I had done. It was a dreadful hustle.

Don and Jean Crowdis posed in front of the Grove Presbyterian manse before the explosion. (COURTESY JEAN CROWDIS MURRAY)

Afterwards, the manse showed all the effects of implosion, collapsing towards the harbour, not away from it. (COURTESY JEAN CROWDIS MURRAY)

All of Richmond's churches were destroyed. The Reverend Charles Crowdis, minister of Grove Presbyterian, had climbed to a higher point on Fort Needham to watch the burning *Mont Blanc*. "Jets of flame and spiral puffs of smoke shot heavenwards," he wrote later. After the explosion he ran back to the manse to see what had become of his family. His two small children, Jean, age five, and Don, almost four, were outside the house, but his wife, Jane, and her two sisters, Marjorie and Marie, were still somewhere in the wreckage. Jean had been upstairs until she suddenly found herself lying almost under the organ, on the floor below; Don was uninjured.

The house had been flattened but had not caught fire, and people began to congregate in the backyard. The church, too, was a pile of rubble. Mr Crowdis found Marjorie, badly injured in the feet and legs. The other sister-in-law, with a few slight head injuries and a broken collarbone, seemed more or less all right. Then he found his wife. Her face was almost unrecognizable, her eyes in a frightful state. Mr Crowdis fetched his wheelbarrow, still usable, from the shed, and he loaded his wife and son into it. With Jean trailing behind, he headed for the nearest hospital, farther north on Gottingen. It was for infectious diseases, but he was desperate. By the time Mr Crowdis got back to the house, both his sisters-in-law had been removed. Nobody knew where. After the children had been taken to a safer area, he set off to find Marjorie and Marie and some lost parishioners.

Mrs Crowdis was operated on that night, and one eye had to be removed. Marjorie, her name appearing later in a list of fatalities, was given up for dead. In fact, she lived until she was ninety-five, though she was never quite free of the pain from her injuries.

St Mark's Anglican Church collapsed, and then it burned; St Joseph's Roman Catholic was damaged beyond repair. All four churches lost a considerable proportion of their parishioners. Kaye Street Methodist lost 91; Grove Presbyterian, 148; St Mark's, about 200; and St Joseph's, 404. Many others were injured or left homeless. The pastors would have their work cut out for them for the next several months.

Richmond schools did not fare much better. At St Joseph's the ceilings caved in, and the windows were blown out. Four girls were killed, and four more later died in hospital. Fifteen girls absent from school that day were killed in or around their homes. The boys, who should have attended St Joseph's in the afternoon, would have been safer at school: fifty-five lost their lives.

Helena Duggan, Evelyn Johnson, and Eileen Ryan attended St Joseph's. Helena, age eleven, had been seated at her desk in a classroom on the second storey when there was a crash and the floor gave way. She ended up in the

This class picture was taken outside Richmond School before the explosion. Many of these children died at home or on their way to school. (COURTESY MERITA DOBSON)

Because Richmond School had been badly damaged, some said it was fortunate that classes had not been in session. (PANS)

basement surrounded by debris but surprisingly little hurt.

Evelyn, about the same age, had arrived early for a music lesson at the convent and had hurried into the cloakroom to take off her coat before going to prayers. Another girl, standing by a window, called, "Come and watch the fire." Clouds of smoke and flames were billowing up. Then, realizing she was late, Evelyn turned to run to class. Her next memory was of picking herself up from among the rubble of the fallen ceiling. Girls were crying, and the nuns were trying to marshall them out of the building.

Ten-year-old Eileen was seated at her heavy wooden desk in the Grade-6 classroom, the stage of the auditorium. She heard two dreadful roars and seemed to fall down through space. She said a quick "Hail Mary" before losing consciousness. Then, through a gap in the debris that surrounded her, she saw her teacher, a German sister, who announced, "There's a German ship in the harbour." Unworthy suspicions flashed through Eileen's mind. Soon she became aware of movement nearby. She heard someone say, "Poor Nellie." But it made no sense.

As classes did not begin until 9:30, only two children were killed at Richmond School. One was Merle Huggins, the principal's eleven-year-old daughter. The Huggins family did not live in Richmond, and Merle travelled to school with her father. Eighty-six other pupils died. Many, such as Alan Pattison and Gordon Driscoll, had been on their way to school.

Helena Duggan was eleven years old in December 1917.

Evelyn Johnson, then Helena's schoolmate, nearly lost her right arm.

Others, such as Catherine Pattison and Tom and Elsie Burford, had still been at home. Because the school had collapsed, some said it was fortunate that classes had not been in session. Given the casualty figures, however, the children might have been safer in the sturdy building, rather than on the streets or in their wooden homes.

The Protestant Orphanage, above the Acadia Sugar Refinery, stood right in the path of the blast. It was reported initially that everyone inside the building had died, but in all, twenty-seven children had been killed, and the matron did not survive. Five children from other schools in the North End lost their lives, but they were either at home or outside. Many teachers suffered severe injuries, including Merle Huggins's father.

Frances MacLennan, daughter of Dr Samuel MacLennan, was thrown onto the floor of the gym at the Halifax Ladies College. (COURTESY FRANCES MACLENNAN)

Nearly every school in Halifax was damaged to some extent. The Halifax Ladies College was situated at the corner of Barrington and Harvey streets. On the morning of the explosion the girls had been lined up for prayers in the gymnasium, where the windows were covered with wire mesh to protect them from basketballs. Mrs Truman, the principal, a dignified widow who always wore a long black dress, stood on the platform. Frances MacLennan, daughter of Dr Samuel J. MacLennan, a surgeon at Camp Hill Hospital, had a place near one of the windows. The girls were used to the sound of blasting, as new railway cuttings were being finished not too far away. "This is the biggest one we ever had," Frances had time to think before she was thrown to the floor. Mrs Truman was hurled off the platform. "She has ankles!" thought Frances, who had never seen them before.

The day girls were sent home. Before Frances reached her house, her mother had become worried and, with no idea of the magnitude of the disaster, had sent her ten-year-old son, Hugh, to try to find her. Hugh and a friend wandered about trying to see as much as possible until a policeman told them to go home.

*　　*　　*　　*　　*

Although the devastation was not nearly so extensive or the fires at all widespread, Dartmouth, largely undeveloped to the north, did suffer considerable damage during the explosion. Twenty-year-old Leighton Dillman worked for the Consumers Cordage Company, usually known as the ropeworks, on northern Wyse Road. He thought that the racket and the roof caving in had been caused by a burst boiler. He was cut in a few places, but when he found his brother, who worked a little farther up in the same building, he was bleeding badly from a huge gash on his face. Leighton took him to the pond behind the works and washed him off as best he could. He wanted to make him more presentable before his mother saw him, as she would be alarmed by all the blood. While they were at the pond, a heavy black rain fell on them, and Leighton tried to clean them off again. Then he helped his brother home.

Their house was located almost opposite where the explosion had occurred. At the time, there were no buildings between it and the harbour: the Dillmans could see right down to the shore and across to Halifax. When the young men arrived home, they found their mother very badly hurt. She had been standing in front of the stove in the kitchen when the roof fell on her. She was lucky to be alive, but her side and her back were injured, and she could not walk. The boys put her in a chair and carried her up into the woods away from the wreckage. Fortunately the Dillman house did not catch fire, though one near it did. So did some in the Mi'kmaw settlement in Tufts Cove, where Leighton sometimes went in summer to buy baskets.

Ethel Mitchell, lying in her bed, between two windows, did not have much of a rest. Mrs Mitchell had been halfway down the stairs when they and the floor beneath them collapsed, throwing her into the basement. Ethel herself was hardly conscious of what had happened after the deafening roar. Amazingly the glass from the windows missed her.

Leighton Dillman, twenty years old at the time, worked at the Consumers Cordage Company, in Dartmouth. He thought that the noise had been caused by a burst boiler. (HALIFAX HERALD LIMITED)

The blankets must have shielded her, but as she made for the door, shards stuck into her bare feet. She was found an hour later, sitting on a biscuit box outside a nearby store, an unknown man's coat around her and large boots on her feet but with some of her own clothes on underneath. She was taken to her grandmother's house next door. It was less damaged, and several people had gathered there, including her mother, who was desperately in need of medical treatment. The stairs in her own house had left a gaping hole, and her room was on the second storey. She had no recollection of getting down, but there had been a long ladder in the garage beside the house. That was a possibility. She never found out who her rescuer had been. It was a miraculous escape for her, but her beloved cat, Buttons, had been killed, and her beautiful rose-pink dress, in which she had looked so pretty the night before, was in shreds.

*   *   *   *   *

As soon as they realized the magnitude of the disaster, people rushed home from all parts of Halifax. Like the Reverend Mr Swetnam, Richmond men were soon heaving away fallen timbers and tugging at twisted wreckage. They used any available implement in an effort to reach a feeble cry or to carry out their dead and injured. Passers-by helped if they could, but many were too bewildered to be of any use. Even children made heroic attempts.

Noble Driscoll's older brother Cliff ran as fast as he could to Duffus Street, where he lived with his bride of less than a year. When the *Mont Blanc* exploded, Cliff was crouched under an engine at the Willow Park railway workshops, at Windsor and Young streets, cleaning the metal. Suddenly it seemed as if all the boilers burst at once. The engine shielded Cliff, but damage to the rest of the yard was extensive. As he made his way home, he met people with blood pouring off them, and the devastation grew worse and worse. He reached Duffus, only to find that the house containing his apartment had become a bonfire; his wife, Annie, was nowhere in sight.

Something told him she might be with his mother. He hurried on, down to Barrington Street, single mindedly ignoring the terrible sights and injuries. Eventually he found her huddling behind the only standing wall of his parents' home, along with other members of his family. Shortly before the explosion she had seen Cliff's brother Al going by on the delivery wagon he drove for Isaac Creighton's general store. She was preparing to give him a letter to mail. She got out, but the others in the house were killed. She was eight months pregnant and was fortunate not to lose the baby. Al Driscoll had a lucky escape, too. His clothes were "just shredded," and his jacket was gone. He must have been unconscious for a short time, but his only injury was a scratch on his little finger. His beautiful chestnut mare was terrified but also unhurt.

Helena Duggan emerged from St Josephs School, and her first instinct was to go home, right down Russell Street to Barrington. But no help or comfort awaited her there. Hardly anything was left. The house was in a pile, and her older sister, Irene, was hanging from a beam by one arm, her face badly cut. Her mother had a large sliver of mirror protruding from the side of her head. She was still recovering from the recent birth of a baby girl and from the death of her smallest daughter, two-year-old Alma, not long before that. She and her children had been standing at a window watching the burning *Mont Blanc*, and the mirror beside them had shattered.

There were soldiers nearby, and one lifted Irene down. Helena helped her mother, sisters, and brother away from the house. A soldier then tried to remove the piece of mirror from Mrs Duggan's head, but luckily he failed: the loss of blood could have been even more serious.

They set off up Russell, with Mrs Duggan talking to Alma, her late child, as if she were holding her hand. When they were out of danger, they stopped and sat on the edge of a sidewalk. Soldiers put a blanket around them. After they had rested for a while and pulled themselves together, they realized they had left the baby behind. Someone went to investigate, but it was too late. The house had burned to the ground. It was reported that a sailor had taken a baby out of a burning house. Was the child rescued? They would never know.

Eileen Ryan tried to make her presence known but failed. When she came to completely, she managed to squeeze her way out, from under the boards and plaster, and to find the side door. She walked up Russell to Gottingen. Only two walls remained of St Joseph's Church. She kneeled on the sidewalk to pray and noticed the stone cross from the top of the church lying between the streetcar tracks.

Her pinafore, or "tire," as they were called, was bloodstained, and she knew she was cut here and there. So far she had met nobody. Then a grocery wagon driven by Mr Perrin, father of Nellie, her schoolmate, came by. She now understood the words she had heard. Part of Nellie's body, her high laced boots, and her clothing stuck out from under a blanket.

Eileen's home, on Macara Street, looked all right from a distance, but as she got closer, she saw that the windows, as well as their sashes and frames, were gone. Her mother and youngest brother were inside. They thought that only their house had been attacked. The boy would have gone to school

The heavy granite blocks of the Richmond Printing Company tumbled like toy bricks that had been kicked over.

in the afternoon and had been preparing to go to church to take confession, as it was the first Thursday of the month. Then her three older brothers arrived. They had seen more destruction and death on their way.

"Boys," Mrs Ryan greeted them, "our home is gone."

"Mother," the oldest answered, "you're lucky to have your life."

Once outside, Evelyn Johnson also headed for home, 12 Russell, near Barrington. She was stopped by soldiers. "You can't go down there," they warned. The lower end of the street was a wall of flames by this time. Instead, Evelyn was told to go to Gottingen and walk south. She hardly noticed the blood dripping from her right shoulder and from cuts on her head and neck until a girl she met said, "Your arm is falling off."

Jack Tappen and his two companions from the *Middleham Castle* assisted whomever they could. Some time after they emerged from the dry dock onto Barrington Street, they came across a house with one whole side blown in. It was beginning to burn. They heard cries for help from a woman and a man holding a toddler. The couple was on the second floor, and the young men stood underneath. Jack and his mates instructed the couple to throw down the child first and then jump into their waiting arms. One of the youths caught the child. Frightened, the woman made the man go next. Even though he landed unharmed, she was still reluctant. Then Jack saw why: she was pregnant. The rapidly approaching flames and the urgings from below helped her overcome her fears, however, and she dropped to safety.

The three young men continued on their way until they reached the Richmond Printing Company. The building's granite blocks had tumbled like toy bricks that had been kicked over. They managed to carry out a few women before the flames got too fierce, but they showed no signs of life. It was only later they realized they were probably dead. At the time, it just seemed important to get them out.

All of a sudden it occurred to Jack that he should go home as fast as possible. His mother and grandmother were alone in the house, between Gerrish and Cornwallis streets. Although it was farther away from the harbour, it might also be damaged. When he arrived, he found every window and most of the doors missing. But both women were in the basement scullery. Before the explosion they had gone downstairs to see to the cat, which was having kittens. Assuming that Halifax was under German attack, they stayed where they felt safest.

As Jack was leaving the printing works, soldiers and firemen were beginning to arrive. More than thirty employees were dead inside, includ- ing Barbara Orr's uncle David. Her grandfather Samuel Orr, Sr, was one of the lucky few left alive. Although more than seventy years of age, he had summoned the strength to heave a granite block off the book-keeper. But he could not save his youngest son, who had called for help but was trapped and out of reach. David, thirty years old, died when a huge block fell on him. His brother Samuel, Barbara's father, had not made it to work that morning. Perhaps he had stopped to watch the fire in the harbour. His body was later found near the former site of Pier 6. The third brother, William MacTaggart Orr, had not arrived, either. He had been seen standing near the Lorne Rowing Club.

Barbara, meanwhile, limped into her aunt Edna and uncle William's home, on Gottingen Street. The house was badly damaged, but at least it was not wrecked or on fire.

Her aunt did not recognize her at first. "Who are you?" she asked the strange-looking figure.

"I'm Barbara."

"But Barbara has red hair," Edna Orr said, looking at the tangled black locks. Barbara convinced her of who she was. Then her aunt asked about the rest of her family. "They're all gone," Barbara answered. She did not actually know if all her family were dead, but she felt it. Her presentiment turned out to be true.

THE ROAD
TO RECOVERY

INITIAL RESCUE
INITIAL RELIEF

IMMEDIATE RESCUE EFFORTS were largely uncoordinated, though policemen, firemen, and soldiers were on hand surprisingly soon after the blast. Vehicles of all kinds—horse-drawn drays, cars, army trucks—transported victims to the closest hospitals, where the living rubbed shoulders with the dead. Doctors and nurses had no idea what was to come. They might well have been at the battlefront.

It was impossible to make lists or find out names. A crying baby snatched from a burning house had to be taken somewhere. A woman bleeding to death could not be left until her husband came. A child badly injured on the way to school needed immediate care. There was no time to be systematic at the beginning of the emergency.

People relied on their own judgment. The night express train from Saint John, New Brunswick, the No. 10, had been about ten minutes late that morning, pulling into Rockingham soon after nine. As it approached the suburb, about two miles north of Richmond, there was an upheaval, and all the windows were smashed. Luckily no one was badly hurt. The engine driver proceeded cautiously until the track was impassable. Soon all the passengers got off the train to see how they could help. The conductor decided that the best thing to do was fill the train with injured and homeless and head back to Rockingham.

Nearly the whole Driscoll family was on that train, together with about 250 others. In fact, Cliff Driscoll had helped load the No. 10. The only one missing from the family was eleven-year-old Gordon, who had been on his way to school. Cliff had searched for him fruitlessly. Two of the family were badly injured: Mr Driscoll had a serious wound on his face and later had to have an eye removed; Art, the five-year-old, had not regained consciousness and lay limp in his mother's lap.

Barbara Orr, meanwhile, was placed on a horse-drawn fish truck and unloaded at Camp Hill Hospital, on Robie Street. Mrs Duggan and her children also arrived at Camp Hill in a horse-drawn wagon. They stayed together in the little room that contained the switchboard. William Duggan, the father, was on duty on a minesweeper in the Atlantic. When the *Mont Blanc* blew up, the crew thought that their ship had hit a mine. But then a message crackled over the radio: "Get back. Halifax is destroyed." He finally got home that afternoon, but only the house's foundation was left; the family pet, a faithful bulldog named Molly, sat on guard, howling. Mr Duggan had no idea if his family was still alive. Nor did Evelyn Johnson. An army truck stopped for her, and a soldier jumped off and lifted her into the back. She, too, was taken to Camp Hill.

Rescuers were doing their level best to put out fires, free trapped victims, and alleviate pain. Then, about ten, a panic occurred that not only threatened to undo what little progress had been made but also caused considerable suffering and probably added to the death toll.

The main military barracks in Halifax occupied a large area between Barrington and Gottingen streets at the south end of Richmond. During the explosion it sustained heavy damage and casualties. Wellington Barracks, as it was called, also contained a large well-stocked magazine with a furnace room nearby. Live coals had been scattered close to the broken wall of the magazine, and if a young lieutenant, C. A. McLennan, had not acted quickly, there might have been a second explosion. He seized a fire extinguisher and played it on the coals. Great clouds of steam and smoke rose, creating panic among those who saw them. They fled, spreading rumours of further catastrophe. The immediate danger had in fact been averted, but some feared that it might come again. Soon uniformed men toured Halifax and Dartmouth, warning of the possibility of a second explosion and ordering everyone to go to the nearest open ground.

Few disobeyed. Only those who believed they were needed stayed put. Firemen remained in their places, and hospital staff refused to budge. According to the Children's Hospital Record of Meeting book, the superintendent of that hospital stood firm. With a cut on her face, she addressed the staff: "No one shall leave this building. It would mean the death of many of the children if they had to be moved to the Commons, and it is the duty of everyone to stand by our post, and if it should be that we are to die, we will die at our post." Not one nurse in the building said a word in objection.

In no time, however, a pathetic stream of humanity, shocked and confused, was pouring through the city, heading for Citadel Hill, Point Pleasant Park, or any nearby field. The sick and injured who could not walk were carried, and many were not dressed for winter. Some clutched a baby;

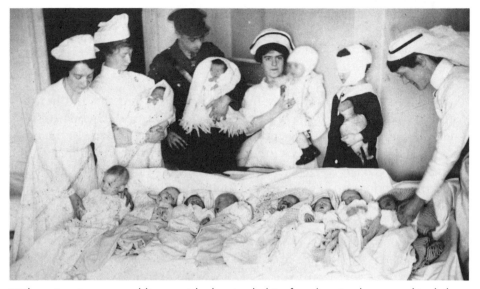

With no time to spare, soldiers snatched crying babies from burning homes and took them to hospital. (MARITIME MUSEUM/KITZ)

others a precious possession, maybe a pet. Most of those from the worst-hit areas took nothing. They just complied with the command. Strangely silent, they left their violated homes, often forever.

Many people who had transport went out to the country. The Wallace family lived on Chebucto Road not far from the North West Arm. A huge, heavy chunk of metal had landed in the garden, just missing some of them. T. J. Wallace, the father, an optometrist, loaded his wife, their seven children, ranging in age from a few months to seven years, and two servants into the car. One of the boys wanted to give up his place for the Newfoundland dog, but Mr Wallace would not let him. The family also picked up a neighbour and then drove to Tantallon, on St Margarets Bay. The journey took a long time, as Herring Cove Road was thick with people, many of them limping and obviously injured. The Wallaces could not make room for anyone else.

In the city Eileen Ryan's brothers had heard that everyone was leaving his house and going to high ground. The family was just about to set out when a group of sailors arrived. They had learned that the Ryans possessed a car, a 1917 Chevrolet, and wanted to find out whether it could still be driven. They got it out of the garage, and it started. The oldest boy, who had a licence, was asked to drive wounded to hospital. Glad to be of service, he quickly agreed. His mother had told him that before he reached home, their next-door neighbour had rushed in to see whether someone could take his daughter to hospital. The girl's jugular vein had been cut, and she was bleeding to death. No one could drive the car or even get it out of the garage, and the little girl died. How the boy wished he had been there earlier.

Mrs Ryan put some valuables into her handbag, and she and her four younger children left for the outskirts of the city, beyond Chebucto Road. They were not alone. Laura went, too, carefully carried by one of the boys. Laura was beautiful, with sleek grey feathers and a crimson tail. She was the pet parrot, which Mr Ryan had brought back from South Africa. The Ryans loved this talented bird, which could mimic bugle calls heard from nearby Wellington Barracks and which could even sound like Mrs Ryan when she put out the cat. On the way, Mrs Ryan's handbag became too heavy, and she hung it on a fence post, walking away and forgetting about it. When they returned, it was still there, untouched. Only life mattered that day, not valuables.

Frank Burford and his older sister, Winnie, made their way to the Commons, behind Citadel Hill. A soldier came by and treated the nasty gash on Frank's leg, the cut he had received from the falling timber. Still carrying his torn schoolbag, James Pattison, with his brother Gordon, was on the North Common. Someone gave them each a coat and James a stocking cap. The cap, crawling with head lice, added to his misery. He could not understand how the lice got through all the oil in his hair, but that was something else that would have to be dealt with later. Local organizations such as the St John's Ambulance Brigade, the Salvation Army, and the Red Cross were roaming the fields, handing out clothing and administering first aid.

Leighton Dillman and his family stayed in the woods above the Dartmouth shore. Ethel Mitchell was high up on the hill behind her grandmother's house.

The crowds endured at least an hour and a half of uncertainty. Then, shortly before noon, the danger passed. Volunteer troops belonging to the Seventy-second Battalion, Ottawa, had flooded the magazine at Wellington Barracks and carried most of the ammunition to the harbour and dumped it into the sea.

Finally people were allowed to leave. The crowds dispersed as silently as they arrived. Those with houses to go to returned home, and those without sought shelter elsewhere. In Dartmouth, Ruth Poole and her family had gone towards Cole Harbour, on the Eastern Shore. As she and her family walked home, they watched the incredible sight across the harbour. "The whole world was pink," Ruth recalled. "Pink arms, pink legs, pink sky, pink houses, even pink water, because the fires in Halifax were reflected in the harbour. Everything was bright."

The Pattison boys were not allowed to go down to Barrington Street, where their home had been. The fires were too severe. Instead, they decided to head for Central Wharf, near the bottom of Duke Street, where they might be able to board the sugar refinery's boat, the *Ragus,* and go to their grandfather's house, near the Dartmouth sugar refinery. They reached the wharf and waited, but no *Ragus* appeared. Finally a government boat drew in and gave the boys a lift to the Marine and Fisheries wharf in Dartmouth. There the superintendent, obviously a worried man, gruffly ordered them to clear out. Then they walked about a mile and a half to their grandfather's house, along the railway track and through the fields of the Mount Hope Lunatic Asylum. He was not home: he had gone to Halifax to try to locate the family. Their grandmother was there, and she cleaned the boys and tried to find out what had happened. Still shaken, James and Gordon could not tell her very much. They had no idea where the other members of the family were.

In time their grandfather and uncles arrived. The Acadia Sugar Refinery, they reported, was a pile of rubble, the loss of life there great. As for the *Ragus,* it had been smashed to pieces, and her crew of five killed. Of the boys' father, mother, sister, Catherine, and brother, Alan, there was no sign.

Charles Upham and his children, Millicent and Archie, along with a crowd of other refugees, had waited in a field behind Dean's Nursery, off Longard Road, until the alarm was over. Most of these people did not know where to go. Then George Grant, superintendent of Rockhead Prison, on Gottingen Street, arrived and offered shelter. Mr Upham sent Archie there and then took Millicent, whose injuries looked worse, to the Military Hospital, on Cogswell. One of Archie's aunts was also at the prison. She had to soak Archie's shirt with water to get it off because the dried blood from his head wounds had run down and glued the shirt to his skin. He was given clothing belonging to one of the Grant boys. The clothes were too big, but appearance had ceased to matter.

Still separated from his family, Reg Rasley, Archie's cousin, also spent a few hours at the prison before being taken into someone's home. He felt a bit better. "I was with people, and I wasn't afraid any more," he said.

Grant had emptied many prison cells to provide refuge for some seventy homeless people, mostly fellow parishioners of Grove Presbyterian Church. Filthy with tar, wearing bloodstained remnants of clothing, and numb with shock, they were a pitiful-looking collection.

*   *   *   *   *

The civilian city of Halifax was not well equipped to deal with a major disaster. The police force, with a chief, a detective, eight sergeants, and twenty-nine officers, had taken on eight temporary men to help handle the wartime increase in crime but was very much overworked. Members of the fire department, which suffered such heavy losses in the explosion, had been employed only on a part-time part basis since 1894, and no change had been made, though the system was altered in 1918 to employ full-time firemen.

Nor were there enough hospitals or morgues to handle huge numbers of injured or dead. Halifax and Dartmouth had four public hospitals: the Victoria General, with 175 beds, already used to capacity; the Nova Scotia Hospital for Infectious Diseases, with 200 beds; the Children's Hospital; and the small facility for infectious diseases on Gottingen Street. In addition, there were seven privately run facilities, such as the Halifax Infirmary, the largest with 30 beds, and four military hospitals, including the one on Cogswell Street, with 150 beds. There were three private undertakers in Halifax—Snow and Company, the Nova Scotia Undertaking Company, and Joseph Spencer—and two in Dartmouth.

Social services were lacking. Private organizations such as the Halifax Association for Improving the Conditions of the Poor, the Charitable Irish, and church groups carried out most of the work in this area. The Salvation Army ran the rescue home, as well as the maternity hospital. Schools for the sight and hearing impaired received grants from the provincial governments in the Maritimes, but most of their funds came from voluntary contributions. There was not even a public safety committee of the type then found in large American cities that could quickly take over emergency operations.

Against this unfavourable backdrop, the City of Halifax launched a large relief effort to begin caring for the victims of the explosion. During the evacuation to open spaces members of council and about twenty other concerned citizens met at city hall to take action. They included Deputy Mayor Henry Colwell—Mayor Peter F. Martin was out of town—Chief of Police Frank Hanrahan, City Clerk L. Fred Monaghan, former mayor Robert T. MacIlreith, legislative council member Richard G. Beazley, Mr Justice Robert E. Harris, and businessman Ralph Pickard Bell. Lieutenant Governor MacCallum Grant chaired the meeting.

The group unanimously agreed to form several committees immediately, all under the name of the Halifax relief committee. The following were

Lieutenant Governor MacCallum Grant (in the top hat) was among the first officials to arrive at city hall. His wife (seated) also helped with relief work, as did his son Eric (third from left), on leave from France. Government House (in the background) gave shelter to injured cadets. (COURTESY MARGARET GRANT)

appointed: executive, chaired by Robert MacIlreith; transportation, by Alderman F. A. Gillis; emergency shelter, by Controller Murphy; finance, by Mr Justice Harris; food, by J. L. Hetherington; and mortuary, by Alderman R. B. Colwell. The meeting adjourned in forty-five minutes, and the committees dispersed to begin work and solicit volunteers. Seldom had so much business been conducted at city hall in so short a time.

Halifax then became a hive of industry. The first task of the transportation committee was to secure automobiles to take homeless to shelters, injured to hospitals, and relief workers to damaged areas. Initially the committee could obtain only twenty-five cars voluntarily and so, without authority, commandeered others whenever possible. (At a meeting in the afternoon Lieutenant Governor Grant gave authorization.) The emergency shelter committee, meanwhile, opened an office at city hall where people offering or needing refuge could register. Members of the committee and volunteers also began touring the North End to seek out people whose homes were inadequate and to find shelter for them. In addition, this committee set up first-aid dressing stations at places such as the YMCA. (Drugstores and shelters also provided this service.) The finance committee, for its part, opened a line of credit at The Bank of Nova Scotia.

At first the food committee concentrated on arranging with wholesale-grocery firms and bakers and dairies for supplies to be delivered to Richmond, emergency shelters, hospitals, and dressing stations, and then it set up a food depot at city hall. With the three private undertakers unable to cope with, or keep track of, the large number of corpses, the mortuary committee had to find a building to house an official morgue. Chebucto Road School, outside the devastated area, or Richmond, was chosen: the upper floors could be used for offices, and the basement, for the mortuary. The building had been damaged, so a company of Royal Engineers were brought in to make the school fit for use. The men covered the empty windows and cleaned the facility. As soon as news of the location spread, bodies began to arrive. They were piled outside until the morgue was ready to receive them.

Before the hastily called meeting at city hall Deputy Mayor Colwell, Chief of Police Hanrahan, and City Clerk Monaghan had approached the military for assistance in emergency work, and they had received immediate co-operation. Colwell had also suggested that the army erect tents on the Commons for the homeless.

Soldiers from the Armouries were the first organized into action. Among them were members of the British Expeditionary Force, waiting to leave for Europe. One soldier, a young American volunteer, wrote to his girlfriend and to his brother, describing some of his experiences. More than a mile from the docks the soldiers saw pieces of armour plate from a ship, too heavy for the men to lift, and on the road they saw a ship's compass and parts of an anchor chain. The men worked among the ruins for hours, making stretchers from pieces of wreckage to carry the injured to tugs that ferried them to ships where they could be treated or given beds. A son of the lieutenant governor, Lieutenant Eric Grant, on leave from France, said that the sights were worse than anything he had seen in the trenches.

One vessel that took wounded was the American hospital ship the *Old Colony*. A hundred sailors had been sent ashore to see how they could help. They returned to the ship with two hundred seriously injured victims, twenty-five of whom eventually died. Barbara Orr's uncle, William Mac-Taggart Orr, found unconscious not far from the harbour, was on that ship, though his worried family was unaware of it. His wife, Edna, continued to search for him, and after a few days he was located.

Colonel Ralph B. Simmonds, a partner in Jas Simmonds Ltd, a large hardware firm, lived in Dartmouth. He offered his services at military headquarters, on Spring Garden Road, and was asked to supply one hundred men. About eleven in the morning they reached Halifax by boat from York Redoubt. Their orders were to clear a passage through the rubble

Lieutenant Garnet Colwell, son of the deputy mayor, had taken Gwen Westhaver to the theatre the night before the explosion. On hearing about the damage in the North End the following morning, he raced to her house, but no trace of it, or Gwen, was left.
(COURTESY LINDA COLWELL)

blocking the entire northern end of Barrington Street. As they heaved and dug, they removed bodies and odd belongings, such as a silver wristwatch with a broken strap, two notebooks with a list of deliveries from the sugar refinery, and a set of keys. Simmonds sent a messenger to his firm to bring back as many labels as possible, to tag bodies and loose objects. All known information was hurriedly recorded. Some labels told where the body or the article had lain; others gave a tentative identification. The official mortuary was not yet ready to take the dead, so Simmonds and his men piled corpses along the side of the road. Family members, meanwhile, were taking their deceased relatives to the private undertakers.

Lieutenant Garnet Colwell, son of the deputy mayor, was in charge of a similar work party, and he took a special interest in the task. Stationed at York Redoubt, he had been home on a twenty-four-hour-leave pass, and the evening before, he had taken a pretty girl, Gwen Westhaver, to the theatre. When he kissed her good night, he tasted tears on her lips. She knew he was due to leave for France shortly. The next morning his father came home and reported that it had been an explosion that had broken their windows, not a German bomb. When Garnet realized that the North End had been destroyed, he sped on his bicycle to Veith Street, but it was unrecognizable, and there was nothing left of Gwen's house. Two days later, after searching ruins for her body, he found her in the Chebucto Road mortuary.

About three hours after the explosion military and naval forces had complete emergency powers. They were acting as police, rescue workers, guards, and transport controllers. They commandeered vehicles if necessary, and they regulated movement into and out of Richmond. They had the authority to deal firmly with any attempt at looting, and many were armed.

*   *   *   *   *

Civilians from the less-affected areas of Halifax and Dartmouth dropped everything to help in the rescue effort. Twenty-one-year-old Joe Glube, who lived on Gottingen Street near North and who owned a busy tobacco and stationery store, had slept through the explosion because he had been up late the night before. His mother and his sister had wakened him, both "hysterical and covered in blood, [though] … their wounds were only superficial." Joe was a bit startled himself when he realized that the roof had caved in. They ran out of the house. A great cloud hovered to the north, and Joe thought that the ammunition dump by Bedford Basin might have gone up. Coal was being delivered next door. When the driver left the coal and took away a body, Joe began to realize that the situation was serious.

Then the Glubes were told to go to the Commons. Mrs Glube suddenly remembered she had left behind her new fur coat. Joe went back for it through the silent, empty streets, but when he returned to the Commons, the crowds were so dense that he could not find his family. He started to worry about his store and had to find out whether it was safe. Other businessmen had had the same idea. By the time Joe reached his shop, on Barrington Street, not far from city hall, people were boarding up smashed windows. He broke up some wooden crates and began doing his own. He had just finished the job when Deputy Mayor Colwell appeared on the Grand Parade. "What are you people doing?" he bellowed through a megaphone. "Do you realize there have been thousands of people killed or hurt? They're starving in the North End. We need help!"

Joe threw down his tools. "Where do we report?" he shouted.

"The Armouries. Bring transport if you have it."

Joe took his second-hand Ford off its blocks and drove to the Armouries. Because of the food committee's efforts, all the grocery warehouses in Halifax and Dartmouth had been opened, and large numbers of volunteers, including members of the Rotary Club, had begun to fill boxes with bread, butter, tea, condensed milk, cooked meat and fish, baked beans, and sugar.

Joe was told to load his car with supplies already at the Armouries and to take the food to Richmond, especially milk for babies.

As Joe drove north, he was shocked to find that the desolation began less than four blocks from his own home. In Richmond he lost all sense of orientation. Some of the area was like a desert, with no buildings standing, and it was impossible to tell one street from another. At first he was overwhelmed by all the bodies lying around, but the job he had to do left no time to be squeamish. In minutes he was actually able to move a dead body out of the way so that he could give a survivor food and blankets. On his return trip, and on many others, he filled his car with injured and took them to already-overcrowded hospitals or the YMCA or some other hastily arranged dressing station.

Joe Glube, a young storeowner in 1917, took his second-hand Ford off its blocks and delivered food to sufferers in Richmond. (RON E. MERRICK)

Two men visiting Halifax had shown extra initiative. George Graham, general manager of the Dominion Atlantic Railway (DAR), had spent the night in his private railcar at North Street Station. Although the car was damaged, no one was hurt. Graham walked the two miles to Rockingham, where he sent a telegram to Kentville, Nova Scotia, requesting a relief train of doctors, nurses, medical supplies, and forty-five DAR track men and bridge builders to repair the railway lines.

W. A. Duff, assistant chief engineer of the Canadian Government Railways, had stayed at the Queen Hotel. After the explosion he borrowed a car and drove to North Street Station to inspect the railway property. The station, a fine building with a glass dome, now stood open to the sky. The farther north Duff travelled, the worse the situation became. Several times he turned back to drive seriously wounded people to hospital, but he finally decided that communication with the outside world was more important. Once he arrived in Rockingham, he cabled Moncton, New Brunswick, relaying the extent of the damage and asking for medical and relief supplies. Later, at the request of the deputy mayor, he sent similar messages to towns in Nova Scotia and to other areas of New Brunswick.

As a result, Truro was expecting the first train of refugees, the No. 10. The train had stayed outside Richmond for most of the morning and then moved as far as Rockingham, where, about one-thirty, the conductor was ordered to take it to Truro, some sixty miles away. The Driscoll family had settled in, but the children had soon complained of hunger. Mrs Driscoll and a neighbour remembered having some Christmas cake in sealed tins. Because their houses had not caught fire, it might still be edible. Cliff went back to the site and returned triumphantly, bearing two large containers. Noble, Al, and Lou filled themselves up on the rich cake.

There was medical aid on board. A Wolfville doctor, a Major de Witt, had been on his way to Halifax for a conference when his train was stopped at Rockingham. He was rushed to the No. 10—fortunately he had brought his medical bag—and he started tending to the most urgent cases. Using only simple instruments, he even performed two necessary eye removals. He had five days of nonstop work ahead of him.

At Windsor Junction, about ten miles from Halifax, a doctor and a nurse joined the train. Finally Dr de Witt had help. He knew them, too: they were his father and his sister. Cliff Driscoll left the train at this point and headed back to Halifax to look for his little brother Gordon and other relatives.

Although the people of Truro had made preparations to receive the No. 10 passengers, they were overwhelmed by their first sight of them. A young teacher, Josephine Bishop, saw them disembark. The state of the children worried her most, black as coal and horribly disfigured. An infant with both eyes gone had also lost its parents. Miss Bishop thought that it might be kinder if some did not survive. On December 7 she wrote to her mother, in Digby:

> I hardly know what or how to write my heart is so full. Yesterday morning we were pursuing the even tenor of our ways when an awful calamity happened in our midst. School had just assembled and I was reading the Bible when two awful explosions shook the building with great force.... Thought at first that the Germans must have opened fire on Halifax. It proved to be as bad or even worse. By ten o'clock trains began to leave Truro with doctors, nurses, firemen, and fire apparatus. At noon came a call for the stricken inhabitants, and at half past three the wounded began to arrive.

About half an hour before the No. 10 pulled into Truro, the passengers on the first relief train from Kentville arrived in Halifax. Stationed at Camp Aldershot, Dr Percy McGrath had graduated from Dalhousie Medical

School in May and, like most of his classmates, had gone straight into the army. On hearing about the explosion, he and his wife, a nurse, gathered all the medical supplies they could find and boarded the relief train, together with other medical personnel and with track and bridge repairmen. Every town along the line had been notified. As the train drew in to each station, waiting passengers climbed on board, carrying bags filled with supplies. The engine driver's home was in the north end of Halifax, and the journey was completed in record time.

Soon after Rockingham the line was blocked, and the passengers had to get off and walk. They struggled through debris until they reached the northern end of Barrington Street, cleared by the military. Dr McGrath noticed bodies "stacked like cordwood," three feet high on either side, and fires dancing all around. Another doctor muttered something about Dante's Inferno. Survivors were still being taken out of basements, and people stumbled by, carrying bundles and baskets, heading for hospitals or mortuaries. Eventually the group reached North Street Station and the King Edward Hotel. The area was roped off, and soldiers were limiting entry. The guards arranged for transport to take the relief workers to city hall for instructions.

The McGraths were sent to Camp Hill Hospital, recently built for returning veterans. It was jammed. Ambulatory soldiers had given up their beds. The injured were lying in the beds, on the floor between the beds, and in any other available space. The windows were gone, and blankets covered the empty frames. The hospital was dark and cold.

Camp Hill doctors had been overwhelmed by the rush of patients. Dr Samuel MacLennan, father of Frances and Hugh, was an ear, eye, nose, and throat specialist. He had been about to operate when the explosion took place. Having served overseas, he and his team knew what to do. They picked up the patient and laid him under the operating table. Then, expecting another bomb, they threw themselves on the floor. Dr MacLennan concentrated on eye work around the clock for several days. When he finally did go home, he brought along out-of-town nurses and doctors. Frances and Hugh were soon sent to stay with relatives in Cape Breton until the emergency was over so that the MacLennan house could be used for visiting medical personnel and their mother and father were free to spend long days on relief work.

The overcrowding at Camp Hill was also hard on the patients. For some time Barbara Orr lay on a stretcher near the entrance to the hospital. The people around her seemed unnaturally still. She waited, but no one came. Finally she called out to a young orderly walking by. He was extremely startled because he had assumed that all in that area were dead. He lifted her up and carried her into a ward. It would be months before Barbara could walk without pain.

Evelyn Johnson, whose arm had been nearly severed from her shoulder, was treated without much delay, her wounds cleaned amid the confusion. At first, however, her prospects appeared grim. Her mother arrived, and a doctor told Mrs Johnson that Evelyn's arm might have to be amputated. Mrs Johnson begged the doctor to do what he could, and Evelyn's arm was saved.

The McGraths had no time to look for someone in authority. They responded immediately to urgent cries such as, "Here. Come over here!" In no time they were in the thick of things. There was bleeding to staunch, broken bones to fix, burns

Linda Colquhoun helped feed the seriously injured at Camp Hill Hospital. Shown here on her wedding day in 1924, she married Garnet Colwell. (COURTESY LINDA COLWELL)

to bandage, and wounds to stitch. The particles of wood, glass, and plaster inside the wounds made them difficult to clean. Then they had to contend with the general state of the skin. No amount of washing was effective. Soon the McGraths lost all track of time and all sense of fatigue and hunger. About six in the evening, relief workers arrived from New Glasgow. Every helping hand was a godsend: Camp Hill had only 280 beds, but an estimated 1,400 patients were admitted on December 6.

Stores of anaesthetics soon ran low. Doctors noted, however, that patient fortitude was remarkable, probably because many were still in shock. It was possible to perform certain operations without chloroform, unthinkable under normal circumstances. Anti-tetanus serum was also in short supply, so it was used only on very deep wounds. Nonetheless, only two cases of tetanus were ever reported.

A sixteen-year-old girl from the Halifax Academy was helping out at Camp Hill. She belonged to C Company, which did volunteer work to help soldiers overseas. Members of the organization had been asked to assist until professional nurses arrived. They followed surgeons around, holding bowls of water containing dissolved blue tablets, probably disinfectant. Some surgeons were removing glass from people's faces. The wounds were horrific: disjointed limbs, oozing burns, and gaping cuts. Several members of C Company had to leave, as they felt too nauseated. Not the sixteen-year-old girl, however. She stayed and even came back the next day.

The military hospitals in Halifax bore most of the burden of medical work, though civilian facilities were also swamped soon after the explosion. The one on Cogswell, like Camp Hill, was quickly overflowing. Uninjured children, especially toddlers, accompanying mothers, as well as streams of people searching for relatives, added to the confusion. It was hard to list the people admitted to hospital, so the only way to locate someone was to look at each patient carefully, and many of them, unconscious, were covered in black grime and suffered facial wounds.

To make matters worse, some facilities were severely damaged. Rockhead Hospital, which held 80 convalescent soldiers, had lost all its windows, and its steampipes had burst or broken. By afternoon, about 90 injured people had been taken in, and the soldiers had dispersed. As quickly as possible the patients were transferred to another hospital. Considering its purpose, Pier 2 Casualty Depot might have been used, but the blast had levelled it. The Pine Hill Military Convalescent Home, with 125 beds, did not fill up so quickly because it was much farther south. After transport was arranged, however, it, too, admitted sufferers. Even the civilian hospital in Dartmouth, the Nova Scotia Hospital for Infectious Diseases, had been damaged. It had lost all its windows, and the ceiling of one ward had fallen in. The small number of patients were transferred to another building, and in the afternoon 150 injured were being treated there.

*   *   *   *   *

The damage lessened outside Richmond, but almost no building in Halifax had gone unscathed: the relief committees calculated that 1,630 had been destroyed and 12,000 damaged, leaving 25,000 people without adequate housing, not to mention the 6,000 who needed shelter, as their houses had been demolished or rendered completely uninhabitable. The evacuation to open spaces had prevented people from tending to their homes, but by afternoon they were finally able to start making their houses, or at least one room, as weatherproof as possible. Those who had delayed installing storm windows now fitted them—if they were lucky enough to find them intact. Stores selling building materials quickly ran out of tarpaper. Cardboard, carpets, blankets—anything that came in handy—covered windows and gaps in the walls. Jack Tappen, from the *Middleham Castle*, cut up a roll of heavy brown paper from his mechanical-drawing class to cover the missing window panes in his family's house.

The Ryan boys shovelled out the debris from a bedroom that had only one window. They nailed a blanket over the space and brought in an oil stove for warmth and for heating water to wash the grime off themselves. On a wall one picture remained, the Immaculate Heart of Mary. Mrs Ryan remembered a bottle of rum, salvaged from a torpedoed ship by her brother. She used the contents now to rub her children, to try to bring some warmth to their chilled bodies. After Eileen stopped feeling cold, the pain in her shoulder grew even more severe. It had troubled her all day, but there had been no time to have it treated. It was at an odd angle, and her mother bound it tightly. That made it less uncomfortable.

Those whose homes were gone found refuge with friends, relatives, and even complete strangers. The Reverend William Swetnam and his daughter, Dorothy, went to friends in Dartmouth. Mr Swetnam had to borrow the fare for the ferry. His money had disappeared with his clothes. The Reverend Charles Crowdis and his children, Jean and Don, stayed in another manse; Joe Glube, his mother, and his sister, with relations.

The Mitchell house, in Dartmouth, was in bad shape. Ethel's father had returned by ferry from Halifax, where he was a partner in the heating-engineering firm Mitchell and MacKay. His wife and daughter were eventually taken to a doctor who cleaned and sutured Mrs Mitchell's badly cut arm. Ethel was still not fully aware of what was going on around her. Then a young friend, Edwin Morash, well known to her parents, appeared in his car. He suggested that Ethel accompany him to his parents' house in Woodlawn and stay there until the Mitchells could find somewhere to live. Ethel was bundled into the car, and off they went. Other friends, from Cole Harbour, offered Mr and Mrs Mitchell a room in their house. Mrs Mitchell went, but Mr Mitchell stayed at the house. During the afternoon he boarded it up as best he could and then decided to camp out in it, to protect his property from looting.

Leighton Dillman, also in Dartmouth, stayed with an aunt and an uncle who lived next door. One room was in fairly good condition. More than twenty people squeezed into that room: there was not too much sleep for anyone that night.

In Truro most of the passengers from the No. 10 were taken to the academy, the courthouse, the fire hall, the civic building, and the old William Street school—all prepared as shelters with medical treatment available. Most of the Driscoll family went to the courthouse, but Noble

The tent city on the Commons remained largely unoccupied on the night of December 6.

and Al went to the experimental farm by horse and cart. They had jumped at the offer, thinking that a farm would be fun. That is, after they had attended to their most pressing need. The first thing the boys had done was look for a washroom where they could throw up quantities of Christmas cake mixed with black oil and dust. Before they nestled between clean sheets that night, however, both boys had a long hot bath and a good scrub.

By nightfall most of the homeless people had found some sort of shelter. The emergency shelter committee had been offered a number of buildings that could be used as temporary hostels: St Paul's Hall, on Argyle Street; the Academy of Music, on Barrington; the Strand Theatre, on Sackville; and the Knights of Columbus Hall, on Hollis. The transportation committee had moved five thousand people, but some, not yet found by rescue squads and their wounds untreated, remained with the pitiful remnants of their houses, crowding apathetically into tiny unsuitable spaces. For others, railway boxcars, halls, schools, and church basements all gave asylum.

About nine the Engineering and Ordnance Corps finished putting up the tents on the Commons, including temporary hospital accommodation for 250. The tents were equipped with canvas floors, cots, blankets, and oil stoves. Medical supplies and personnel waited, but patients refused to be transferred there. Nor did many uninjured occupy the tents that night. After the events of that morning tents probably seemed much too flimsy.

The military had worked long and hard all day. Then an American troop transport, the *Von Steuben,* arrived in port and discharged a work party. Two hundred and fifty fresh, eager sailors were more than welcome to replace exhausted workers. (Ironically the ship, the former *Kron Prinz Wilhelm,* had belonged to the North German Steamship Line. It had been seized in an American port at the outbreak of the war and later had been taken over by the United States Navy.) Relief supplies and workers, including firemen and fire equipment, also arrived from Moncton, New Brunswick, and Amherst and Springhill, Nova Scotia, giving local men a chance to rest. Some of the hoses, however, were a different gauge and could not be used. (This later led to the standardization of fire hoses throughout the province.)

That night few homes contained all their residents. Families split up in the confusion felt lost, and hallucinations were common. The cuts and bruises were much easier to bear than the feelings of loss and bereavement. Even so, a curious detachment was prevalent among the refugees. Many of the seriously injured died during the night. At the same time, babies came into the world in the cold and the discomfort of temporary shelters or overcrowded hospitals. Premature and still births had been brought on by shock, falls, and injuries. Fires and torches gave heat and light in the devastated area, now without power of any kind. Candles and oil lamps also cast a kindlier glow on disfigured faces.

NO REST FOR
THE BATTERED CITY

DAYLIGHT ON FRIDAY, December 7, crept slowly through heavily overcast skies. Anyone who remembered the Maritime forecast for Friday in *The Halifax Herald* of December 6 would not have worried unduly: "Moderate westerly winds. Fair and colder." *The Amherst Daily News* had offered a more pessimistic outlook: "North and north-west winds. Mostly cloudy and cold. Local snowfalls near the Nova Scotia coast."

Unfortunately the Amherst newspaper was closer to the truth, though still much too optimistic. As the day wore on, an increasingly ferocious blizzard hampered emergency work and penetrated every tear and crack in the makeshift repairs to the houses. The morning also brought sensational headlines in local newspapers. "HALIFAX IN RUINS," proclaimed *The Morning Chronicle*. "HALIFAX WRECKED," announced the *Herald*. The *Herald*, in fact, produced only a hand-printed bulletin. Every window in its building on Argyle Street, in the city centre, had been blown out, and the printing press filled with broken glass.

By afternoon the streets were clogged with snow. The narrow tracks cleared through the rubble of the devastated area were quickly blocked. Troops now had the added tasks of shovelling snow to try to keep a passageway open and of digging through deep drifts covering the ruins to find what lay underneath. In the harbour high winds caused great turbulence, loosing ships from their moorings and flinging around wreckage. Despite the violent storm, naval crews worked to secure drifting vessels and to remove heavy flotsam endangering shipping. The British *Picton*, its cargo of ammunition still on board, was being tossed around in the heavy waves. The ship was moved to the Eastern Passage, beyond Dartmouth, the next day.

The telephone service had been severely disrupted by the explosion. Lines were down, and poles had been snapped off throughout Richmond.

The day after the explosion the worst blizzard in years struck Halifax, bringing further misery to the stricken city.

The main toll lead had been blown to pieces, cutting off all communication to the north and the east of Halifax. By one o'clock on December 6, there had been limited service, and repair work was under way. By night two hundred of the eight hundred disconnected lines had been cleared. The blizzard on December 7, however, knocked them out of commission again and seriously delayed resumption of normal service in the less-damaged parts of the city. The telephone company requested that until the end of the emergency, only urgent calls be made. The cable between Halifax and Dartmouth had been badly damaged, probably by the *Imo*. An attempt was made to lay a new cable, but the storm forced its abandonment.

The snowstorm, raging throughout Nova Scotia and New Brunswick, slowed down relief trains or stopped them altogether and stalled repair work on the lines. Deliveries of food, fuel, and blankets became harder and harder. The weather discouraged people from seeking medical attention, and exhausted relief workers had to struggle to get home for an hour or two of rest. The transportation committee's report outlined some of the difficulties. Practically every car eventually broke down, and for those rescued from snow drifts, there was no safe, protected building to accommodate them. Even horse-drawn sleighs had difficulty getting through.

Nevertheless, relief volunteers persevered. The St John's Ambulance Brigade, for example, began district visiting, and the Red Cross supplied 150 voluntary aid department (VAD) nurses to military hospitals. The

British sailors helped search the ruins for bodies and effects.
(CITY OF TORONTO ARCHIVES/JAMES, 2449)

Halifax School Board promised to mobilize public-school teachers to help in the relief effort. City council and a group of citizens once again convened to plan the day's strategies. As the blizzard was beginning to rage outside, four more committees were created: clothing, chaired by Mrs William Dennis; medical relief, by Lieutenant Colonel Paul Weatherbe, of the Royal Canadian Engineers; fuel, by Richard Beazley, a member of the legislative council; and Dartmouth relief, by A. C. Johnston. In addition, Arthur S. Barnstead, secretary of Industries and Immigration and deputy registrar general of Nova Scotia, was appointed chairman of the mortuary committee, with Alderman R. B. Colwell continuing as vice chairman. Barnstead's father had performed a similar task after the *Titanic* disaster some five years earlier. The Chebucto Road mortuary opened later that day, and the City agreed to pay private undertakers for coffins and burial.

The clothing committee began its job in earnest. It set up a clothing and footwear distribution depot at the Green Lantern Restaurant downtown. Like all buildings used by the committees, it had to be repaired and cleaned. Once the committee opened the doors, however, there was heavy two-way traffic: one line up of people donated clothing; the other took it. Meanwhile the fuel committee secured supplies of coal to deliver to homes, shelters, and hospitals. "Lack of warmth," Richard Beazley wrote, "would have added another cross to the already heavily burdened."

The Dartmouth relief committee received aid from the Imperial Oil

Company. The company turned over three bunkhouses for use as shelters, and about two hundred people moved in. It also donated ten thousand dollars and provided a trained nurse and some caretakers.

The previously formed committees continued their work. The emergency shelter committee converted more buildings into temporary living accommodations that had cooking facilities, and food-committee volunteers, as well as restaurants such as the Tally-Ho and the Green Lantern, provided supplies. In a short time twenty-one shelters were set up in places as divergent as the Union Jack Club and the Salvation Army barracks. These, in addition to private homes and to refuges in other towns, housed and fed approximately six thousand people in the week following the disaster. The food committee secured more depots near the affected area, such as St Matthias Hall, Alexander McKay School, and the Oddfellows Hall. Food began to arrive from outside Halifax; for example, Christie Bros, an undertaking company in Amherst, Nova Scotia, filled many of the coffins it supplied with food before shipping them. As well, registration of survivors became more centralized, though it was still haphazard and done by many of the committees. Card files were kept at city hall and the YMCA, and in Richmond, volunteers with notebooks trudged from house to house.

During the afternoon additional volunteers drove to every badly damaged home in the North End to persuade the inhabitants, particularly the elderly and the ill, to leave for places where they would be more comfortable in the violent storm. By evening most of those cars lay abandoned on the roadside, but many lives had been saved, and nearly one thousand more people had been accommodated.

Joe Glube, with his Ford, had reported to the Armouries again. He was asked to assist a doctor in administering first aid. Dr Philip Gough was not a physician, but a veterinarian. He and Joe went from house to house, dressing wounds. If Dr Gough thought that a case was too serious for him to handle, he made arrangements for transport to a hospital. Often they drove people themselves—through the blinding snow. In the hospitals physicians and nurses such as Dr Percy and Mrs McGrath hardly knew what day it was. There was a never-ending stream of patients.

In the meantime, despite the storm, Prime Minister Sir Robert Borden arrived at city hall by sleigh. He had been attending meetings in Prince Edward Island in preparation for the upcoming federal election. (Voting for this election did not take place in Halifax. As a result of the explosion, it was first postponed, and then two candidates withdrew, allowing the other two to be elected unopposed.) A native of Nova Scotia and a former Halifax lawyer and MP, the prime minister had cancelled all further meetings when he could not get accurate news of the damage. He promptly met with city council and promised whatever federal assistance was necessary. Mr Justice Robert Harris, chairman of the finance committee, reported that about $30 million would be needed to rebuild the broken city. Subsequently he and Borden launched a nationwide appeal for funds.

*   *   *   *   *

One of the most pressing matters, blizzard or no blizzard, was locating missing victims. The snow, heavy and damp, clung to the clothing and blurred the vision of rescue workers who searched ruins with cold, stiff fingers. More than three hundred servicemen worked continuously, giving up only when another group marched in to replace them. People were still probing the remains of their homes, but their hopes of finding anyone alive grew less and less.

There were miracles. Late in the morning a soldier, Private Benjamin Henneberry, thought he heard a sound from the cellar of a house in the Flynn Block, where his family had rented an apartment. His wife had been buried for five hours the previous day before being rescued and was now in hospital. Five of his children were still missing; two had survived. In response to his shouts for help, troops rushed to assist. Under the still-smouldering debris they found a girl of about two. She was under a stove and sheltered by the ashpan, burned but alive. The rescuers and Henneberry, who had just returned from overseas, assumed she was one of his children. Given the state she was in, it was hard to make out distinguishing features. News of the discovery spread and lent urgency to the searches.

Several days later the child was lying in Pine Hill Military Convalescent Home when she saw someone she recognized. She cried out, and the woman turned around, stared for a minute, and rushed over to the bed. It was the little girl's aunt. She hugged the child and then noticed

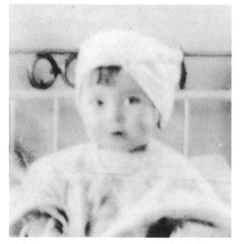

Little Annie Liggins was a miracle child. Twenty-six hours after the explosion she was found alive under the rubble of a collapsed apartment building.
(COURTESY ANNIE LIGGINS WELSH)

that there was a label on the cot with the name Henneberry on it. "That is not a Henneberry child. That is a Liggins!" the aunt cried. And so it was. The little girl, who had endeared herself to the staff with her happy nature, was Annie Liggins. The Liggins family had rented an apartment in the Flynn Block near the Henneberrys. Annie's mother and brother had been killed, and her father was serving in France. Annie Liggins, now Annie Welsh, still treasures a photograph of herself in hospital. On the back is written, "Annie Liggins. (ashpan baby). Rescued after being buried for 26 hr under debris of house. Compliments of Co. Sgt Major Davies. Machine Gunner. 63rd. H.R." According to newspaper reports, Davies had been in charge of the party that had dug Annie out. Although she was too young to remember him, he must have visited her in hospital and taken the photograph.

Having found his wife and children in Camp Hill Hospital the day before, William Duggan was trying to trace his relatives. Life was more static in 1917, and it was common to find one generation of the same family living near another. Mr Duggan went first to his mother's home. Her body had been dug out of the ruins and set aside to be taken to the mortuary. Soldiers were still shovelling, and next they found his brother's wife, holding her baby in her arms. His father, brother, and two sisters were also brought out. Other relatives had been killed not far away.

With his son, Archie, in Rockhead Prison and his daughter, Millicent, in hospital, Charles Upham had gone by sleigh to search for his relations. It seemed he had lost a large number of them. That afternoon his father-in-law, Archibald Rasley, was buried at Fairview Cemetery, after a brief service conducted by the Reverend Charles Crowdis. Mr Rasley's son was the only relative there. The others were dead, in hospital, or searching for those who might be alive.

Many spent the day plodding from hospital to hospital, with the mortuary always a last resort. The heavy snow hindered tired, aching limbs and blinded eyes already dimmed by tears. Crowds surrounded newspaper offices, hoping for information. Already lists of the dead had appeared in *The Morning Chronicle*. The lists of the missing were even longer. It was especially difficult for families that had lost men working at the waterfront. Some men seemed to have disappeared, possibly swept away by the tidal wave. It is not easy to determine to what extent the wave contributed to the deaths and the damage. A soldier who was detailed to work in the devastated area wrote to his father: "Down by the waterside ... [there was] not enough left to make a fire. Besides it was pretty well soaked and buried in mud from the bottom of the harbour."

Reporters were going to all known shelters and hospitals and compiling lists of survivors. This was a time-consuming task, as thirty-six official locations and many private homes had to be checked. Jim Gowen's father, with *The Halifax Herald,* was one of them. When a reporter located someone believed lost, it brought a flash of pleasurable excitement. Generally, however, it proved a harrowing experience, even for a hardened newsman. Surrounding towns that had received victims promised to send names as soon as possible.

For those waiting for news or waiting to be found, every hour seemed to go on forever. James and Gordon Pattison still did not know what had happened to their father, brother, or sister. Their grandfather and uncles spent the day searching and at last found the boys' mother, taken to the YMCA by an American sailor. She was badly injured, but the discovery gave the boys a little hope for the others.

Barbara Orr, in Camp Hill Hospital, watched silently as people filed through the ward looking anxiously for a familiar face. Would anyone look for her? Helena Duggan had seen her father, and she was feeling well enough to walk around. She passed the time wandering through the hospital to see what was happening. She looked into a bucket and saw human eyes. That finished her curiosity.

In Truro, Noble and Al Driscoll received no information about their brother Gordon, and they felt lonely being separated from the rest of their family, at the courthouse. That morning, when Al got up, Noble stared in horror at the bedclothes, spotless the night before. "I thought you had a good bath the same as I did," he said indignantly.

"So I did," Al retorted, but a bit worried. Then Noble moved, and Al cried, "Just look at your own side of the bed!" The sheets and pillow slips were completely soiled with oily soot. It would take many baths before the boys were clean again.

The blizzard was still raging at nightfall. Sixteen inches of snow fell on Halifax on December 7, but at least it softened the starkness of the blackened ruins. Once again people huddled together for warmth. Eileen Ryan and her family, in their one room, received supplies of food, delivered by flat wagon, and later in the day were taken to the Majestic Theatre, on Barrington Street near Spring Garden Road. There they had the use of a backstage dressing room, and Eileen slept on a pile of army blankets. With other children billeted there, it was fun playing on the stage, where they had never been allowed to go before. The Ryans were soon moved to the Knights of Columbus Hall, behind Government House. Meals were served by Red Cross volunteers in the grand council chamber, big enough to be a ballroom. Eileen's shoulder still troubled her, and she stood up to take her meals, as it was more comfortable. That refuge did not last long, either. The next was much farther away. They were taken to Antigonish, on the way to Cape Breton. Even the aisles of the train were crowded for the long ride. The young man next to Eileen had lost his entire family, and it made her feel that she had got off lightly. As they travelled up the side of Bedford Basin, Eileen, wearing mismatched clothing from the Red Cross, looked back at Halifax. Flames burst from under some of the ruins. On arrival in Antigonish they were escorted to the Royal George Hotel. At last Eileen's shoulder received professional attention. Her collarbone had been broken, and had started to knit improperly. A retired physician named Dr MacIsaac rebroke and bound it so that it could heal normally. Eileen suffered less discomfort after that.

Ethel Mitchell was settled into the Morash household, in Woodlawn, and the numbness of shock gradually disappeared. Lieutenant Commander Percy Ingram, who had taken Ethel to the party on the HMS *Highflyer,* had gone to Hester Street, but the Mitchell house was boarded up, and there was no sign of the family. He asked around and finally went to the police. He found out she was alive but, in the chaotic conditions, could not contact her. His own naval duties, with nine crew members of the *Highflyer* dead and fifteen others injured, were demanding, and his ship was due to sail with the delayed convoy in a couple of days. Ethel later tried to find out where the *Highflyer* was so that she could get in touch with him, but no such information was given out during wartime. Months elapsed, and finally she received a postcard from him saying he was just about to go into hospital but giving no reason. She heard no more.

Bertha Bond and her sister, Ethel, who had helped rescue the Reverend William Swetnam and his daughter, were staying with distant relatives in the South End. Bertha, in a letter to her fiancé, summed up the feelings of many others: "We can hardly realize yet what it means. So many of our friends and relatives are gone, and … all our end of Halifax is … burnt to the level, but we are looking at our trouble with never a waver because there are so many worse off than we are."

*   *   *   *   *

The severe weather, rare in the Maritimes until after the New Year, did not let up for several days. On the morning of December 8 the snow stopped, and a few flickers of sunshine appeared in the afternoon. But it was only a brief respite. On Sunday, December 9, it changed from winter to spring, causing a sudden thaw and turning sixteen inches of snow into filthy slush. All movement became laborious and uncomfortable. Houses developed leaks, and more hasty patching had to be done. The transportation committee had to secure more teams of horses to try to keep things moving, but they were so slow that the narrow streets were in danger of becoming completely clogged. A number of women volunteers now kept a lunch-room at city hall open day and night for the drivers. Sunday was normally a day of rest, but it had been decreed a normal working day because of the emergency.

Monday, December 10, brought another violent snowstorm. It seemed that there would never be any relief for the battered city. Cold temperatures succeeded the blizzard, but people were thankful that at least nothing fell from the sky.

The war took a back seat. The news that Jerusalem had surrendered to Britain occupied a small, insignificant paragraph in the newspaper. Casualty lists from overseas were much shorter than those from the explosion. Blackout restrictions were forgotten, and leave for all servicemen had been stopped. No further embarkation for Europe was to take place until the end of the emergency period, which lasted until December 27. The Dominion government then suspended local call-up until February 4, as all males were needed to help restore services. Large numbers of men were still required to search among the ruins, hacking at ice with picks, digging through the snow.

Soldiers were told to shoot, if necessary, anyone attempting to steal from unattended houses or shops or from the dead, and newspapers warned that transgressors would be shot if they resisted arrest. Wild rumours circulated. The body of a looter was supposedly seen hanging from a lamp post. No doubt some with criminal intentions profited from the situation, but no record exists of anyone being shot. Chief of Police Frank Hanrahan, on the evening of December 9, said he had heard of one case of possible attempted burglary. By December 12 a mounted armed guard surrounded the devastated area, bolstering the number of troops already screening move-ment through Richmond. Passes were issued to anyone with official permission to enter and had to be shown. Otherwise entry was forbidden.

Anti-German feeling also ran high. Somehow or other, it was felt, the Germans had been responsible for the tragedy. On December 9 sixteen people of German birth were arrested. Since the outbreak of war they had been reporting to the police once a month. Following a military inquiry that day, some were released; others, in a few days. Windows of one or two houses whose owners had German-sounding names were smashed, but there was really too much to be done to waste time on revenge.

Most citizens had come forward to offer assistance. Women who had always relied on maids now worked harder than they ever had. They helped in hospitals, made home visits, did clerical work for relief committees, and took in victims and out-of-town relief workers. Canteens set up for the military and for relief workers were staffed by volunteers, largely women. There were no more dinner or bridge parties, and the usual pre-Christmas entertaining was forgotten. Theatres were closed, and restaurants helped supply meals for the homeless. Leisure activities were, for most people, a pre-explosion luxury.

There were others, however, who took advantage of the situation. Some tradesmen adhered to union rules and demanded overtime rates for extra work. Bricklayers refused to allow plasterers to help repair chimneys, as it was bricklayers' work by union rules. Some landlords allowed their unoccupied properties to be used free of charge, while others demanded exorbitant rents. Some merchants did not charge for goods, while others boosted their prices. On December 12 Deputy Mayor Henry Colwell issued a proclamation warning that profiteering would be rigorously punished. People were encouraged to inform on transgressors, but the only reported conviction was that of a soldier accused of selling relief supplies.

Lists of the missing and the dead continued to appear in local papers. Families clung to the hope that a loved one might have been taken to an unknown destination. December 8 saw hundreds of names of those in the different hospitals. "Barbara Orr, Camp Hill" was one of them. Later that afternoon, as she scrutinized every face that went past, Barbara saw one that was familiar, her aunt from Dartmouth. Barbara called out, "Aunt, it's Barbara." The woman looked doubtful. "I'm Barbara Orr."

"Oh, no, no, you're not Barbara. She has red hair." That bright-red hair was always a distinguishing feature. Barbara's was still black, and her face was cut and discoloured. Her aunt came to her bedside, almost afraid to put her arms around the girl for fear of hurting her. She arranged to take her niece home to Dartmouth, though Barbara could still not walk without assistance. Later her uncle told her that most of her family had not yet been found and that it was assumed they were dead. Unknown to Barbara, another uncle, William MacTaggart Orr, was also at Camp Hill, taken there from the USS *Old Colony*. He was not fit to be moved until December 13, and later he identified some members of her family. Barbara worried about the two little ones. Maybe they were somewhere but could not tell their names. The house had burned to the ground, so it was unlikely, but the thought often haunted her.

On the same page as Barbara, "Mrs V. Patterson" was listed at the YMCA, where her father had already found her. The name was misspelled: it should have read "Pattison." As soon as she became well enough, her father took her to his house in Dartmouth to be with her two sons. Her hand had been

City of Halifax No. 11258

Pass for Devastated Area

Allow Bearer within Devastated District

NAME _____

FRANK HANRAHAN
Chief of Police

Anyone with official permission to enter Richmond received a special pass.
(COURTESY NELLIE ADAMS)

badly injured, crushed and cut, and blood poisoning developed. It required medical attention for a long time, but she did regain the use of it.

Near Mrs Pattison's listing, there was a notice: "Pattison Allan [*sic*], 8 years old, missing. Pattison Catherine, 10 years old, missing. Pattison, V. J., missing, adv. R. F. Grant, Victoria Road, Dartmouth." The advertisement appeared for the next four days. On December 12 it was announced that Alan had been identified at the Chebucto Road mortuary. A day later Catherine's body was found. Both children were identified by Mrs Pattison's brother. But there was still no word of Mr Pattison. Hope was fading rapidly, and Mrs Pattison grew more despondent every day.

On December 9 *The Morning Chronicle* asked for help in locating the missing. A large number of sailors had not been accounted for—many never would be. Three members of the Burford family were listed: Elsie, age nine, Lou, age thirteen, and Frank, the father, age forty-four. Charlotte Burford, the mother, was very ill. It took some time to sift through the ruins of Flynn Block, where the family had lived, and approximately sixty people had been killed there. Eventually the two children were identified, and on December 10 Mr Burford's body was recovered at Hillis & Sons Foundry. It was fortunate that the younger Frank had been sent on an errand.

A paragraph concerning the Driscoll family appeared on December 12: "Walter Driscoll, 1549 Barrington Street, his wife and several children are in hospital in Truro. Wife and children practically uninjured. Driscoll's injury is severe. Enquiring for Gordon Driscoll, 11 years old, who is reported to have been seen by several people. If any information is received I will be pleased to have it communicated to me. H. O. MacLatchy, Truro." Gordon was never identified, and it was months before Art, the five-year-old, who had been unconscious on the train, recovered the power of speech.

For weeks advertisements filled the pages of Halifax newspapers. The following are some examples from December 13:

The owner of the girl baby about 2 months old which was handed to a young lady on Gottingen Street, being previously picked up on Almon Street by a soldier, in a pasteboard box covered with an older child's check coat, can get same by applying at 1461 Shirley Street.

Missing. Donald Cameron. Answers to Donnie, 4-1/2 years, fair hair, dark grey eyes. Wore red sweater or night gown. Was moved on first ambulance from Roome Street on Thursday morning. Father anxious.

Would the soldier who rescued baby from unconscious woman's arms on Longard Road the morning of the explosion return baby to its parents, 9 Longard Road.

On December 16 Bertha Bond once again wrote to her fiancé. She described her friends' houses: one whole family was living in the kitchen; another house did not look too bad from the outside, but inside, the door frames were out of place, mantels had been thrown across the room, and glass stuck straight out of the walls—"just churned up." A friend was grieving dreadfully, as her son, who had been at the Richmond Printing Company, had not yet been found. Another had just had word that her daughter was alive in Truro.

Then came a real cry from the heart. Bertha had received a Christmas card from Sandy, and it was one of her most cherished possessions. "You know that is now the only letter of yours I have," she wrote. "Those little things you sent me for safe keeping, and all you had given me but my ring are gone, and I did prize them so much."

The loss of possessions seemed of minor importance at first, and those that meant most were often the ones that could not be replaced. Cameras were rare in 1917. Families usually had professionally taken photographs of special events such as weddings, but few had snapshots. Many survivors were left with only memories of their loved ones. Barbara Orr, for example, had not one photograph.

RELIEF FROM
NEAR AND FAR

IT WAS DIFFICULT for the rest of the world to find out exactly what had happened in Halifax. With telephone and telegraph connections broken, information came in driblets and was often inaccurate. Some out-of-town newspapers received their first telegraphic news via Havana, Cuba. Radio stations on the Atlantic coast were under strict wartime regulations, and wireless communication had proved unsuccessful. After they did manage to restore partial service, both telegraph companies, Western Union and Canadian Pacific, were restricted to official messages only. As soon as those restraints eased, the wires carried press messages all over the world. Sometimes they were distorted—casualty figures ranged from fifty to fifty thousand—but a more accurate version was soon released.

Over the following weeks financial aid from many places poured into Halifax. The Dominion government appropriated $6 million (its contribution would ultimately reach $18 million). The Strand Theatre in Truro donated a day's ticket sales. The Australian government gave $250,000; the City of Chicago, $125,000; and the Province of Ontario, $100,000. Britain was especially generous. The Imperial government voted £1 million, then worth $4,815,000. The Lord Mayor of London set up a subscription list, and results were printed daily in *The Times*. The fund eventually reached $600,000. The British Red Cross gave $125,000, and King George V sent a personal donation of £5,000. On December 20 it was announced in *The Halifax Herald* that the Compagnie Générale Transatlantique, owner of the *Mont Blanc,* had donated $10,000. Local newspapers reported financial gifts from Newfoundland (still a British colony), the West Indies, South America, China, and New Zealand, as well as other parts of North America and the United Kingdom. Sir John Eaton, president of T. Eaton Co., arrived in Halifax with his own train, food, sleeping car, staff, and medical unit. He opened a clothing and supply depot that carried building materials and other necessities. All goods were given free to anyone with a requisition from their pastor or a committee chairman, and the staff was made up of experienced, efficient department heads. Although the exact amount of Eaton's contribution was never calculated, it certainly ran into the six figures. Many others sent practical gifts such as clothing and furniture. Relief of all kinds was arriving hourly, as were letters of sympathy and offers of assistance and accommodation from as far away as Vancouver and Washington, D.C., not to mention nearly every town in Nova Scotia. Indeed, relief committees had to request that donors check with them first before sending more supplies.

Boston displayed tremendous generosity, holding various benefits and memorial services. The *Herald* later outlined the history of "ancient ties of blood and kinship," which explained Boston's "splendid outburst of help and sympathy for this city." At a luncheon Harry Lauder, Scottish singer and comedian, pledged $1,000 of his own money; other guests donated a further $1,203. Dame Nellie Melba, Fritz Kreisler, Dr Karl Muck, and the Boston Symphony Orchestra gave a concert for "The Relief of Sufferers from the Recent Disaster in Halifax." It began with the American national anthem, followed by the overture "In Memoriam" by Sir Arthur Sullivan.

What first comes to mind for most survivors, in fact, is the instant and unstinting aid from the State of Massachusetts. That government subsequently contributed, in both goods and money, a total of more than $750,000. On receipt of the news of the disaster, about eleven on the morning of the explosion, Governor Samuel W. McCall sent a telegram to the mayor of Halifax offering unlimited assistance. Naturally, as all wires were down, he did not receive a reply. That afternoon a meeting of the Massachusetts public safety committee, composed of one hundred men from all parts of the state, was held. By ten o'clock that same night a fully equipped train was ready to leave. A. C. Ratschesky, vice president of the public safety committee, was in charge of the expedition. A prominent banker, he was now devoting all his time to the war effort. On the train were thirteen surgeons and doctors (all members of the Massachusetts State Guard), six American Red Cross representatives (each with a different specialty), nurses, railroad officials, representatives of the press, and quantities of medical supplies.

About ten-thirty the train left Boston. The passengers had no idea what lay ahead, but when they arrived in Saint John, New Brunswick, they soon found out. Ratschesky immediately wired Boston for a trainload of glass, putty, and other building materials. Relief workers from Saint John joined the train, bringing along further medical supplies.

FOOD

FIRST AID
CLOTHING
BEDDING

HALIFAX

G. BAXEY.

(HALIFAX HERALD LIMITED)

John F. Moors, chairman of the Boston Red Cross civilian relief committee, together with his colleagues, had spent the first part of the journey working out a plan to supplement the organization of relief in Halifax. It was agreed that certain areas would need addressing, in particular, care of the homeless, the sick, and the injured, as well as specialized supervision of children and rehabilitation of victims, especially the handicapped.

According to a report of J. Prentice Murphy, secretary of the Boston Children's Aid Society, Mrs Frederick H. Sexton joined the train at Saint John. She had been at a meeting, had heard news of the disaster, and was now anxious to return home. Her husband, principal of the Nova Scotia Technical College, was also the eastern Canada vocational director for rehabilitation of returned soldiers, in charge of fourteen hospitals for handicapped veterans. As a result, Mrs Sexton, involved in the Canadian Red Cross and various other organizations, was familiar with city institutions and its health and welfare problems. She provided names of people who could help with rehabilitation, and she emphasized the importance of Halifax as a military port.

To illustrate the type of situation the city was capable of handling, she recounted a terrible tragedy that had received no newspaper attention. A British ship carrying West Indian troops had twice lost a rudder and had been carried ever farther north. Many of the men had suffered frostbite and the ship had to dock at Halifax. Some 350 amputations, mainly of feet, had to be performed. These soldiers, who had never reached the battlefield, were now being re-educated in vocational hospitals in eastern Canada.

On the way from Saint John to Halifax, people stood at every station, eager to board the train. Doctors and nurses were given preference, and soon every place was filled. Snow and gales also met the train, and heavy drifts caused stoppages. Then the engine broke down, delaying it even further. On Folly Mountain, difficult terrain about seventy-five miles north of Halifax, the railway line was completely blocked. When the purpose of the train was made known, every man in the area got to work, shovelling, ramming, and using brute force. Amid loud cheers, the train finally got through. It arrived in Rockingham early on the morning of December 8 and made its way slowly around the city, along the barely finished tracks to the South End Station, therefore avoiding Richmond.

Work began almost immediately. All painters and glaziers were asked to attend a meeting at the city engineer's office to discuss plans for reconstruction. Meanwhile Lieutenant Colonel F. McKelvey Bell, the new chairman of the medical relief committee and the head of military hospitals in

Halifax—along with some local doctors and an American major named Giddings, who had come on the train—searched for a suitable building to convert into a hospital. They chose the Bellevue Building, on Spring Garden Road near Queen Street. It was home to the Officers Club, and hardly a window or door was intact; the pipes had also burst from the cold. In the next few hours American sailors and Canadian and British soldiers worked wonders. That night the American hospital of Bellevue, Stars and Stripes flying, opened its doors to sixty patients. In twelve hours its operating room was the scene of complicated surgery. Charlotte Burford, Frank's mother, had arrived for treatment, still unaware that her husband and her two younger children were dead.

As Bellevue was being made ready, other members of the Boston party toured Richmond. They watched as rescue workers dug through the mounds of snow. J. Prentice Murphy later jotted down some of his impressions in his report. He was struck by one sight in particular: "A team of horses was caught in the full blast of the explosion and probably killed outright through suffocation, yet they were partly erect and covered with a sheathing of ice so that the horses looked like a piece of statuary."

On the afternoon of December 8 about fifty people met at the City Club, a social club in downtown Halifax. Prime Minister Sir Robert Borden attended, together with the mayors of Halifax and Saint John, prominent citizens, including leading clergymen, A. C. Ratschesky, and the members of the Massachusetts Red Cross. They reviewed the current state of relief organization and discussed ways to enlarge and streamline it. One of the Americans' suggestions, quickly followed, was that other buildings be used for committee offices, as city hall had become extremely congested.

In response to a suggestion from former mayor Robert MacIlreith, the group agreed to appoint a managing committee to co-ordinate relief work. MacIlreith was made chairman; businessman Ralph Bell, secretary. Twenty other Haligonians joined as members. In addition, a registration committee was created, and it soon compiled all the previously assembled files and printed detailed forms enabling the recording of comprehensive information and the arranging of appropriate relief. Eventually it organized an index file that was divided according to street; the registration forms were sorted by number.

Medical and general supply committees (a medical supply depot had already been opened, at the Nova Scotia Technical College) were added to the list. A reconstruction committee was also formed. A lawyer, G. F. Pearson, was named chairman, and an army colonel, Robert S. Low, was made manager; members included owners of local construction companies.

This committee, the largest, had an enormous task ahead of it. It immediately began maintaining detailed ledgers that summarized, street by street, the damage to individual properties. The ledgers also listed the state and assessed value of each one before the explosion, as well as the amenities, such as sewage and water systems, and whether it had had a finished attic or a cellar. It would be some time before all the information could be compiled and an accurate assessment reached.

Furthermore, a temporary employment bureau was opened. It soon received more than six hundred applications for paid positions. Five hundred people were placed, including housekeepers, carpenters, teamsters, stenographers, glaziers, and nurses. The bureau also collected names of volunteer workers.

By the end of the City Club meeting there were twelve committees. Members had changed, and so had several of the original chairmen, some of whom were now on the managing committee. (Boston relief workers became advisers.) At first women were not to be on any of the committees, even though a few were already members. Clergymen insisted, however, and names were added. A list of the committees and their members, including office addresses and telephone numbers, was released to the press.

*   *   *   *   *

The medical relief committee, formed the day before, had urgent work to do. Of the more than nine thousand injured victims, the majority received attention in twelve emergency dressing stations and in doctors' offices and through home visits. More than twenty-five hundred people packed local hospitals. (Others were in surrounding cities.) On December 8 Dr Percy McGrath was on his third day at Camp Hill, and the first rush of emergency patients was still being treated. When a doctor relieved him, he spent a few days making home visits by sleigh before returning to Camp Aldershot.

Given these conditions, the opening of emergency hospitals was essential. Eight were opened altogether, providing beds for about one thousand patients. Besides the USS *Old Colony*, a Truro facility, and Bellevue, the YMCA, the Halifax Ladies College, and St Mary's College were in operation as hospitals by December 9. One in New Glasgow, Nova Scotia, opened the day after, and the Waegwoltic Club, in Halifax, was receiving patients by December 24.

Buildings such as the Halifax Ladies College and St Mary's College,

By the end of December the medical relief committee had opened several temporary hospitals, providing beds for approximately one thousand people.
(MARITIME MUSEUM/KITZ)

already equipped with kitchens, dormitories, and bathrooms, were better suited to this purpose. In one day the ladies college—now known as the Maine Military Hospital—was cleaned, with tarpaper fitted over windows and stretcher beds put in place of desks. The domestic-science kitchen was converted into a dining room, and the science laboratory transformed into a spotless operating room. The college catered to 159 patients.

On December 9 Red Cross ambulances discharged more than one hundred injured victims. Doctors, nurses, and Red Cross volunteers worked to heal the sick, while many of the college's teachers, students, and maids stayed on, cleaning, cooking, and making bandages. In a few days the senior corridor became home to the first baby at the college, born in Room 34. He was moved to the new nursery, and he and his mother stayed until early January. He was well supplied with warm clothes when he left.

To staff the emergency hospitals, and to supplement personnel in permanent facilities, Halifax relied on hundreds of doctors and nurses from out of town. American doctors, numbering 120, worked mainly at Bellevue, at the ladies college, and on the *Old Colony;* 102 Canadian physicians came from other cities, mostly in Nova Scotia and New Brunswick. The number of nurses from outside was even higher: 459. Every one of them was needed. Lieutenant Colonel McKelvey Bell later reported that 522 eye and 224 fracture cases had been treated and that more than 250 eye removals and 25 amputations had been performed over a period of about two weeks. These were only the tip of the iceberg, however: his figures did not include similar cases treated in doctors' offices. The state of the injured left many relief workers with gruesome memories. *The Halifax Herald* told of one doctor from Sydney, Nova Scotia, who could not deal with the tragedies of the explosion. When he returned home, he talked incessantly of the horrors he had seen. Unable to keep them in his mind any longer, he committed suicide.

Once emergency hospitals opened, patients were transferred to facilities whose treatment was more suitable. Millicent Upham went to St Mary's College. She needed additional attention for her facial wounds, including her empty eye socket. Her brother, Archie, joined her there. His head injuries were much more severe than they had first appeared. During an operation lasting eight and a half hours, doctors removed twenty-two pieces of glass from the boy's head. Then they inserted a silver plate, a new technique only used overseas at the time. Two years later, when taking out the plate, doctors found another piece of glass.

Evelyn Johnson, her shoulder on the mend, had been moved from Camp Hill to the YMCA. An uncle visited her there. "It's a pity about your father,"

Archie Upham (centre) was later taken to hospital, where doctors removed twenty-two pieces of glass from his head.

(COURTESY HELEN UPHAM MATHESON)

he said. Evelyn looked puzzled, and he quickly changed the subject. When her mother came in the next day, she was wearing black, and Evelyn realized what her uncle had meant. Her father had been killed at Richmond railway yards, but a few days had passed before he was found, and identified by his older son. Evelyn's other brother, Jerry, had been seriously injured and was in another hospital. Her mother and the older boy, meanwhile, were living in a room at a cousin's house. The Johnson home was no more than a heap of ashes.

A few of the relief committees were still setting up distribution depots around the city. The clothing committee, for example, opened five centres in Halifax and Dartmouth, with the one at the Green Lantern Restaurant remaining as headquarters. Trains and ships were delivering full loads of clothing and footwear. So much footwear arrived, in fact, that the committee had to introduce a special department at the Royal Mail Steamship Company on Granville Street.

Leighton Dillman, in Dartmouth, picked up a new overcoat at a school. "Boy, did I look sharp!" he recalled. "It was grey herringbone tweed, a lot better than the new one I had lost. There was one mass of clothing in the room, and all volunteer help, of course. I just took one look at that coat, and that was that."

Helena Duggan went to the Green Lantern. "I got a black imitation-sealskin coat," she said. "I was so happy with it. And I had a stocking hat." Helena and her sister Bessie were staying with different families in the South End, Helena with a kind woman named Mrs Eaton, and Bessie at a doctor's house. Sometimes children who needed only a little medical treatment had been sent to hospital with a badly injured mother. The hospital was no place for them, and they lived temporarily with other families. "These were good people who came around just till we got organized better," Helena said.

"Mrs Eaton kept me for quite a time. She was lovely."

Ten-year-old Jean Hunter, a Richmond School pupil, lived in a boxcar at the Willow Park railway terminal for twelve days, as her home on Agricola Street was badly damaged. One corner of the car was a makeshift bathroom enclosed by a curtain. Boards, beds, a stove, and dishes, cracked and broken but usable, were along one wall. "It was too high to get in and out," said Jean, "so we just stayed in—my grandmother, my mother, my brother and myself, my aunt and her boy, all in one boxcar." They did have an outing, however, to St Mary's Hall for some necessities. They spent one night there, had a bath, and got some clothes. Her aunt received a lovely, warm coat, and Jean a pretty corduroy-velvet one. It was much too long but better than the combinations she got, which were so tight that she could hardly sit down. She wore the coat on her journey to Massachusetts, where she stayed with relatives for six months, until her family's home was repaired.

Some victims were astonished by the generosity of individuals. Al and Noble Driscoll, now with their mother, were still in Truro. They looked much better, except for their hair. Mrs Driscoll gave them a dollar to go to a barber and have it cut. When the barber touched Noble's head, he winced. The man looked more closely. "Ah, you're from Halifax," he said. He spoke briefly to the other barber, who was just about to start on Al. They gave the boys a comprehensive treatment: one shampoo, then another, all done extremely gently. Occasionally the barbers removed small splinters of glass and wood. Another customer arrived but was turned away. After a while Noble got worried. All they had was a dollar for all this work. Finally the men seemed satisfied. When Noble timidly held out the dollar, his barber laughed. "Follow me," he said. He took the boys over to the clothing store across the street and bought each one a complete outfit. When they tried to thank him, he just patted their shoulders kindly.

At first the committees that managed the distribution of clothing, food, and fuel enforced few rules and kept no records. Then they took a more organized approach. Clothing, for example, was sorted into departments, and efforts were made to control its distribution. It proved difficult. Richmond residents had lost everything, and they needed complete outfits. With damaged houses in other parts of Halifax and in Dartmouth, as well as bad weather, half the population had been left without adequate apparel. The clothing committee's report of February 1, 1918, showed just how difficult regulation had been in the first few weeks: "We had applications for clothing from those who were not entitled to it, but rather than hold up the work of relieving the sufferers we felt it better to clothe everyone by accident than to allow one of the sufferers to go without." Although all committees stressed the concept "charity, not relief," some victims were too proud to ask for help. Volunteers tried to ensure that all needy got their share of the bounty. Before long, people had to present a requisition form to get clothing. Soon the food and fuel committees followed suit and introduced their own safeguards. By the end of December the rehabilitation committee gave out purchase allowances, stopping distribution of food and fuel altogether.

The rehabilitation committee had been formed on December 12 to deal with the welfare of people, not property. At its first meeting, on December 13, the chairman, Dougald MacGillivray, manager of the Canadian Imperial Bank of Commerce, announced the probability of a royal commission being established

Jean Hunter lived in a boxcar for twelve days. She eventually became a secretary for Colonel Ralph Simmonds, in charge of military rescue work after the explosion. (COURTESY JEAN HUNTER)

to study the whole problem of restoring the city. (After two weeks J. Harry Winfield, general manager of Maritime Telegraph and Telephone, became chairman.)

From its establishment, the rehabilitation committee encompassed the registration committee, which now employed 121 people, more than half paid by their own organizations, and used 250 volunteers. The workers canvassed every house, hospital, and shelter—the aim was to register every affected family, not only those requiring relief. Up to January 31, 1918, the workers completed 4,953 registrations. Although they tried to visit each household only once, duplications did occur, and complaints were often heard about the multitude of well-meaning visitors, not always welcome in stricken homes.

The severe weather in the ten days after the explosion hindered the work of the emergency shelter committee. More than forty cities had offered accommodation for the homeless; for example, Lunenburg, on the south shore of Nova Scotia, pledged food and shelter for five hundred; Berwick, in the Annapolis Valley, offered to take thirty orphans; and Montreal volunteered three 5-room flats, rent free until May. With the high number of family fatalities and injuries, in addition to the desire to look after property interests, the majority of homeless preferred to stay in Halifax or in nearby towns. As a result, the emergency shelter committee, in conjunction with the reconstruction committee, concluded that repairs to the exterior of houses that could be made inhabitable should be done first. Frozen mortar, high winds, blizzards, and sudden thaws, however, created arduous conditions for workmen. Approximately eight hundred people with no alternative had to stay in shelters that were hastily fitted with cooking and sanitation facilities. Eight thousand more remained in damaged houses or went to other homes. The chairman of the committee subsequently reported that in the first two weeks after the explosion 16,700 blankets and 1,800 quilts had been distributed.

Not only the human population of Richmond had been left homeless. Many animals had suffered the same fate. The Society for the Prevention of Cruelty (SPC) had been working from the start, destroying those animals injured beyond help, giving or finding shelter for others, and repairing barns. Horses, cows, pigs, and hens, as well as dogs and cats, needed protection. SPC accommodation was soon overflowing. People were asked to take in an animal or to offer spare sheds or barns for others. The Boston Society for the Prevention of Cruelty to Animals sent two inspectors and one thousand dollars, and donations marked for animal care arrived from many other sources. Cliff Driscoll found the family cow in the care of the SPC, but when he claimed her, he was asked to contribute to her board and lodging. Cliff demanded to know what had happened to the cow's milk yield and was finally allowed to remove her without payment.

*   *   *   *   *

Throughout the month of December help continued to arrive daily. Army units and other provinces and towns provided motor vehicles, and the Ford Motor Company of Canada donated three touring cars. The transportation committee, at the height of its work, received as many as three thousand calls a day for automobiles and roughly twenty-five hundred for teams of horses and trucks.

On December 12 the *Calvin Austin*, from Boston, docked with $200,000 in supplies, as well as glaziers and engineers. The *Northland,* also from Boston, arrived soon after with a cargo worth $100,000.

Among other relief workers who came were repairmen and operators for the telephone and telegraph systems. As news of the disaster had spread around the world, messages, incoming and outgoing, flooded the wires. By the night of December 9, in spite of the deplorable weather, three hundred telephone lines were restored, and emergency lines were hooked up to all the relief centres. From then on, the service improved daily. For days people lined up outside the St Paul telephone office, on Salter Street, anxious to make long-distance calls to worried relatives. Operators worked incredible hours, so relief was happily received.

Western Union, even with twelve extra operators, could scarcely handle the volume of telegrams, which averaged five thousand a day during December. Bertha Bond sent a cable to Sandy Wournell, her fiancé. The telegram, "SAFE WELL BERTHA BOND," reached him in Boulogne, France. In the early days some cables took strange detours. From certain parts of Canada, the most direct route to Halifax was through London, England.

Leo Campbell, twenty-one years old, worked in the Western Union office on Hollis Street. "We worked night and day," he said. When the lines were down in the first few days after the explosion, a man took outgoing telegrams by train to Truro. There he picked up the ones for Halifax and brought them back on the next train. Then the problem of locating the recipients began. Boy scouts, and youths from other organizations, had been asked to help find them. But they needed passes to enter the devastated area: the military was not too keen to have message boys wandering around. If an official Western Union worker, not a young volunteer, tried to make a delivery, he might be permitted past the guard line. Once inside Richmond, the worker first had to find the street. Then, if houses were still standing, he had to search for the number. If no one was there, he tried other ways. "We would ask the neighbours and anyone we saw," Leo recalled. When that failed, they went to the office of the information committee, set up on December 10 to keep track of the whereabouts of survivors. "We would deliver to shelters and wherever people were," he said. "If that did not work, we would put notices in the papers, with the names of the people. The telegrams came for years—people not hearing and then thinking that their relative might have been in Halifax. We really did our best to locate someone who could find the right person."

The 1918 Halifax City Directory illustrates vividly the problems in finding addresses. For Barrington Street it lists all the names and addresses on the southern end. Then, at number 1190, at the edge of the northern end, or Richmond, it stops. Instead of numbers are two words, "Devastated Area." Other whole streets—Rector, Roome, Russell—have the same description. Not a single house number is given.

WHAT ABOUT
THE CHILDREN?

A S THE DAYS WENT BY, special problems became evident. More than fifty old people whose homes and families had been wiped out were discovered in various emergency shelters. Some could go to relatives in other places, and others to the Home for Aged Men or the Old Ladies Home.

Even more serious were the cases of numerous children. Many had been orphaned, and more had lost one parent. Countless others, with parents hurt or homeless or permanently disabled, were being cared for in shelters or in private homes, and children suffering from injuries were in hospital. Registration of the injured, the homeless, and the dead was taking place with some speed but was much less effective for children than for adults. Identification of infants, for example, was often difficult, and tragic mistakes were occasionally made. Amid the initial confusion unauthorized adoptions even took place, causing years of uncertainty and misery. This practice was quickly stopped, and appeals were made for the return of such children. Most cases were probably resolved, but it has never been established how many there were.

On December 11 a special children's committee was formed to deal with the grim situation. Given his background, Ernest Blois, provincial superintendent of neglected and delinquent children, was named chairman. He had written a code that became legislation giving the Province fairly sweeping powers to remove children from homes that were considered unsatisfactory and to place them in institutions. Altogether, there were thirteen people on the committee, including a doctor and two judges. Each children's institution was asked to send a representative, and a number of teachers from city schools were invited to take part. Social workers from Boston and Toronto gave advice. The committee, part of the rehabilitation committee, was to make every effort to reunite children and parents or

The Protestant Orphanage was eventually rebuilt, and many explosion orphans ended up there. (PANS)

Children needed warm clothing for the cold winter nights in damaged homes.
(MARITIME MUSEUM/VAUGHAN)

relatives and to avoid the permanent placement of normal children in institutions.

In 1917 there were half a dozen orphanages in Halifax, financed largely by private donations and churches. There were two Protestant homes: the Protestant Orphanage and the Halifax Infants Home. (The Protestant Orphanage had been destroyed in the explosion, but it soon reopened in temporary accommodation and was eventually rebuilt.) And there were four Roman Catholic institutions: the Home of the Guardian Angel, St Joseph's Orphanage for Boys and Girls, St Patrick's Home for Boys, and the Monastery of the Good Shepherd. Not all children in these institutions were orphans but for many reasons needed care. If parents were alive, they had to pay board, usually three to four dollars a week, depending on the child's age. The war, with so many fathers away in the forces, had seen an increase in the orphanage population. If a mother had died, a father, unable to cope, might board his children for a time. Adoptions did take place. One stipulation was that the religion of the adopting family match that of the natural parents.

The plans of the children's committee, though admirable, took longer than expected to put into operation, and unhappy situations continued. J. Prentice Murphy, from Boston Children's Aid, recorded some examples in his report:

> 1) Three Protestant children, full orphans, in good physical condition. No place was open to them so they continued to stay in a very unsatisfactory hall where there were numbers of detached adults as well as family groups.
>
> 2) Families of children who were well, but whose parents were ill or injured. e.g. Four children, mother dead, father blind. Three children, father dead, mother badly injured; the children very attractive and very ill at ease in the crowded shelter where they lived.

Sometimes mothers or children were maimed or killed and fathers serving overseas, but compassionate leave was not granted speedily. One woman with four children had been living in the heart of Richmond while her husband was away. Three of the children were killed, and the fourth was never found. The mother was unconscious when removed from the ruins and spent time in hospital with a concussion. She later tried to trace her lost child but never did. The uncertainty increased her nervous depression. In August 1918, still tense and run down, she had not yet seen her husband. He had applied for leave but, like so many others, seemed to have been overlooked.

Blois, chairman of the children's committee, drafted his first report about three weeks after the explosion. The work undertaken by the committee during that time would daunt even today's social workers with their more sophisticated techniques:

> After effecting an organization the Committee has been dealing with the following matters: *first*, getting urgent temporary repairs made to existing children's institutions, *second*, investigating cases to ascertain if children were in proper custody and being properly cared for, *third*, procuring necessary articles of clothing, etc. for children, *fourth*, hunting for "missing" children, identifying "unclaimed" children, and restoring children to their parents, *fifth*, interviewing hundreds of people who were (a) hunting for lost children, (b) wishing to adopt homeless children, (c) arranging for the care of children, *sixth*, attending to a large correspondence mostly regarding the adoption of children,... *seventh*, arranging for and supervising the transfer of children from hospitals, shelters, etc., the Committee in most cases having sent someone to accompany the children, *ninth* [*sic*], arranging for temporary maintenance, permanent care, pensions and compensation or allowances for children, including finding of permanent homes, *tenth*, locating and referring to the proper agencies a number of wounded children, *eleventh*, getting possession of children unlawfully taken possession of by improper persons, *twelfth*, arranging for the proper guardianship of certain children.

By the end of December the committee, working closely with the registration committee, had come into contact with 500 families and more than 1,500 children. Of those children, 200 had needed hospital treatment for injuries, 8 others were completely blind, and 48 were suffering from eye injuries. In 13 other cases the mother had been blinded, and the fathers of 3 more had lost their sight; 4 others had been left with a serious physical handicap. The explosion had created 70 orphans, 120 motherless children, and 180 fatherless children. In 111 instances the father was overseas, and in some of these the mother had been seriously injured or killed. There might well have been others whose cases had not yet come before the committee.

Serious injuries sustained by parents meant that children had to be boarded by the committee until a parent was fit to cope again. Often, in this case, either the father or the mother had been killed. A father, alone and having to work long hours, sometimes found it more convenient to board his children and to visit when he had time.

Circumstances that did not fit the usual categories also emerged.

Grandparents frequently took children whose parents were dead or separated, and some of these grandparents had been killed in the explosion. "Coloured or feeble minded orphans," the committee believed, constituted a special problem that would have to be dealt with. Some children who had lost a mother or a father already had a step-parent. Special provisions or proper guardians would probably be necessary for many of them as well. The "disobedient or incorrigible" boy or girl would need to be considered in a different light.

The committee, furthermore, wanted to protect the children from the social ills of the day. For example, parents were often inclined to put children out to work at too early an age, and it was possible that conditions after the explosion would increase this tendency. This held little promise for the future, when the child could be left without proper education and with few means of earning a livelihood. The children affected by the explosion, Blois and his colleagues believed, were owed more than any other victims:

> In conclusion we would point out, it is a comparatively easy thing to dispose of children. Almost any one would give a child food and clothing and no matter how poor the food, how ragged the clothing or how unfit the shelter the child will soon regard it as a home and respond in character to its environment. Change in family life most wonderfully affects the character and physique of the child. Therefore, it is of great importance to fully realize now, before it is too late, the tremendous change which this disaster has wrought in the lives of so many Halifax children, and to provide, in so far as human wisdom can, every safeguard, every advantage and opportunity for the children.

*　　*　　*　　*　　*

A month after the explosion the children's committee compiled an annotated list of eighty names. It appeared in local papers under the headline "INFORMATION WANTED REGARDING MISSING CHILDREN." Persons with knowledge of the whereabouts of these children were assured that all communications would be kept confidential. A few of them were found, but most of the names appeared later on a list of the dead in the 1918 Halifax City Directory.

Three of the children described belonged to the Moore family: Hazel, age nine, Gerald, age five, and Hilda, age six months. On the morning of the explosion they had been at home, on the harbour side of northern Barrington Street, with their mother, grandmother, and aunt. The burning *Mont Blanc* seemed to be pretty close to their window. Then a man banged on the door and yelled, "Get out! That ship is going to explode!" But the

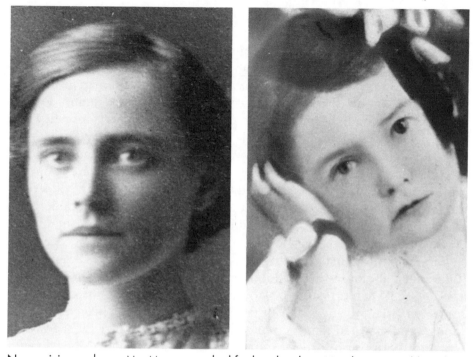

Never giving up hope, Mrs Moore searched for her daughter, Hazel, son, Gerald, and baby, Hilda, for years. (COURTESY PEARL MOORE CLATTENBURG)

warning came too late to do much good. The grandmother and aunt took the children and rushed to the door while the mother grabbed some clothes. Just then the *Mont Blanc* exploded. The mother was pinned under the wreckage, and soldiers later rescued her, but they did not find any more bodies. Her husband, an amputee who had lost both feet in an industrial accident, was working at North Street Station, and he was, surprisingly, unhurt. As soon as she left hospital, the mother scoured Halifax for her children. Her hopes soared when she read the names Hazel and Gerald Moore on a ledger from a ship that had given refuge to survivors; Hilda was just a baby and could not have given her name. But that was the only trace of them. The mother, never giving up, travelled for years to different parts of Canada and even to Massachusetts—to wherever she heard that Halifax children had gone. "Maybe they are living with someone. If they are, I hope she is being good to them," Mrs Moore would say to her daughter, Pearl, who was born after the explosion. Although their names were on the 1918 list of the dead, no bodies were ever found, and no proof of death ever established. "Had I known they were dead," she would muse, "I could have put it to rest in my mind." But it haunted her all her life.

For the first few weeks the committee's work was temporary in nature. Children were placed as satisfactorily as possible, but permanent arrangements and supervision would be essential. The committee wanted orphans to go to private homes if at all feasible, but with housing conditions as they were, it sometimes seemed better for a child to be placed in an institution temporarily, not a crowded, insanitary, and poorly heated home. People who wanted to adopt, relatives or others, were carefully investigated, especially if the child was permanently handicapped in any way. Sometimes it was possible, if a brother or a sister was old enough, for orphaned siblings to continue to live as a unit. In one family, for example, where both the mother and the father had been killed, the eighteen-year-old girl took over the responsibility of three younger children. Relatives who became legal guardians sometimes felt that the child was better off in an orphanage, and they paid the required board.

The committee first tried to place orphans with relatives even if the children did not know them. Blood ties, it was felt, would ensure a happier upbringing. When orphans had no next of kin in Halifax, the committee contacted distant relatives. In one family, two children had been orphaned, and it was discovered that the only relatives lived in an east-coast town in Scotland. With war in progress, investigation was difficult. Nevertheless, letters were sent to the relatives and to local authorities. In the end the Scottish family was considered unsatisfactory.

Some relatives were not acceptable for other reasons. The registration form for one soldier's family read: "Daniel, soldier, killed. Mary, his wife, missing. Anna, 9-1/2, O.K. Kathleen, 11, missing. Helen, 7, missing. Ethel, 5, killed. Gerald, 3, killed. Michael, 1, killed. Everything destroyed." Relatives from another town offered to take Anna, and committee inquiries produced satisfactory results. The child went to stay with them, but one question had not been resolved. Were they the same religion? It turned out they were not, and the local church made objections. The child was brought back to Halifax to the appropriate orphanage.

Only after all avenues had been exhausted would the committee consider placement outside the family. Even though it took time, committee members wrote to children's welfare societies or to organizations such as the Red Cross to secure information and to ascertain the suitability of a family before a child was released.

Newspaper reports, many with exaggerated estimates of the number of children left parentless and destitute, aroused public sympathy. More than one thousand offers to adopt explosion orphans came from all over North America. Children with blue eyes and fair hair were the most sought after. One gentleman was willing to take two healthy children, a boy and a girl, aged ten to twelve, with happy dispositions, good family backgrounds, and pleasant manners. However, children with red hair, turned-up noses, or weak chins, he intimated, would not be welcome. An official from a southern American state wrote, "Send fifty colored girls at once." This request could certainly not have been filled. Nor would it have been considered.

From Charlottetown, Prince Edward Island, came a telegram dated December 14: "HAVE SIXTY PRIVATE HOMES FOR CHILDREN MOSTLY PROTESTANT/SOME FOR PERMANENT ADOPTION/REST WILLING TO HOME INDEFINITE TIME." Charlottetown authorities even offered to send a committee to handle the situation.

Some requests were touching. A Dutch immigrant living outside Edmonton, Alberta, wrote, "I hope you excuse mine writing but I am only four year in Canada ... and I cannot explain myself the way I wanted, but I do feel sorry for all the poor little ones. Please let me know, I was an orphan child myself and know what it is, to be without a home." A letter from a couple in Pittsburg, Texas, explained that as they had given their only boy, a nineteen-year-old, to the navy, they wanted to take one or two orphans and raise them as their own. They had considered Belgian war orphans but decided that Halifax children were more in need of help. The only stipulation was that the children should not be afflicted in any way or have any tuberculosis in their backgrounds. Tuberculosis, in fact, was a commonly mentioned fear.

A nurse who had come from Calais, Maine, to assist in relief work was asked to speak of her experiences when she returned home. After her talk, about a dozen families came forward with offers of good homes, and the nurse offered to make immigration arrangements.

Committee members answered every letter or telegram. Although some people, who requested strong boys, obviously wanted only cheap labour, most applications were sincere.

Despite the flood of requests, the committee decided that homes in Nova Scotia were preferable, as the children would be among their own people and the province would not lose its youth. It would also be easier to maintain supervision. Generally, those orphans who did leave the province went to close relatives or moved at a later date.

A high proportion of children were fortunate to be legally adopted by caring relatives or suitable families. They made the necessary adjustments and settled down. Some had a choice of several homes, as uncles, aunts, and grandparents came forward. Barbara Orr was old enough to choose where she wanted to go. She had offers from three families of relatives, and she decided to live with her aunt Edna and uncle William MacTaggart Orr, who had children about her own age. She completed her education with her cousin and friend Gladys and felt as if she had found another brother in her cousin Bill. She never forgot her sad experiences or losses, but she did not dwell on them. "Sometimes," she said, "it seemed as if it had all happened to someone else."

Other orphans, less well placed, had no chance to settle happily. In the emotional aftermath of the explosion relatives hastily offered a home, only to find later that they could not cope with extra children. Behavioural problems sometimes arose, or houses were overcrowded. Once in a while children moved from relative to relative, and brothers and sisters were frequently split up. The results were often unhappy, and orphans ended up in institutions, which, in many instances, provided a more stable life. Some children's lives were always unsettled and difficult: they could not hold down a job or maintain a steady relationship. Perhaps the children's committee tried too hard to place the children with relatives or in Nova Scotia. Some of them might have been much better off with one of the kind, genuine offers from farther afield.

IDENTIFYING
THE DEAD

FROM ABOUT NINE in the morning, when it opened, until ten at night, when it closed, the mortuary in the basement of Chebucto Road School drew thousands of anxious searchers. Every day mortuary workers issued lists of identified bodies and detailed descriptions of the unidentified to all local newspapers. Some people may have recognized a name or a description; others were doing the rounds to find missing family. They checked the newspapers, the shelters, the hospitals and, finally, the morgue, which one *Halifax Herald* reporter described as "a place of soft going feet and lowered voices."

A soldier or a volunteer worker escorted each person to the mortuary. If the seeker was female and obviously distressed, a sympathetic woman accompanied her. To keep out the morbidly curious, a volunteer interviewed each person before permitting entry. Once inside, people first studied the unclaimed bodies considered easily identifiable. Next, as the sheets were gently lifted, they gingerly scanned the less-recognizable bodies. Finally, they examined the effects and the descriptions of bodies mutilated beyond possible recognition. The morgue released no body without a burial permit. No vague "I think it might be my brother-in-law" would do. In the days immediately following the explosion, not finding a loved one brought fresh hope that he or she was still alive. But as time went on, people felt relief when they identified someone and could give the person a proper burial. Mourning and sorrow are usually better dealt with right away, not always kept at bay.

Initially every morgue in the city had been filled at random. In a few days, however, administration became methodical, with the Chebucto Road mortuary as the official morgue. Under the able direction of provincial civil servant Arthur Barnstead, the difficult work of the mortuary committee was carried out largely by military personnel and by volunteers. An embalming professor, R. N. Stone, and an undertaking expert, A. A. Schrister, came

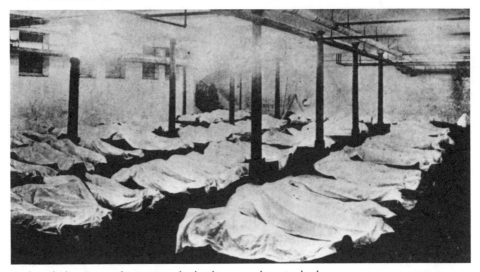

At the Chebucto Road mortuary the bodies were kept in the basement. (MARITIME MUSEUM)

from Toronto, and they took charge of mortuary procedures. Many bodies were embalmed, especially those of children who were not too disfigured. So many people were injured and in hospital or had been taken to other cities that the mortuary committee wanted to keep bodies for as long as possible in order for identification to take place.

The committee placed a notice in local newspapers stating that all deaths other than in hospital had to be reported. It also asked all private undertakers to send unclaimed bodies to Chebucto Road. The bodies were stripped and washed with water from nearby homes. (Although the school had been hastily repaired, the water supply was not yet reconnected.) Clothing was kept if possible, but most of it was in too bad a state. Everything found in pockets, all rings or other jewellery, and all objects collected from the vicinity of a body were placed in a carefully labelled cloth bag. Many of the bodies sent from hospitals did not have effects or clothing with them, and this added to difficulties in recognition. The effects, the descriptions, and the bodies themselves were all given the same number, and every effort was made to identify corpses, with office workers upstairs filling out specially prepared forms on each one.

Mortuary workers tried to be as exact as possible about where the body had been found—both the address and the actual spot. They also noted approximate age and any pertinent remark. In many cases, only vague assumptions could be made. Descriptions such as "3 lots from … Veith Street, possibly Mrs … and two children" were common.

Meanwhile rescue squads—working with five members of the mortuary committee, under the direction of aldermen R. B. Colwell and W. G. Foley—attempted to label every body: "Lady at N. W. corner of basement, Flynn Block. Lying with children." The snow and the wind and the rain, however, blew labels away or erased the writing. Often workers could not determine how many bodies there were, so they resorted to general descriptions such as "charred remains." Relatives, too, carried pathetic remnants of humanity to the mortuary in all sorts of containers. They did not know what else to do. One tag read, "Remains of three or possibly six bodies brought in a clothes basket." Another said, "Two or possibly three children." The sadly essential tasks of the mortuary workers, most of whom were soldiers or volunteers, not professionals, were difficult and distressing.

Troops were not relieved from the gruesome duty of removing bodies from the ruins until January 11, 1918. Along with the bodies, they were instructed to gather all personal effects lying nearby. Assigning belongings to corpses was not easy. One team of soldiers, for example, dug through a basement of a two-storey house inhabited by six families. It had collapsed and burned. A packet of letters, bills, and receipts had, surprisingly, escaped damage and was lying near a child. It was sent with the boy. Someone from the same church identified the boy and the rest of his family, and all were buried at Mount Olivet Cemetery. As there were no close family members left alive, the contents of the mortuary bag were never claimed, and the papers stayed in the child's cloth bag in the mortuary. They had actually belonged to a woman, Irish by birth, whose body had probably been in the vicinity, as had that of her only child, a girl. Her husband was in France and reached home four months later. Safe after two years in the trenches, he now had neither a home nor a family. Because the papers had remained as the effects of the child who had been buried in December, the man never saw them. Would the soldier have wanted his own affectionate letters, so much cherished by his dead wife? Would he have received any comfort from them and from reading the poem she had cut out of a newspaper and kept with them? Each verse ended, "The song he sang in the trench that night,/Was the song of a girl back home."

Strict sanitary conditions prevailed in the mortuary, but for public health reasons, bodies could not be held indefinitely. On December 17, ninety-five unidentified, badly charred bodies were buried. The corpses had been carefully numbered and described, and their places of burial had been noted in the event that a relative did turn up and want to visit the gravesite. Some of these bodies had carried only one clue to their identity: "No. 548. Charred remains of man with part of collar unburnt. Mark on collar—

Tooke—17—Hunt Club. Laundry mark thought to be R 106 or S 166. Buried Dec. 17, 1917. Fairview." The mortuary kept the piece of collar in the man's numbered bag in case of future identification.

The effects of others offered a more complete picture: "No. 480. Headless. Age uncertain. Brown or blue sweater. Heavy blue pants. Black and white undershirt. Heavy grey socks. Black working shoes. Effects. Keyring with four large keys. Penknife. Crucifix and Roman Catholic emblem. Buried Dec. 17, 1917. Mount Olivet." The emblem found on that man's body determined where he would be buried. Catholics were laid to rest at Mount Olivet, off Mumford Road, and others, nearly all Protestant, at Fairview, off Windsor Street.

The funeral held on the afternoon of December 17 for the ninety-five unidentified dead took place in the Chebucto Road schoolyard. The weather was similar to that of December 6: cold, clear, and calm but with snow-covered streets. Before the service began, a haze settled over Halifax, softening every hard outline. About three thousand people gathered well before 3:30, when the service was due to start. The crowds stretched more than a block on either side of the school. They waited quietly, many of them wondering whether any of those charred heaps of bones were all that was left of their own loved ones. While soldiers carried the caskets, each surmounted by a wreath, from the mortuary and laid them in rows, the band of the Princess Louise Fusiliers played the funeral march.

A Protestant service was held first. Led by the band, the huge crowd sang, "O God, Our Help in Ages Past." In his address the Anglican archbishop of Nova Scotia said, with great feeling, "It is not by the hand of the Almighty these unfortunate human beings have suffered, but by the mistakes of others." He also reminded his listeners of the importance of caring for the children who had survived. The audience was all too conscious of the dead children, whose small white coffins lay on the ground in front of them. That service ended with the singing of "Abide with Me."

The Catholic service followed, conducted by Father McManus and Father Grey of St Joseph's, the parish so hard hit. No hymns were sung, but the intoned, responsive reading was deeply moving. The services ended with everyone, Catholics and Protestants, singing "God Save the King."

The caskets were then lifted onto large trucks. The two processions left by different gates, each preceded by a band playing "The Dead March in Saul." Then, followed by various dignitaries and hundreds of citizens, one walked solemnly to Fairview Cemetery, the other to Mount Olivet. No such procession had "ever trod the streets of this city," *The Morning Chronicle*

No. 75. James Fraser, the boy who carried these, would have attended St Joseph's School in the afternoon.

No. 411. The girl who wore this locket was probably a pupil at Richmond School. She was never identified.

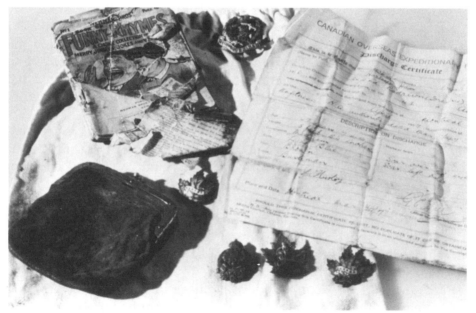

No. 209. John Hurley, a crew member from the British *Calonne*, had just been discharged from the service. He kept his certificate in his pocket. (ALL ARTEFACTS MARITIME MUSEUM)

The band of the Princess Louise Fusiliers played the funeral march at the burial of the unidentified dead on December 17. (CITY OF TORONTO ARCHIVES/JAMES, 2453)

reported, "and the prayer of all people here, of all creeds or no creed, must be, 'God grant so sad a sight may never be witnessed here again.'"

Burial of the unidentified dead continued until Christmas Eve. Up to fifty soldiers and many other men worked in the cemeteries, as the number of graveyard employees was too small to handle the rush. They placed the number assigned to each body inside the coffin, outside the coffin, and on a slab at the head of the grave. A chart of the graves was made, showing the position of the numbered bodies, so that in the unlikely event of identification, a relative could find the exact place of burial.

Given the descriptions of some of the bodies, it was surprising they were never recognized: "No. 1074. Female about twenty years. Dark brown hair. Fair complexion. White waist. Brown striped underwaist and chemise. Short corsets. One black petticoat, one blue petticoat. Light ribbed pink underwear. Long black stockings. Patent leather no. 4 laced boots. One narrow plain band gold wedding ring. (No marks). One Tiffany style gold ring. One gilt brooch, open bar pattern with heart at centre and blue stone in centre of heart. Note states: Found at 14 Duffus Street. Buried Fairview A Cemetery, December 24, 1917."

That the mortuary kept her body for almost three weeks indicates that the committee thought she would probably be identified. Had she lodged at the house on Duffus Street? Had she been visiting, perhaps seeing her young husband off to the war? The brooch seems to have sentimental value, and the rings look little worn.

Four families had lived in that house. One was a couple in their sixties, with one son at home, one overseas, and a third married and living elsewhere in the city. The wife and son were killed, and the husband was injured in the knee. He stayed with his married son and recovered, more or less, after two weeks. Then, depressed, he moved to the country, never settling in one spot and treating his painful knee himself. He was tired of strange doctors. "I don't feel like seeing the place again," he said of his former home. Less than a year later, during the 1918–19 influenza epidemic, his son died. A young British family had rented the second apartment. Both parents and one child were killed. The two survivors were a boy, age seven, and a girl, age twelve. The girl "was rescued from a house of ill fame," where she had been given shelter, probably kindly meant. Her brother was found in hospital in Truro. Both were adopted by an aunt who lived a long way from Halifax. A family of five had rented the third apartment, and the mother, the father, and two of the children were killed. The lone survivor, a seven-year-old boy found wandering in the street by a relief worker, was taken to a children's home. His grandmother, living in a town more than seventy miles away, came for him. All four members of the family in the other apartment had been killed. A woman and her baby, lodgers in one of the apartments, died. No wonder a visitor in that house could have remained unidentified.

The body of Vincent Pattison, James's father, was recovered in the spring of 1918. (COURTESY JAMES PATTISON)

Not only clothing, hair colour, and physical features appeared in descriptions. A sailor from the British *Picton*, subsequently identified as twenty-five-year-old Charles Dunn, from Scotland, had other distinguishing marks. On the back of his right hand was a tattoo of the head of Buffalo Bill and, on top of his right arm, a serpent and a butterfly. Another sailor, never recognized, had the Norwegian flag tattooed on his heart alongside a female figure. On his right arm appeared a horseshoe and the words "Sailor's Grave" and "Good Luck."

There were military paybooks and leave passes, as well as reminders of the war in the effects of civilians. An unidentified woman wore a brooch made up of the British and French flags, with the maple leaf in a shield in the centre. A boy of seven, also unknown, carried a Canadian soldier's coat button and one marked "N.S. Forces," in addition to a shoulder insignia, "CANADA." Another boy carried some strips of paper stamped, "Buy Victory Bonds." He must have had a printing set and had also made a list of his favourite film stars. Mary Pickford and Douglas Fairbanks were numbers one and two. He was about twelve, with brown hair and a thin body. He wore a blue jersey-style sweater, white fleece-lined underwear, a narrow black-leather belt, black stockings, and black laced boots. On his finger was a brass ring with an oval Union Jack. First he was documented as unidentified, but later it was changed. The names of his mother, father, and four brothers and sisters also appeared on the list of the dead in the 1918 Halifax City Directory. They lived on the harbour side of Barrington Street, close to the explosion site.

In the two months after the explosion the mortuary committee made substantial headway. Its report of February 4, 1918, stated that 1,400 victims had been identified, while 150 unclaimed bodies had been buried unrecognized. Hundreds of bodies had not reached the Chebucto Road mortuary, however. Countless more were found months later, particularly in spring, when the ground was softer, making excavating easier. Workmen, clearing sites for future building, came across bodies in the rubble. At that time Charles Upham, father of Millicent and Archie, decided to search the foundations of his own house. He did not want strangers to find his family. With the help of his brother and Archie, he shovelled through the ashes and cinders. "All we found of my mother, two sisters, and brother, we put in a shoebox—just a few bones," Archie said. "They were buried in Fairview in that shoebox, but by then it was nearly summer." The family had lost thirty-three close relatives.

It took about four months to clear away the wreckage of large factories. The body of James Pattison's father, buried under the ruins of the huge Acadia Sugar Refinery, was recovered in April 1918. His effects were returned to his wife, including James's pocketwatch. His father had borrowed it because his own was in for repair. The watch had stopped forever at 9:10 a.m. It had always been a few minutes fast.

CHRISTMAS

LOSS AND MOURNING, long hours of relief work, and care of the injured and the homeless occupied many citizens in Halifax and Dartmouth. Newspapers were filled with articles related to the explosion and to the war. It seemed too frivolous even to contemplate Christmas shopping or holiday festivities.

Nonetheless, on Monday, December 17, the first appeal appeared on the front page of *The Daily Echo* (Halifax). It suggested that children who had suffered should be given some joy at Christmas. The children's section of the newspaper, The Sunshine Club, was inaugurating a fund for the sick children in hospitals or in institutions, to give them "the best Christmas they ever had." Cousin Peggy, editor of The Sunshine Club, told one tale of kindness. One "wee maiden," she wrote, had given up her birthday celebration and had taken the ice cream and the gifts to the Children's Hospital. Cousin Peggy invited all boys and girls, especially those in rural areas who had not had the chance to help, to send toys or money, to share their Christmas with the less fortunate.

At that time it was common for children's clubs in newspapers to hold appeals for poor children. This Christmas, however, there was much more urgency. The explosion had badly affected about ten thousand children, who were left, according to the newspaper, without a proper home or a proper family. Their well-loved dolls and teddy bears and the Christmas gifts bought ahead of time had been destroyed. Marjorie Drysdale, who lived on Veith Street, was always glad she had secretly peeked at a hidden package. Otherwise she would never have known that her parents had bought her the toy piano she had so longed for.

Another headline on the front page of the *Echo* may have brought the spirit of the season home to some readers: "TURKS COULD NOT DRAW BRITISH FIRE." The war in Palestine had reached Bethlehem, and the British artillery, under bombardment, could not return fire without endangering the site of the nativity. A strategy had to be deployed. The British troops moved away during the night, cutting off the Turkish line of retreat. This caused the Turkish commander to withdraw hastily. The British capture of the city was effected without damage, and Bethlehem was once more in Christian hands before the celebration of the birth of Christ.

December 17, however, was also the day of the burial of the ninety-five unidentified dead from the Chebucto Road mortuary. Identifications of victims were still being made, and for people who did not yet know the fate of their loved ones, Christmas, let alone the salvation of Bethlehem, had little meaning.

For others it seemed like a suitable time to lighten the gloom. On December 19 the *Echo* reported that toys, books, and money were arriving quickly. The girls and boys of Mount Pleasant School in Milford, Hants County, Nova Scotia, for example, decided that instead of giving gifts to one another, they would donate them all to the children in hospital. On December 20, stores, most of which had been generous with goods after the explosion, began to advertise. Wentzells, a big store on Barrington Street, at Buckingham, appealed to sentiment: "Mister, do you think Santa Claus will be around this Christmas? Many and many a little kiddy has asked that question in the last few days. Is he going to come around to your home? Don't darken the kiddies' Christmas any more than you can help. Don't let them 'know' more than you can help. Life's trials and sorrows enter only too soon into their lives. When you are ready to buy your Christmas supplies, we are ready." Since the explosion, Halifax merchants had suffered a staggering blow to trade. *The Halifax Herald,* for its part, urged Nova Scotians to help the economy of the city by cutting out mail orders to central Canada and by shopping at local stores.

On the evening of December 20 numerous people attended a meeting at the Halifax Board of Trade, including representatives from The Sunshine Club, The Farmer Smith Club (the children's section of *The Evening Mail,* Halifax), and various organizations. Santa Claus Limited was launched with a public appeal for money, workers, gifts, and automobiles. It set up a special account at the local branch of the Merchants Bank of Canada to take donations and an office and two telephone numbers at the Halifax Academy, the only school undamaged during the explosion. About five thousand dollars was needed to purchase ten thousand packages. The following day the *Mail* carried the appeal, using the photographs of six wounded and homeless children:

Although the people of Halifax have performed veritable miracles, greater efforts must be made. Tangible Christmas cheer must enter every home over which hangs a shadow cast by the great disaster. A Christmas package containing fruit, cake, candy is to be delivered to every child in the city who has lost a home in the explosion. It is hoped that 250 ladies will report for duty. Fifty cars are needed for distribution. You can't refuse THEIR call.

The *Echo,* through its Christmas fund, felt confident that it could supply gifts and stockings for one thousand children for Santa Claus Limited. Two hundred women had come forward to help with its appeal. On December 22 the paper reported that a crowd of volunteers had turned up at the academy, at the corner of Sackville and Brunswick streets, and that $183 had already been donated. Under the headline "SANTA CLAUS LIMITED" the paper printed the following poem:

Old Santa Claus was sailing in his aeroplane so swift,
When, poof! there happened something that gave him quite a lift;
He was passing over Halifax with Yankee children's toys,
And it clean upset his balance with its rattle and its noise.
Down, down, he tumbled madly till those presents out he tossed;
And they'll need them, laughed old Santa, to replace the ones they've lost.
And so that good old Merryman can always see a way
To make a MERRY CHRISTMAS out of the darkest day.

An advertisement directly above the poem indicated how local companies planned to capitalize on the explosion in time for Christmas. H. H. Marshall advertised *The Halifax Catastrophe,* a book of forty views of the ruins. Single copies by mail cost fifty cents, and wholesale prices would be supplied on application. Marshall's was not the only publisher to bring out a book of photographs. *Views of the Halifax Disaster,* issued by Royal Print & Litho, sold its first ten thousand copies by December 25. The advertisement for *Devastated Halifax,* a book of fifty views, published by Gerald E. Weir, claimed, "This book is interesting and instructive, and one you will be glad to have in later years—a book that your friends will be delighted to receive—especially the boys at the front. Mailed to any address in Canada, United States, or overseas." Some companies produced series of postcards. Cox Bros Co. advertised, "Postcards of the Ruins! 2 for 5 cents, postage prepaid, 12 for 25 cents. If desired, a full set of Thirty Different Views will be mailed to ANY ADDRESS in Canada or U.S.A. on receipt of 60 CENTS."

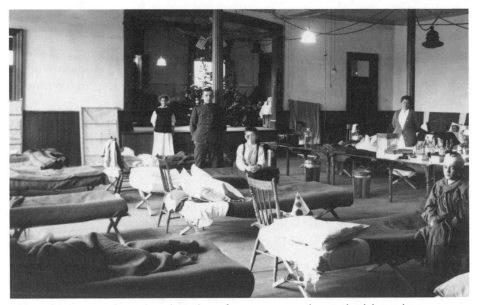

Although Christmas brought only sadness for many, every hospital celebrated it in some way. (CITY OF TORONTO ARCHIVES/JAMES, 1785)

The MacLaughlan Studio, on Barrington, produced fine panoramas. They sold for one or two dollars, depending on size, and many were framed. At least three broadsheets of poems related to the disaster were sold, ranging in price from ten to fifteen cents.

On Christmas Eve the *Echo* reported that The Sunshine Club's appeal had raised more than thirteen hundred dollars, as well as gifts of every kind. Santa Claus Limited put up the first Christmas tree, at the YMCA. By the end of the day a tree shone in most large hospitals. At the Waegwoltic Club, now a temporary hospital, the tree was enjoyed as much by an eighty-five-year-old grandmother as it was by an eleven-month-old girl who had lost one eye. Camp Hill, to have gifts and music, was one of the only hospitals without a tree: it was so large and crowded and the children too dispersed throughout the wards.

Santa Claus Limited's bank account continued to climb, augmented by collections taken in rural schools, from concerts, sales, and pupils who had voluntarily given a week's pocket money. Names of contributors were printed in the paper, and many were children's. Local students whose schools were closed, such as some of the girls from the Halifax Ladies College, were happy to help collect toys and make up parcels.

Automobile owners did not disappoint Santa Claus Limited, either. Fifty assembled at the Halifax Academy to distribute parcels and stockings to hospitals, shelters, and homes. To help locate children in private homes, nurses at dressing stations had supplied names. Many clubs and organizations contributed decorations, food, gifts, and volunteer help. By the end of Christmas Eve, it was hoped, thousands of stricken people would be brought some measure of happiness.

In many families, Christmas Eve brought only grief. Another large burial of the unidentified took place, and several identifications had been made the previous day, including those of a young mother and her four children. The search for lost relatives continued, and lists of the missing still appeared daily. Anxious eyes watched as each ruined home was excavated.

*   *   *   *   *

People had protested that the Christmas of 1917 should not be a time of rejoicing, and generally it was not. All theatres were still closed, and few hotels or restaurants served festive meals. But those who spent their day helping in institutions such as crowded hospitals—where many lay swathed in bandages and some could not see their gifts—said it was by far the busiest and the most meaningful Christmas they had ever spent.

Doctors and nurses helped with decorations, and some began the morning rounds with carols. Most young patients woke to find a well-stuffed stocking on their bed, and Santa Claus visited every hospital. Evelyn Johnson, at the YMCA, received her presents from a very jolly Father Christmas. He was actually her favourite doctor, an American relief worker, and he could always make the children laugh. At St Paul's Hall, Dr Samuel Prince, a professor and writer, donned a red gown instead of his usual black robe and played Santa Claus with gusto. Children's fears that the lack of chimneys might deter Santa quickly evaporated.

Fire halls, relief centres, and churches, which also held services, all had Christmas trees and dinners or teas for homeless or injured children. Organizations entertained groups large or small. The Overseas Club, a social organization, invited twenty-four destitute children aboard the *Lord Kelvin,* docked in the harbour. There was a turkey with all the trimmings, followed by ice cream. Then, from behind the tree, the hosts brought out a "mystery box" for each child. At the Imperial Oil Company shelter in Dartmouth the Red Cross and the local clergy supplied a Christmas tree and gifts. At the food depots the food committee dispensed a luxurious lunch, including roast beef, tinned peas, and potatoes.

One of the most elaborate celebrations was held at Mrs Michael Dwyer's residence, on Spring Garden Road. Mrs Dwyer had donated part of her large house to the Princess Louise Chapter of the IODE for use as a temporary home for children leaving hospital; she had also helped finance the project. The IODE had already seen to it that toys were available for the children. Mrs Dwyer's granddaughter Eileen had donated her doll house, a fine fully furnished one with glass windows. It was a great success with both boys and girls.

At Christmas the IODE created a rose-coloured world, shading each lamp in pink. On Christmas Eve, each child hung a stocking by the fireplace, and in the morning every one was filled. A giant Christmas tree twinkling with stars yielded a multitude of beautifully wrapped parcels, and one by one the children received their gifts as their names were called. One father, whose wife had been killed, even managed to leave hospital to visit his children for the first time.

For other children Christmas was quiet and sad. Frank Burford was staying with relatives outside the city. There were no presents. He had just received a letter from his older sister telling of his father's death, and his mother was still in hospital. "We had nothing to rejoice about," Frank said. Nor did James and Gordon Pattison. For them it was a "blank day" as they thought about the family gathering of the previous year. There was still no word of their father, but they knew now that there was absolutely no chance he was alive. "It made you sensitive to other people's anguish, too," James said.

Christmas, with small presents, none costing much, and the Sunday-school picnic in summer, were always the main treats of the year for the Driscoll children. They had left Truro and were now staying in South Uniacke, except for Art, who was in hospital, and Gordon, who was never found. They celebrated Christmas together but much more solemnly than usual—and with no Christmas cake.

Altogether, the Christmas of 1917 was unusual. There were more trees and gifts and parties for children who were not accustomed to them, and fewer for those who were. Hardly anyone complained. One woman, though tired and foot weary after hours of volunteer work, perhaps summed up the overall feeling: "I think that today brought me to a greater understanding of the true meaning of Christmas."

MEDICAL–SOCIAL
SERVICE

A S SOON AS the first flood of emergency medical work subsided, it became clear that some form of continuing care would be necessary. Lieutenant Colonel F. McKelvey Bell, chairman of the medical relief committee, was anxious to clear military hospitals so that they could return to their original purpose. It was not possible, however, simply to discharge people, most of whom were not completely cured, when adequate housing and supervision would have to be arranged. This type of care was lacking in Halifax: in 1917 the Victoria General Hospital, for example, did not yet have an outpatient department. With the large number of people requiring help, steps had to be taken.

Consequently, the rehabilitation committee established a medical–social service, at first staffed almost entirely by volunteers from Boston. There were five social workers initially, with Ruth Emerson, of the social service department of the Massachusetts General Hospital, in charge. Soon a sixth was added, and a number of Halifax women helped as volunteers. In the beginning the service concentrated on the hospitals, as the medical relief committee had already introduced district-visiting nursing. Run by a Miss O'Bryan, also from Boston, it had taken charge of all visiting in homes, dressing stations, and shelters.

The medical–social service worked closely with relief committees to ensure that each discharged patient had suitable shelter and clothing. (After the first week the Canadian Red Cross assumed responsibility for clothing.) The staff interviewed all patients, short term or long term, to gather sufficient information for registration and to pinpoint any pressing needs. They prepared medical statements on the injured, and they tried to reunite families scattered in different hospitals, keeping careful statistics and accurate records on each. The purpose of the medical–social worker—the link between the hospital and the outside world—was to help explosion victims resume a normal life to the greatest possible extent.

When the service began, about twelve hundred explosion victims were still in hospital in Halifax, and by December 16, approximately three hundred had been discharged. Continuing medical care was essential. Wounds and burns had to be dressed daily, and many had the potential for complications. Given the substances blasted into the wounds, the incidence of blood poisoning was also high. Depression and perplexity at the sudden loss of family, home, and friends made formerly capable people unable to cope. A man, sixty years old, had been comfortably settled with his wife; their son, his wife, and their two children lived nearby, and two other sons were overseas. During the explosion the older man's wife was badly injured, requiring the amputation of most of her right arm. More of it would have to be removed when she was strong enough. His daughter-in-law and his older grandchild were killed, and the younger one, a three-year-old girl, was badly cut. Both the father and the son were seriously depressed and needed encouragement, as well as consultation on the long-term medical needs of the family. A social worker spent time with them, and her patient, clear explanation of the wife's condition and her hopeful prognosis for the child helped the men "regain their courage."

Many people discharged from hospital went to family, friends, or relatives, but others were more difficult to place, especially when their social problems were as grave as their medical needs. A family of five concerned the medical–social service deeply. The father had been killed, the mother blinded. One daughter, age twenty-one, with one eye enucleated, required medical supervision to save the sight in the other eye. The other daughter, age seventeen, had one leg amputated below the knee. The youngest, a boy of nine, had lost one eye, had bad prospects for the other, and suffered a severely mutilated face. The mother would be in hospital for a long time, but the children were fit to leave if proper care could be obtained. After a great deal of investigation, a solution was found. The older girl went to her employer's family, interested in her welfare. A convent, where she knew one of the sisters well, gave shelter to the other girl; a relative took the boy.

A period of convalescence was essential if some patients were going to regain full health. There were no civilian convalescent hospitals in Halifax. Part of the YMCA temporary hospital, however, had been adapted for this purpose. One young wife, whose husband was overseas, had serious cuts that needed careful dressing over a period of weeks. She planned to go to her mother-in-law in Amherst, near the New Brunswick border, where the closest medical care was eight miles away. Her two children were in separate shelters, and she was too worried about them to consider her own injuries. She thought that if they went to Amherst, they could at least be together.

A social worker collected the two children and took them to Amherst, to their grandmother. The woman was then quite happy to go to the YMCA.

Social workers found that injuries requiring follow-up care fell into five categories: fractures, eye damage, deep wounds and lacerations, burns, and amputations. They conducted a census and divided the injured into three groups: permanently handicapped, recovering, and doubtful prognoses. This last group, the largest, would need constant encouragement to take advantage of all the medical facilities available. To this end, the service established contacts with relief committees, individuals, or organizations that could help, such as the Victorian Order of Nurses (VON), the Imperial Order Daughters of the Empire (IODE), and the Rotary Club. It also kept track of patients being transferred from military and temporary hospitals to other facilities. By mid-January many temporary hospitals, including the Halifax Ladies College, the New Glasgow facility, and St Mary's College, had closed down. In addition, the majority of American surgeons and the Massachusetts Red Cross unit had returned home, leaving the Boston social workers behind to continue their work.

*   *   *   *   *

It was not long before the medical–social service drew complaints. For many explosion victims the service was just one more irritant. Survivors were visited by registration workers, district nurses, and now another set of volunteers with their questionnaires. No one was used to being asked personal and seemingly prying unnecessary questions. If a family had a problem, they went to their minister, not a stranger who did not fully understand local conditions.

The service, however, was not the only relief component causing discontent. Complaints were widespread concerning the distribution of relief supplies, and committee outlets were charged with inefficiency. People maintained they sometimes had to visit depots three times before their orders were filled. In particular, the distribution of clothing in hospital was considered unsatisfactory. Red Cross volunteers did their best to supply discharged patients with proper apparel. They even took measurements. But the fit of the garment was not the main objection. The problem was, with so many people in mourning, there was not enough black clothing. One young woman who went to fetch her widowed mother from hospital found her in tears, holding the brightly coloured outfit she had been given. The girl rushed out and, with the last of her money, bought her mother a black dress.

In the midst of all this the rehabilitation committee decided to cut food allowances by one-quarter to one-half. People not receiving them had protested that recipients were getting more than they actually spent on food. One man reckoned that it had cost $12.00 a week to feed his six-member household. Full board for a child was about $2.00 a week, and board *and* room for a working man was $3.50–$4.50. A widow who ran a small store put in a claim for $50.00 for her entire stock. So it did seem to much of the population that food allowances were higher than necessary. The weekly food rate for an adult dropped from $3.50 to $2.50; for children over ten, from $3.00 to $2.00; for five- to ten-year-olds, from $2.25 to $1.25; and for babies, from $1.00 to $0.75. The decreases were unfortunate. John E. Godwin, one of the aldermen for Ward 6, in the North End, wrote to *The Halifax Herald* concerning the $3.25 allowance for one adult and one child. "I would like to see the menu card possible on this," he demanded.

On January 14 Halifax mayor Peter Martin called a public meeting to hear grievances. Richmond residents suggested that north-end representatives be placed on relief committees, and the mayor himself demanded that no more second-hand clothing be issued and that food allowances be increased. Relief organizers claimed, in turn, that much of the criticism was unjustified. They believed that the discontent had been generated by meetings in the North End that had expressly requested complaints. Newspaper accounts of vast sums of money and of huge quantities of relief goods, they said, had raised people's expectations too high.

Nevertheless, action was taken. Social work became more systematic, with repeat visits occurring rarely. No more used clothing was issued, except in a few instances where it was believed that new garments would be inappropriate to the former financial status of the victim. If suitable new clothing was not available, a money order was given so that proper apparel could be purchased at a local firm. When it came to food allowances, however, relief organizers refused to compromise.

*   *   *   *   *

Despite the criticism, the medical–social service was proving its worth. The reality was, many injured people needed it to readjust to their unfortunate circumstances. One fifteen-year-old boy working at the dry dock had suffered injuries that led to the amputation of his right arm to above the elbow. As he had also suffered a fracture of his right leg, his physical recovery would take time. His emotional problems were equally serious. Both his parents had been killed. The boy, unlike his brother, was not keen to live with an aunt in the city. He also required vocational guidance and sympathetic care until he could cope for himself. Finding a home for him was not difficult, but his rehabilitation was another matter.

Another boy, motherless for some time, had had his feet so badly crushed on the tug *Stella Maris* that both had to be amputated. After discharge from hospital he needed a wheelchair until, in a few months, artificial feet could be fitted. A social worker arranged for him to live with an uncle.

Altogether, there were thirty-one amputees. The machinery for re-education in this area was already in place because of the war. After treatment and certain adjustments some were able to continue work, but others needed retraining. The Invalided Soldiers Commission, headed by Frederick Sexton, principal of the Nova Scotia Technical College, under-took most of the work in this field. The commission provided artificial limbs, taught their use and care, and offered retraining.

Other cases filled social workers' dockets. A severe fracture of the skull left one fifteen-year-old, treated by a skilful surgeon, with no mental impairment but a deep gully in his head. Part of his brain was covered only by membrane. His left arm had been fractured and required bone plating. As a result, he could lose the function of his left hand. Supervisory care would be vital for at least a year.

A different type of case, where proper follow-up would prevent permanent damage, was typified by a seven-year-old girl. Both parents had been killed, and suffering from shock, the girl had been taken to hospital. "Her condition was pitiable," the social worker noted, "when spoken to she merely cries in a dazed fashion and trembles violently." The child was unable to speak or walk and ate practically nothing. Rest, quiet, and proper hygiene, all in normal surroundings, were advised. The girl's grandmother wanted to take her, but when the social worker investigated, she found the conditions more than unsuitable. Eleven people, including eight noisy children, lived in three rooms, an environment that would have had serious consequences for the girl. The grandmother argued that the child should be with her own relatives, but the worker persuaded her that for six months, placement in a private home with a good family would be better. After that, she would probably be well enough to return to her grandmother's, where improvements could be made in the meantime.

On January 15 the service presented its early findings to representatives of interested groups: the Halifax Medical Society, the rehabilitation, the children's, and the medical relief committees, and nursing associations. Social workers had scrutinized 2,846 medical records and dealt with 861 cases, of which 302 had been handed over to other committees, and others needed no further medical supervision; 261 people were under the service's care. Moreover, the Boston workers were leaving at the end of January, and the service strongly recommended that a trained social worker be appointed for at least several months.

This recommendation was amply carried out. Five full-time workers, including two nurses and a Dalhousie graduate in charge of neurological cases, two part-time district workers, a stenographer, and IODE volunteers carried on the work of the medical–social service.

THE RELIEF COMMISSION ARRIVES

ON JANUARY 22, 1918, relief organization underwent further structural changes. The Dominion government appointed the Halifax Relief Commission through an order in council under the War Measures Act. Its mandate: "to take over all unexpended funds, to assume Relief work of the voluntary committees, to report as to the extent of damage and to make such recommendations as it might think best in view of all circumstances as to the disbursement of the Relief funds, and the best method of restoring or assisting in the restoration of the area affected." The commission consisted of a prominent Halifax lawyer, T. Sherman Rogers, chairman, a Nova Scotia county court judge, William Bernard Wallace, and an Oshawa businessman, Frederick Luther Fowke. Ralph Pickard Bell, a local businessman already involved in relief work, was appointed secretary.

As early as mid-December there had been mention of establishing a government body to oversee rebuilding. The Halifax Board of Trade had written to the mayor recommending that a conference of provincial and Dominion authorities be held to discuss the "wise" disbursement of relief funds. On December 14 the Halifax Board of Control, the paid executive body of city council, urged similar action.

Subsequently Nova Scotia premier George H. Murray called a meeting of provincial and city officials "to consider and report upon the form of Commission proposed to take over and carry on all work instituted and to be undertaken in the rebuilding of Halifax and vicinity and the rehabilitation of citizens following the destruction of life and property by the disaster of December 6." On December 28 a further meeting was held, this time with Dominion government representatives. The result was a report that made several recommendations asking the Dominion government, among other things, to appoint an agency of not less than three and not more than five members to hold office until relief work was completed. The commission, the report proposed, should have wide powers: "a) The work of furnishing temporary relief. b) The support of those incapacitated. c)The maintenance of those dependent on people who lost their lives. d) Compensation for injury to property and person, and loss of life. e) Reconstruction of devastated area, including any change of location deemed necessary. f) Rehabilitation of citizens who have so suffered in health or property as to render assistance of this nature necessary." It should also take over certain municipal responsibilities: "a) To enter upon and clean up all properties, in order that public health may be conserved. b) To condemn and raze all buildings not in their opinion worth repairing. c) To make temporary repairs. d) To provide temporary housing. e)To appraise and estimate damage. f) To act as public administrators. g) To expropriate. h) To receive, appropriate and expend all contributions public or otherwise."

By the time the relief commission was appointed, much of the work of the individual committees had slowed down. After more than six weeks of arduous work, members were happy to transfer their responsibilities to the commission and to return to their daily lives.

Before the takeover, each committee submitted a report outlining what it had accomplished. The transportation committee, which had been moving homeless, injured, workers, and corpses around the city, announced that it had organized the construction of a building to house vehicles: "Today we have probably one of the finest equipped garages in Eastern Canada ... and are returning cars to their owners in such shape that they are quite satisfied to take them on without further trouble." The general supply committee reported that more than 10,000 entries had gone through its books. The coal situation, according to the fuel committee, was well in hand. Various mining and coal companies throughout the province had been generous, but deliveries would have to continue for 936 families.

The clothing committee, for its part, estimated that about 25,000 people had required assistance, and the emergency shelter committee reported that it was still operating eight shelters. The information committee had accumulated a file on 18,378 persons and had answered 6,377 letters and telegrams, some from as far away as Australia. The finance committee, in turn, had inaugurated a book-keeping system "that would stand the test of the most rigid examination." By January 31, though promises of further funds had been made, $3,380,470.89 had been received and $731,166.01 had been disbursed. Work at the Chebucto Road mortuary had petered out, with the clerical workers moving to Arthur Barnstead's office, on Hollis Street. The registration committee had faced an enormous workload, carrying out some 20,000 visits. Registrations now numbered 4,953, representing 229 out of 328 streets in Halifax. They ultimately reached 13,844; from No. 9600 on, all were claims only and were placed in a separate folder. By July 1918 the 121 employees were down to a supervisor and two clerks.

Lieutenant Colonel F. McKelvey Bell, chairman of the medical relief committee, returned to military duty on January 23. In his final report he stated that in addition to the hundreds of eye, fracture, and amputation cases, 3,754 other wounds had been treated in hospital. Bell, already the author of one book, had an idea for a novel, *A Romance of the Halifax Disaster*, that would be published later in the year. He dedicated it to "the self sacrificing band of men and women of Halifax, from other parts of Canada and from the United States who so nobly assisted the victims of the disaster...."

Across the harbour the Dartmouth relief committee had closed food and fuel depots at the end of December but had augmented hospital accommodation. Artist Henry Rosenberg had offered his home for this purpose, and later the Dartmouth Coal and Supply Company donated Parker House for long-term patients and convalescents. Dartmouth relief, however, did not come completely under the authority of the relief commission until the autumn of 1918.

Some committee members and relief workers stayed on as paid employees or as volunteers for the commission, which created four departments with permanent staffs. The largest department was rehabilitation, responsible for restoring people to "their former condition of living." The other three were reconstruction, medical, and finance.

One of the first things the commission did was introduce cash allowances to cover funeral and medical expenses, transportation costs for explosion-related travel, and general living expenses. General living allowances were based on household income prior to the explosion, with current income taken into account. Foremen at the docks or railway, for example, had made about $110 per month; stevedores, $70–$80; and labourers, $50–$60. Women working in factories had earned about $25 or less. Rents ranged from $5 to $20 a month, with most families paying about $10. Allowances also varied according to the number of dependent children. One woman with four children received $25 per week; her husband's wages had been $120 per month.

To be eligible for allowances, explosion victims had to sign affidavits and fill out a variety of claim forms. Ministers such as the Reverend Charles Crowdis, formerly of Grove Presbyterian Church, were in constant demand to witness affidavits and to help figure out puzzling questions. They also acted as character witnesses for people who had lost their personal papers in the blast. It helped to have an honest reputation. On one occasion a woman's food allowance was withheld when it was learned she had been guilty of shoplifting. After an inquiry it was discovered that an error in identification had been made, and the voucher was processed. Cases of this kind were rare, however, and relief money was usually dispensed without any problem.

The commission gave assistance in other areas. In a number of cases men could return to work—if they had a workplace to go to. Some, however, had been widowed and were too busy taking care of children or repairing damaged homes. Occasionally the commission paid for a housekeeper to relieve the father. Many men were also too seriously injured to return to work right away, and they received short- or long-term disability allowances; the maximum weekly amount was twenty-five dollars.

Hundreds of wage earners had been injured or killed, leaving their families without adequate income. If a worker had been on the job at the time, the Workmen's Compensation Board paid the family 55 percent of the person's former salary. (Nova Scotia had established the board in 1915, the second province to enforce compensation for people killed or injured on the job.) This required more paperwork and more verification. If a body had not yet been found and most of the co-workers were dead, it was difficult to prove that someone had been at work, especially for families of men who had been employed on the docks. There were special cases. A young teamster had been driving at the time of the explosion. He passed a house that had caught fire, and a distraught mother was outside, her baby inside. The man ran into the house to rescue the baby but was trapped and killed. As he was not on the job, or driving his team, at the time, Workmen's Compensation would not pay an allowance to his widowed mother. After the intervention of his former employer, William MacTaggart Orr, of the Richmond Printing Company, the decision was reversed. Families, often with the help of their minister, made every effort to obtain compensation but not always with positive results.

*   *   *   *   *

The relief commission also oversaw the medical–social service, whose work was still a high priority. Clinics opened in Halifax to deal with the service's referrals. A neurology clinic was operating at the YMCA. Run by Dr William McDonald, a Massachusetts neurologist, it treated victims with damage to the nervous system and with psychological problems. In

February 307 patients were under the clinic's care. Dr McDonald stayed in Halifax until the end of that month, when his colleague Dr Judson Graham, a local physician, took over. In his report Dr McDonald stressed that people suffering from emotional trauma needed rehabilitation as much as those who had been physically injured. He quoted one woman afflicted with depression who had said, "I try to be brave and I realize that I am better off than many who have lost their eyes, but it is hard to walk about Halifax and pass many of my old friends without being recognized." Dr McDonald continued: "You who have seen so many of the gashed and disfigured faces in Halifax, need no description of the woman who spoke thus, to understand how she, no less than the sightless, must begin life anew under circumstances for which her experience has not trained her. So it is with the bereaved and the sick in mind and body."

By early February the YMCA hospital also housed a general clinic that was soon providing treatment for 1,236 patients. (In the three weeks following the disaster, relief doctors had given their services free of charge. Subsequently all medical costs were paid first by the medical relief committee and then by the commission.) Staffed by four local doctors, the clinic contained x-ray, massage, and electrical-treatment facilities. But some patients refused to take advantage of them, even though transportation could be provided. They had seen too many different doctors and too many well-intentioned social workers and had filled out too many forms. One woman would not go for further massage treatments because she had to undress partially, and there were men in the room. Blind veterans performed some massages, and others were being trained, but she did not realize they could not see her, and no one had informed her.

Conflicts arose at times between the medical relief organizations and the City Health Board. Authority overlapped, and the board accused the clinic's doctors of being overzealous and of exaggerating some conclusions, especially regarding public health. Recommendations for treatment did not always coincide with those of other physicians who had already examined a patient.

Once in a while the medical–social service had to intervene, such as in the case of a young dressmaker. She had sensory paralysis of the right hand and was referred to the clinic by the district social worker. A clinic doctor advised her to have an operation to restore the hand's function. She refused, satisfied with her family physician's diagnosis and her treatment at the Halifax Infirmary. Her social worker brought all the parties together, and she consented to the operation. The prognosis was excellent.

Apart from the YMCA clinics, public health care in Halifax was minimal.

A young stevedore had been gassed while looking for relatives in the ruins, and later he was diagnosed as having incipient tuberculosis. The doctor recommended transferral to a sanatorium to prevent the young man from becoming a helpless invalid.

Unfortunately the closest T.B. sanatorium was in Kentville, more than sixty miles away, and it always had a long waiting list. There was a small, poorly equipped hospital in Halifax, with room for twelve T.B. patients but no proper sanatorium. Tuberculosis was already a serious problem in Halifax, causing about 125 deaths in 1917. The annual mortality rate from T.B. was twice that of Toronto, a city more than nine times the size.

Conditions after the explosion contributed to incidence of the disease. Exposure, colds, pneumonia, and sharing crowded rooms with T.B. cases made it one of the long-term concerns of the medical community. At one home, about ten weeks after the explosion, nine people, a widow and her eight children, were still living in two rooms. Much of the plaster was down, and the windows had no glass. Barrels of mixed and unmixed plaster lay around. It was bitterly cold, with one small fire in the kitchen giving off the only heat. Clothing covered the windows, and one child was barefoot. To make matters worse, the oldest daughter had T.B. Perhaps the family, still stunned by what had happened, had been unaware that they could apply for relief. In addition, a social worker did not visit the house until well into February. On February 26 the medical–social service filed a report with the relief commission. The whole family was tested for T.B. and then monitored. The commission issued a cash allowance for essentials and repaired the house.

Medical relief workers had been urging the City for some time to establish a T.B. sanatorium. In June the commission opened its own, buying Parker House, in Dartmouth, but only after eleven patients had died. The cost of much of the furniture for the sanatorium was covered by the Massachusetts–Halifax relief fund. (This fund, amounting to $500,000, had, since the departure of Massachusetts workers, been administered by a committee of Halifax citizens. The Massachusetts–Halifax relief committee still had headquarters in Boston, and the local committee met frequently.) At a daily per-capita cost of $2.17, twenty-two patients could be cared for at the sanatorium, and improvement in their health was noted in a short time.

Specialized care for blinded victims was progressing well by the time the commission opened the T.B. sanatorium. Much earlier the rehabilitation committee had set up a special committee to supervise the recovery of people with eye injuries. More than one thousand eye cases had needed attention, and skilled eye surgeons, many from out of town, had performed a great deal of fine sight saving. Fortunately figures given in the press for the total number of completely blind were exaggerated, but the reality was bad enough. Thirty-seven people—eight men, twenty women, and nine children—had been left sightless, though many of the dead had been in this condition. Two hundred and six survivors had lost one eye and needed monitoring to ensure that vision was retained in the other. Two hundred and sixty more people still had glass embedded in their eyes and had to be kept under observation.

Halifax already possessed a fine school for the blind, where some of the injured had been cared for soon after the explosion. Sir Frederick Fraser, its director, had engaged extra staff and opened a clinic to receive eye patients immediately after they left hospital. He also taught many how to cope with their disability.

On January 15 Fraser launched an appeal for $500,000. The income would, he said, "bring to many a one now helpless and hopeless new opportunities to fit himself or herself for the battle of life." The fund received donations from around the world, and by April it reached $72,000.

The cases Fraser cited in his appeal were heartbreaking. In one family of seven the husband and two children had died. Two other children had been badly cut but survived. The mother, blind, was in one hospital, while her nine-year-old daughter, also sightless, was in another. A woman of eighteen, husband abroad in the army, could still distinguish day from night, but the prognosis was not good. She was in "a bad mental state," and she was four months pregnant with her first child. How was she going to take care of a baby she would never see?

Serious eye injuries were frequently accompanied by other head and facial wounds, requiring long hospitalization. Eyelids had been damaged by glass splinters, and artificial eyes could not be fitted until after plastic surgery had been performed, sometimes as long as a year later. The sudden change from being self-supporting and independent, from being a breadwinner or a busy wife coping with housekeeping, cooking, and children, was hard for most of the blind to accept. To make matters worse, few could return to their own homes, where they could have felt their way among familiar rooms and objects.

While the explosion blind were still in hospital—in many cases until February or later—they had several visits from relief volunteers and social workers. Some tried to help them adjust; others arranged clothing, cash allowances, and accommodation. Specialists also wanted to assess suitability for retraining. One woman obviously grew tired of the whole situation. Her prayer was loudly expressed: "God, our Heavenly Father, destroy the Beast that is still defying Him through the Halifax Relief Commission, Social Service and Secret Service as well."

Social workers and volunteers continued visiting the blind after they returned home. Few had enough confidence to leave the house except for medical appointments, and even then only if they were escorted. The false cheer some had managed in hospital faded to despair when the awful truth of their altered family situation and their helplessness struck home day after day.

Living conditions for some were deplorable, and they moved frequently, never developing familiarity with their surroundings. Overcrowding led to ill health and frayed nerves. There were instances of blind women being ill treated and neglected by their husbands. One case, where a man physically abused his blind wife, went to court, and the man was prosecuted. Families, understandably, were irritable, and drinking among husbands of blinded women and among some of the lonely widowers became noticeable.

The medical–social service and the School for the Blind tried hard to improve conditions. Social workers and volunteers supplied raised playing cards and dominoes and taught some women how to do simple knitting. They encouraged those who were well enough to attend the school, which provided classes in self-reliance and Braille. Most were reluctant, however: they were afraid and proud.

In April the relief commission hired Mr and Mrs Joseph Murphy, from New York, to come and take charge of blind relief. She was a public health nurse specializing in eye work, and he was partially sighted, which probably contributed to their success in gaining the confidence of the explosion blind.

On arrival the Murphys made an assessment of the situation. Mrs Murphy reported that practically all the twenty blind women were idle and that it was important to re-educate them so that they could resume household responsibilities. With money from the Massachusetts–Halifax relief fund, the Murphys purchased equipment. The women learned how to use sewing machines, washing machines, bread mixers, and other domestic appliances specially adapted for the blind. Mrs Murphy visited each woman regularly, giving instruction in the arrangement of furniture and in baby care and offering all sorts of tips on how to cope. Classes and social gatherings where the women discussed their difficulties and achievements became popular. Darning was not a favourite, but cooking, though potentially dangerous, was a constant source of interest. The meetings even roused some healthy competition. "Mrs H said she managed to bake a pie," one woman reported. "I went home, determined to try one too. The family said it was great."

Various local women's groups took considerable interest in the blind women after they realized the great need. They, together with the Murphys, arranged outings for individuals and for groups. Picnics, boat rides, musical evenings, and sales of goods made by blind women all helped morale. More learned Braille. There were a few exceptions, such as the woman who remarked, "I didn't like to read when I could see." Of course, setbacks occurred. Artificial eyes led to infections, and all too often they broke, sometimes even when in the socket. The commission supplied replacements free of charge, but only one set per year unless the

Like so many others, Eric Davidson was standing in front of a window when the *Mont Blanc* blew up. He was only two and a half years old when he was blinded by flying glass. (RON E. MERRICK)

eye had been defective. Poor health, too many new babies, or poverty prolonged the adjustment time, which was usually about two years.

Three of the eight men who had been blinded were soldiers, so they were under military care. Of the five others, one returned to the family farm and took little advantage of rehabilitation facilities. Another, an older man of fifty-five who had been a carpenter, suffered months of setbacks and unhappiness. Then he received two Braille lessons a week at home and took to it immediately. The Murphys gave him a phonograph and records, and adjustment soon followed. He became a voracious reader, ordering books from the Canadian National Library for the Blind. He did puzzles and played games with raised cards and checkers with friends, who called regularly.

After overcoming their initial apprehension, the three other men, two in their twenties, one age thirty-two, attended the School for the Blind. They took gymnastic lessons, which seemed ridiculous at first. The classes, however, gave them confidence, as well as strength. Mr Murphy taught those classes, and he later received a letter from one of the men, who had typed it himself. "You showed me how to find myself by methods I must confess I at first thought foolish and unnecessary," the man wrote. "Now I realize that by no other method could I have overcome that stiffness and timidity so peculiar to the newly blinded. Now I am able to walk along as loosely and easily as when I had my sight." The three men took Braille, typing, chair caning, piano tuning, and shoe repairing—classes aimed at developing career skills. All of them, for a time, earned money at shoe repairing. The retraining seemed successful despite further operations and ill health.

Several of the blinded children required prolonged medical treatment before they could receive schooling. Three contracted tuberculosis, and one had to learn to walk again. Two were not yet school aged. Family circumstances often determined the degree of success. Those orphaned as well as blinded took a longer time to adjust than those who had loving parents to help. Eventually most of the children boarded at the School for the Blind, where they received exceptional care. Music was an integral part of the program, both instruction in appreciation and in playing instruments. Country holidays were arranged in summer, treats throughout the year. Practically all missed school from time to time to have operations, usually some form of plastic surgery, and troubles with artificial eyes abounded.

Eric Davidson was two and a half when the explosion occurred, and he was blinded by flying glass. When he was old enough, he became a weekly boarder at the school. After he turned twelve, he insisted on finding his own way home on weekends. He got lost a few times but could eventually make it by streetcar and on foot. When he was in his teens, he became interested in motor mechanics. No books on the subject were available in Braille, but whoever had time read aloud to him.

Not all the children at the school were totally blind. Millicent Upham, who had lost one eye, was a weekly boarder and then a day pupil, going home to her aunt and uncle's at night. She had to take care not to strain her other eye but had no serious difficulties. In her last year, when she was seventeen, she helped teach the younger students.

Two other boys studied at Dalhousie University, with other students reading aloud to them when no Braille books were obtainable. Millicent used to help them, too, but found it hard to make economics sound interesting. One of the girls became a teacher at the School for the Blind.

The rehabilitation of the blind saw victories and defeats. Not all responded to retraining. Some were unwilling, or poor health or lack of transportation or overwhelming family problems prevented others from reaping the benefits. One blind woman simply had no energy to take part. She had several children, her husband was out of work, and for a few years her pension was the only income. Family support played a large part in the successes. A few women took only the re-education they felt was necessary and did not often join in the classes or the social occasions, but they managed reasonably well.

When the Murphys returned to New York in August 1919, one blind man wrote, on the typewriter Mr Murphy had trained him to use, "I feel as if I am losing the best friend I ever had. You found me a Blind Man utterly and hopelessly lost in the little World of Darkness in which I was suddenly dropped in December 1917.... The Murphy Brand of Blind Men are no joke."

Over the years social workers kept in touch, and the relief commission paid for medical treatment if it was explosion related. In 1922 one more survivor lost his sight, bringing the total number of the blind up to thirty-eight. Five blind survivors died of TB. within five years of the disaster, and several more were treated for the illness. The influenza and the smallpox epidemics of 1918 and 1919 also affected the sightless as much as those who could see.

ONE APARTMENT
EVERY HOUR

I T HAD NOT TAKEN the reconstruction committee (now the reconstruction department) long to decide that the best way to accommodate
the homeless was to build tenement-style apartment buildings. These
could be quickly erected—and torn down—in rows on large public sites,
not on individual lots that would be needed for permanent rebuilding.

The committee had decided to repair salvageable houses first and to clear
the devastated area. To complete the task, it brought in enormous quantities of supplies, large numbers of horses and wagons, and approximately
twenty-two hundred workmen, who were housed in hastily erected barracks on the Exhibition Grounds. Local construction firms also hired more
than fifteen hundred men. Their barracks were on Isleville Street and were
known as Cavicchiville, after the company that was given the contract to
prepare the land for rebuilding. Although this influx boosted local trade, it
also contributed to social ills and health problems. Medical authorities, for
example, expressed concern that some men might have come from areas
where smallpox was prevalent. Vaccinations, however, were not compulsory
at that time, so workmen from out of town were given medical examinations.

Three thousand repairs were completed by January 21, allowing hundreds of people to return to their homes. But five thousand survivors still
had no accommodation. Again military advice was available. Colonel
Robert Low, who had designed military camps at Borden and Valcartier, had
arrived from Ottawa to manage the reconstruction committee. Under his
guidance and example—he was on-site fifteen hours a day—troops built accommodation for one thousand on the South Common, above Citadel
Hill, in thirty days. Early in January, now with local workmen and those
from out of town, construction got under way on the Exhibition Grounds,
off Almon Street, and the Garrison Grounds, off Sackville. Workmen built
40 two-storey buildings, containing 320 apartments, on the Exhibition

In the dead of winter the temporary houses did not look at all inviting.
(MARITIME MUSEUM/VAUGHAN)

Grounds in thirty-two days and four blocks of 16 apartments each, as well as temporary stables, on the Garrison Grounds. Construction was taking place at such speed that the reconstruction department reckoned that one apartment was being built every hour.

The buildings, intended to last for five years, were constructed of wood and tarpaper, the inside finished with Beaverboard. Workmen also equipped them with water and electricity. They hooked up sewage lines and built roads, all in the dead of winter. Only a few brief strikes delayed construction. Unions objected to men not sticking to their own trade; for example, plasterers laid chimney bricks for the sake of speed. Men were also not paid overtime for working on Sundays. But the Halifax Relief Commission promised them that such conditions would change when housing was no longer a dire necessity.

By mid-March the first apartments on the Exhibition Grounds were ready for occupation. The settlement, known as the Gov. McCall Apartments, was divided into five avenues: Endicott, Maine, Rhode Island, Massachusetts, and Fredericton. Approximately twenty-two hundred people moved into the apartments, which ranged in size from two rooms, for a couple, to four rooms, for a family.

Rents for temporary housing, including water rates, depended on the size of the flat. Four large rooms with bath cost $12.00 a month; four small rooms with bath, $10.00; three rooms without bath, $7.50; and two rooms without bath, $5.00.

The Massachusetts–Halifax relief fund paid for the furniture, except for fixtures such as stoves and bathtubs, which were provided by the rehabilitation department. The local committee that oversaw the fund placed bulk orders. The furniture, of excellent quality, was purchased in Massachusetts and shipped by rail, duty free, to Halifax. The goods were stored in a warehouse on Windsor Street, and tenants in the temporary apartments could go there and choose what they wanted. (It was policy to have a variety of styles.) Thereafter, the furniture belonged to its new owner, who could then take it to his permanent home.

Other people could qualify for furniture if they registered with the committee, which considered each request on its merits and issued a voucher for deserving cases. Jean Hunter's family, who had stayed in the boxcar, received furniture after their house was rebuilt on its original site, on Agricola Street.

Typical orders from the committee were fairly long:

4 beds	1 oilcloth square 6ft by 9
4 springs	Complete outfit of kitchen utensils
4 mattresses	1 complete dinner set
4 bureaus	20 blinds
4 commodes	20 curtain rods
12 sheets	1 Morris chair
18 pillow slips	1 parlour table
4 pairs flannel blankets	1 wardrobe
4 bedroom squares	1 Boston couch
1 dining table	1 refrigerator
10 dining chairs	12 knives
1 buffet	12 forks
1 congoleum square 9ft by 12	12 teaspoons
8 mats 27 in by 60	12 tablespoons
1 3-piece parlour suite	12 tumblers
1 kitchen cabinet	12 bath towels
1 parlour carpet	12 towels
4 kitchen chairs	1 clothes wringer
1 kitchen table	1 bread box

Cribs, baby carriages, sewing machines, clocks, rocking chairs, and tools were all given out free. A Mi'kmaw, for example, received a pair of snowshoes to go hunting. (The warehouse also dispensed items for institutions: a piano for a music teacher, organs for churches, typewriters for the blind, furniture for orphanages, and invalid chairs.) It was common-

The Massachusetts–Halifax relief committee dispensed furniture from this warehouse. Residents in temporary accommodations could choose what they wanted. (PANS)

Massachusetts governor Samuel McCall, wearing the bowler hat, visited the apartments named after him. Charles Vaughan, a future mayor of Halifax, is in the baby carriage. (MARITIME MUSEUM/VAUGHAN)

sense aid at its best: recipients obtained possessions similar to the ones they had before the disaster.

Many satisfied customers sent letters of thanks to the committee. "I might say, dear sir," wrote one, "that the one bright spot in this awful year of trouble has been what those generous people of Massachusetts have done for us." Another was delighted with a "beautiful and splendid piano." The delivery appealed to a third: "I think it was just grand for you to bring them around yourself."

Not everyone approved, however. The relief commission began receiving numerous complaints from people not benefiting from Massachusetts generosity. By spring the commission was paying small claims for lost household belongings, even to people who had already received furniture. First of all, no one was forced to take the items, and some people preferred to provide their own. Second, others were not eligible. It seemed unfair that people receiving free furniture also got financial compensation. Before long the value of the goods was deducted from monetary claims, even though the Massachusetts–Halifax relief committee had intended that the furniture be considered a gift from the people of Massachusetts. The committee agreed, however, that it would be fairer to subtract the value from claims, especially when it became apparent that items were being sold. As five hundred dollars worth of furniture bought in Massachusetts, where prices were low, would cost one thousand dollars in Halifax, buyers could usually be found.

* * * * *

Tenants in the temporary apartments tried to make their accommodations as comfortable as possible. The Burfords—Frank, his mother, Charlotte, and his older sister, Winnie—moved onto the South Common, Apartment 11, Block 4. "We lived there winter and summer," Frank recalled. "We had two big bedrooms and a lovely big front room and a nice bathroom. I built a cupboard there, and I still have it after all these years." Evelyn Johnson, her two brothers, and her mother also lived on the South Common. They rented an upstairs flat with two bedrooms.

The communities, however, were not without problems. With so many people living at close quarters, infectious diseases were a real danger. In the summer of 1918 a smallpox epidemic affected the Exhibition Grounds and the South Common. Vaccinations were recommended for everyone, and the scare ended. (Minor outbreaks of smallpox were not uncommon in Halifax, with so many seamen and transients. It was not, however, considered a high-risk area for the disease. Houses were placarded, and affected families isolated.)

The settlements also lacked recreational amenities. In the summer of 1918 money from the Massachusetts–Halifax relief fund, the Rotary Club, and other organizations supplied two fully equipped playgrounds, one on the Exhibition Grounds, the other on the South Common. There were swings, slides, seesaws, and room to play ball.

It had become clear as well that organized activities were needed. The Exhibition Grounds contained more people than many a Nova Scotia village but in much more crowded conditions and with no entertainment nearby. At the suggestion of Mrs F. H. Sexton, who had joined the Boston relief train at Saint John, New Brunswick, and who was still involved in voluntary social work, the relief commission built a community centre on the Exhibition Grounds, the first of its kind in the city. The Christian Science war relief fund, which had been quietly helping in Halifax since December, in the area of education in particular, offered four thousand dollars to furnish the building; the new Halifax Welfare Bureau, its headquarters on Brunswick Street, paid for the upkeep. Other groups, such as the IODE, the Halifax School Board, and the YMCA, helped with activities.

Members had to pay an annual fee of twenty-five cents, which allowed them access to a daily kindergarten, clubs for children and adults, dressmaking, cooking, and dance classes, a library, movie nights, and other events. Six months after it opened, the centre's membership totalled four hundred, and the atmosphere on the Exhibition Grounds improved.

APPRAISALS
AND CLAIMS

SHORTLY AFTER the explosion insurance-company notices began to appear in every newspaper, asking clients who had suffered loss to come forward. It was common in those days to have small life insurances, even for children. They were a way of saving for the future. These claims were paid promptly on proof of death. But it was not so easy to collect property-insurance payments. Most homes and their contents were insured against fire but not against explosion, though it did not take long for enterprising firms to offer this option. Underwriters repudiated liability for buildings destroyed by fire, as the explosion had caused the original damage. It would be difficult, they said, to assess the proportion of damage attributable only to fire. They also argued that the disaster had been created by war, and therefore the money to compensate for it should come out of public funds.

The Halifax Relief Commission sought a compromise to avoid long and costly litigation. It appointed a five-member appraisal board, the majority of whose members were suggested by fire-insurance underwriters. Melvin S. Clarke, owner of a prominent real-estate business, was chairman. With F. S. Whittaker, a Saint John, New Brunswick, insurance broker, he prepared a complete and detailed appraisal of the damage in the North End, followed by one of the rest of the city. After some negotiation insurance companies agreed to pay 20 percent of private-housing and small-business losses and 35 percent of large-company losses.

While the board oversaw property cases, two courts dealt with smaller claims for personal belongings, including clothing, furniture and, in the case of a business or a store, supplies or merchandise. Set up by the rehabilitation department, these courts started sitting on January 30. Hearings were held twice a day, afternoon and evening, and were presided over by barristers. Claimants who filled out forms for amounts of less than one hundred dollars were notified of the time they could attend. No more than ten minutes was devoted to each case, and the claim was usually paid the same day.

Few received the amount asked for, as a percentage of the total sum was nearly always deducted. Those modest in their demands and recognized as honest, upright citizens were more likely to have their claims met speedily and fully. A young woman whose clothing had been destroyed by glass, soot, and snow filed the following claim for seventy-five dollars:

1 Plush coat—$10	1 silk dress—$15
1 summer dress of chiffon—$10	1 silk blouse—$5
Pair of boots—$7	1 winter hat—$5
1 serge skirt—$7	

"As I am only a working girl," she wrote, "I would like for you to give this your immediate attention as I had to work hard for what was destroyed." The woman received seventy dollars.

Claims for sums larger than $100.00 sometimes required more than one visit to court. The original appointment was made by letter, then the adjudicator made an offer, and if it was too low, the claimant could appeal. Those with little time or patience often gave up. One small businessman made a claim for $1,429.50. On his first visit he was told that items valued at $975.00 had been disallowed. That left $452.50. On his second visit he was offered $252.50. He argued and was told he could appeal. That would have meant a third appointment, and he had already lost hours of work time. He was not content but accepted nonetheless.

A family who had lived on Kane Street was more successful, possibly because of their dire circumstances. The wife had been injured, a wage-earning son, one of five children, killed, and the house destroyed. Initially three children were in a shelter, the mother was in one hospital, and one boy, with a serious eye injury, was in another; the father was staying with a relative. They were given a flat on the Exhibition Grounds, and in July the family received full settlement for their claim: $559.35.

People sometimes did not file for compensation as soon as it was advertised. Many were widows whose husbands had handled all financial affairs. One woman did not submit a claim until March. Her husband had been killed, and she had four small children. "My losses in the explosion were so great," she wrote, "that I am just beginning to think of what I did lose." Part of her claim showed the kind of rural life that many people in Richmond had led:

97 Fowls, Rhode Island Reds, Orpingtons, Leghorns—$97
1 Cyprus Incubator—$20
10 Bushels Potatoes—$12
40 Quart Bottles Preserves—$20
15 Bottles Pickles—$4.50
15 Bags Portland Cement—$18.75

Claim forms were not easy to fill out accurately. Under normal circumstances few today could list all the contents of their houses or wardrobes. At that time many claimants were grief stricken and still not fully recovered in health. They only began to remember details of lost belongings months later. For an elderly widow, alone and homeless, all the forms and all the courts were too confusing, and she could not manage without help. An engineer who returned home found his house on Veith Street burned to the ground. His wife and his five sons, ranging in age from seven to sixteen, had all been killed. His house was insured against fire, but he was hardly in the mental state to be able to recall its furnishings.

Others did not even know they could get reparation. A social worker was trying to find a family that had not registered. She finally located the place where they had lived. The man, a soldier who had been given ten days' leave, was busy building a shack behind his wrecked home. He was surprised, and grateful, to learn he could receive compensation. His only son had been killed, and his wife, whose hearing had been affected, was staying in a shelter. In March they received a settlement of $400 and lived in the shack until their house was ready. Later, when they became aware of the claims others had put in, they made further requests. Another soldier, who had been abroad for two years, came home four months after the explosion. As his family had moved, he had never seen the apartment his wife had rented in the Flynn Block, and most of the furniture had been new. His wife and daughter had died, as had many of the people who had lived nearby. He did not know who might be able to describe the apartment's contents, but then he thought of the priest. In May he accepted a settlement of $480. The courts' work was far from straightforward.

The courts did not consider loss of actual cash or objects of "pure luxury" such as fur coats, jewellery, paintings, ornaments, or pianos. Cars could be included in a claim, but many expressed resentment because they felt that cars, too, were pure luxury.

Claims involving clothing of the dead were also disallowed. Difficulties arose when all the adults in a family had been wiped out and compensation had to go to the next of kin. Relief commission officials questioned relatives,

The owners of the Acadia Sugar Refinery received about $190,000 in compensation. Vincent Pattison had been buried under these ruins.

friends, landlords, and ministers about the contents of houses and about their condition. Reports often conflicted. As word spread of how much various neighbours had received, so did feelings of discontent or satisfaction. Exaggerations of the magnitude or the paucity of awards added zest to the tales.

Next of kin did not always gain by pushing too hard for settlements for relatives' possessions. In one case, where an entire small family had been killed, the relations making the claim were fairly well off. The victims, on the other hand, had lived in a small, poorly furnished apartment. After acrimonious correspondence and visits to the landlord and the neighbours, the claimants were told that they could take out administration papers but that this would also make them liable for the large debts the dead family had incurred. The claim was dropped.

Overall, adjudicators decided on 16,422 claims, totalling $3,494,730.11; the amount paid out was $2,570,048.60. There were also 1,156 traders' claims, equalling $337,338.18; $258,327.05 was paid out.

*   *   *   *   *

The appraisal board, meanwhile, was assessing property claims. First the board dealt with claims of less than five thousand dollars, those of private homes and small businesses. Claimants with damaged or destroyed build-ings also had to fill out itemized forms, giving all the details about their property: barns and outbuildings, state of repair, date of most recent repairs, assessment, mortgage, and taxes. If all papers had been destroyed, this was difficult. Few had the advantage of legal advice, so ministers, doctors, and aldermen helped if they could. (It was also hard for assessors if forms were incomplete.) Once the forms were filled out, they had to be notarized and filed with the board. The board then sent out a property inspector and made an assessment.

If a house had been completely destroyed, the owner had a choice of having it rebuilt at the expense of the relief commission or of receiving a lump sum equalling the appraised value. If a house had been damaged, the owner could sell it to the commission, which paid off any existing mortgage so long as it did not exceed the appraisal. The commission also had the power to expropriate.

When repairs were feasible, the owner could choose between having commission labourers do the work or hiring someone privately. Many did the latter, assuming that it would be faster and preferring to hire local firms. In the first year about ten thousand houses were repaired. A reconstruction labourer earned thirty cents an hour; board in the camp cost four dollars a week.

All work was inspected before the commission paid a private contractor, to prevent either the owner or the contractor from cutting corners. By August the appraisal board employed about ten property inspectors, who also examined work in progress. In one case, where a shoddy job was being done, the contractor received a letter warning that unless improvements were made immediately, all inspectors would be informed of the dubious quality of his firm's work and would be especially diligent in future inspections.

Naturally, mistakes were made, and complaints frequent. The value placed on homes that had been totally destroyed was often insufficient, not taking into account escalating costs for replacement. Tenants were advised to withhold rent until repairs were completed. Landlord–tenant relations suffered when, in some instances, rents were deliberately not paid for reasons that had nothing to do with the explosion, and false charges were presented to the commission. In other cases, rent increases were demanded because there was a scarcity of housing. The commission tried to deal with all such complaints. In fact, some people thought that officials would never stop knocking on their doors.

In the early summer of 1919 a special commission of the appraisal board began to deal with claims of more than $5,000, none of which was for a private home and all of which were negotiated by lawyers. In July the board heard the case of the Acadia Sugar Refinery, whose owners had claimed $474,149. The refinery had been up for sale at the time of the explosion, to pay off debts, and the company lawyer argued that it would have been sold if it had not been destroyed. Even though it had not been in operation, it had been used for storage and had still employed a large number of men. The board decided on compensation of $187,138.90, and the company accepted.

For the badly damaged Provincial Exhibition buildings, whose site had been taken over for temporary housing, the claim was $224,593; the settlement was $135,000. Government property was not eligible for compensation; shipping was covered by marine and war-risk insurance.

March 3, 1920, was the cut-off date for the filing of claims. As an incentive to improve the appearance of the city as quickly as possible, the board issued no settlement until repair work had been done. City revenue had dropped sharply, as more than $18 million worth of property was exempt from taxes. For this reason, too, it was essential that the return to normal take place without delay.

IT MUST HAVE BEEN THE GERMANS

FIXING
RESPONSIBILITY

WHILE THE SOCIAL MACHINERY was trying to get Halifax back on its feet, the legal machinery was trying to establish who was to blame for the explosion. The press had demanded to know how such a catastrophe could have happened. As early as December 7, 1917, *The Truro Daily News* had called for blood: "The party or parties responsible for such a needless collision with clear water, in broad daylight, should be hung in good old fashioned style at the yard's arm." It had taken two more days for headlines such as "FIX RESPONSIBILITY" to appear in Halifax newspapers. "Let justice be done tho' the heavens fall," concluded *The Halifax Herald*.

Rumours of sabotage, inefficiency, and carelessness abounded. Aimé Le Medec, the captain of the *Mont Blanc*, had put himself under police protection, but Francis Mackey, the pilot, had remained at work in Halifax Harbour. He and two of the crew had been interviewed, and their story, blaming the *Imo*, reported in the press. Their account maintained that the *Mont Blanc* had been on her own side of the channel. In a later story the *Imo*'s crew agreed but insisted that the *Mont Blanc* had then cut in front of their ship. The collision, the men claimed, would have been fairly minor if the French steamer had not been carrying explosives. Crowds of people had watched the accident take place, and conflicting stories were rife throughout the whole Maritime region. Surely the promised legal inquiry before the Wreck Commissioners Court would set the record straight.

The inquiry opened at the courthouse on Spring Garden Road on the afternoon of December 12, only six days after the explosion. Presiding was Mr Justice Arthur Drysdale, local judge in admiralty for the Nova Scotia district of the Exchequer Court of Canada. He was assisted by Captain L. A. Demers and Captain Charles Hose, of the Royal Canadian Navy, acting as nautical assessors. William A. Henry, KC, appeared on behalf of the

Dominion government; Humphrey Mellish, KC, and J. P. Nolan, of New York City, for the owners of the *Mont Blanc;* Charles J. Burchell, KC, for the owners of the *Imo;* F. H. Bell, for the City of Halifax; Crown Prosecutor Andrew Cluney, KC, for the Nova Scotia Department of Attorney General; and T. R. Robertson, KC, for the Halifax Pilotage Commission. It was an impressive array of legal talent.

The hearing of evidence began the following morning, with members of the press the only spectators. The surroundings were a grim reminder of the previous week's events. The courtroom had "aged plaster dropping from the walls, which showed here and there large sections of bare lath," the *Herald* later reported. "The whole [was] dimly lighted by two feeble electric lamps ... and the remainder of the window [was] roughly boarded up." A large harbour chart and the models of two ships were available for witnesses to illustrate their testimony. Unless under examination, however, all witnesses had to wait in another room. The only exception was Andrew Johansen, steward of the *Imo*, who was bilingual and might be useful as an interpreter for his ship's crew. It was an empty, gloomy scene.

Le Medec, captain of the *Mont Blanc,* was the first witness. *The Evening Mail* (Halifax) described him as short in stature, with a broad forehead and snapping dark eyes; his black beard was long but neatly groomed. Under examination by Henry, counsel for Ottawa, Le Medec, speaking through an interpreter, Louis d'Ornano, described the ship's cargo and how it had been loaded. Henry asked whether Pilot Mackey had been "imbibing freely" the night of December 5. Le Medec replied that since the war, no liquor was permitted on French ships. Then the lawyer turned his attention to the movement of the *Mont Blanc* in the harbour on the morning of December 6. Le Medec said that his ship had kept a reasonable speed from the time it had left anchorage, off McNabs Island, and that visibility had been good. At 8:25 he sighted the *Imo* emerging from the Narrows, cutting across his course, her starboard side facing him. The *Mont Blanc* signalled with one whistle blast, indicating that it would veer slightly more to starboard, or to the right, towards Dartmouth. Le Medec testified he had ordered the crew to slow the engines.

The *Imo* had replied with two blasts, indicating that it was going to port, or to the left. (As it was coming from the opposite direction, from Bedford Basin, that meant it was moving towards the Dartmouth shore, or into the *Mont Blanc*'s channel.) The *Mont Blanc* gave a second single blast and again edged closer to the Dartmouth side. Le Medec ordered the engines stopped, and the *Imo* gave another two-blast signal and continued towards the *Mont Blanc.* The *Mont Blanc* could go no nearer to shore, as there was no room. The ships were now 150 metres apart, the land 60–70 metres

There were plenty of witnesses from the *Mont Blanc* who could testify at the inquiry.

away. The *Mont Blanc*, heavily loaded, could not stop quickly and was still making headway. When it seemed that a collision was unavoidable, Le Medec gave orders to the helmsman to bear hard to the left, thus swinging towards Halifax and across the bow of the *Imo*. At the same time, he issued two short, sharp blasts. Now the two ships were parallel, each with the other on its starboard side, about 50 metres between them. Le Medec said he had thought they could now pass safely. The *Imo*, however, blew three blasts, meaning "full speed astern!" As she was light and still had some speed, her bow, under reverse propulsion, swung towards the starboard side of the *Mont Blanc*. Immediately, realizing that a collision was imminent, Le Medec also ordered full speed astern in an attempt to prevent the *Imo* from striking Hold 2, where the TNT was stored. He succeeded. The *Imo* hit Hold 1, penetrating 3 or 4 metres, reaching the barrels of picric acid. Smoke began to rise immediately.

When he saw flames, Le Medec thought that the ship was going to blow up at once. It was impossible, he said, to do anything to stop the fire. In order not to jeopardize uselessly the lives of more than forty men, he gave the command to lower the lifeboats. After all the crew had boarded, he ordered them to leave, and they headed for the eastern shore. On arrival, after they had left the water's edge, he had the first officer take a roll call. Just then the explosion took place. They were all thrown to the ground, and one crew member was seriously injured. He estimated that about twenty minutes had elapsed since the collision.

Burchell, lawyer for the owners of the *Imo*, continued the examination.

He asked whether the *Mont Blanc* had flown a red flag. Le Medec replied that international rules required a ship to fly a red flag only if explosives were being handled on board, not just carried. What was the ship's position after the crew had left? The captain said she had been in mid-channel at the point of collision but that the impact had pushed her towards the Halifax shore. Then Burchell wanted to know why Le Medec had not stayed with the ship and tried to change her course. The captain insisted that he had tried to stay but that the first officer had pulled him towards a lifeboat, saying he could do no good. Even if he had remained, he said, he could not have seen where the ship was heading. The smoke was too thick.

Burchell questioned the chain of command between Le Medec and Mackey. The captain and pilot had stood on the bridge, fairly close together, separated by the rope that worked the whistle. The captain said that the pilot had given orders, but that at all times under French law, the master was in command of his ship. He took advice from the pilot and transmitted it to the helmsman, in the wheelhouse, and to the officer working the telegraph to the engine room. The lawyer asked whether Le Medec and Mackey had spoken much. Le Medec replied that it would not have been possible. He did not speak English, and the pilot did not speak French. He insisted, however, that there had been no misunderstandings: he knew words such as *port, starboard, slow, stop,* and *full speed ahead.* The pilot, too, understood the necessary French terminology. Le Medec had been at sea for twenty-five years and was well aware when orders were being carried out and the correct moves being made.

Burchell's persistent questions frequently sounded censorious. As all questions and answers were transmitted through the interpreter, Le Medec's replies sounded calmer in English than they did in French. Burchell asked whether the captain had seen the pilot go back to the wheel before he left the ship. Le Medec had not, but he had ordered the helmsman to straighten the wheel, that is, put it amidships.

"Did he think of changing the helm to run the ship into some place where it would not be so dangerous to the city—did he think of running it up into the Basin?" Burchell asked through the interpreter.

"No, sir," Louis d'Ornano answered for Le Medec, "he says that if the explosion was to take place ten metres one side or ten metres the other side it was bound to happen."

"Ask him if any signals were given to the engineer after the collision—on the telegraph?"

"He stopped."

"Who gave that?"

"The captain."

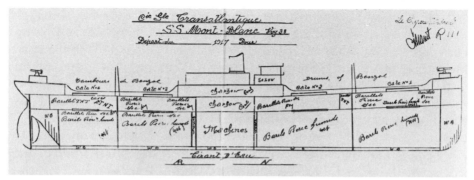

Exhibit M.B.R.1, showing the storage of the *Mont Blanc*'s cargo, was introduced early in the inquiry. (RECORD OF PROCEEDINGS)

"Does he know if it was obeyed or not?"

"Yes, sir," replied d'Ornano, "and he says the proof is that when they got into the boats they could not get away—they had to push themselves with the oar."

City Solicitor Bell was curious about what the men had done to put out the fire. He asked whether they had tried to open the seacock, to let water in. Le Medec did not actually know but said that it would have taken half an hour to open. Then Bell asked whether anyone had tried to quench the fire with pumps. Le Medec explained that the amount of water the pumps could give out was insignificant in such a fire and that spraying water on benzol was not safe.

The first witness from the *Imo* was Peter B'Jonnas, second mate. B'Jonnas had been in the forecastle stowing away the anchor when the collision occurred.

Again William Henry tried to ascertain the condition of the pilot. "Was the pilot drunk or sober that morning?"

"He cannot say," the interpreter, Andrew Johansen, answered after consultation with B'Jonnas, who, after more questioning, conceded that the pilot had looked all right.

For the most part B'Jonnas's evidence was inconclusive. Like many other survivors from the *Imo*, he was not certain about the sequence of events. First of all, he had not witnessed much. He had not been on the bridge and had not been in a position of command. The shock of the explosion and of his ship being hurled across the harbour, as well as of being left semiconscious from a chest injury, made the details leading up to the collision less vivid. B'Jonnas often replied with a simple "I am not sure" or "I did not notice."

What evidence he did give was sketchy at best. He thought that the captain, pilot, and helmsman had all been on the deck the whole time. He also recalled the *Imo* issuing two whistle blasts and then one, and he was fairly sure that the *Mont Blanc* had replied with one. Then the ships had each given three blasts, the *Imo* first. They were now about one hundred metres apart and drawing closer. He did not notice the *Imo*'s engines reversing or the ship changing course. The *Imo* struck the *Mont Blanc*'s starboard bow with little shock, as the *Imo* was moving slowly. He also said that there had been a one-blast signal given earlier by the *Imo* that had been answered by one from a tugboat. (Later, crew members of the tug *Stella Maris* denied this.) "Was he there to listen for whistles?" Burchell asked later. Listening for whistle signals, B'Jonnas replied, was not one of his duties.

Under closer questioning by Captain L. A. Demers, B'Jonnas admitted he did not know why the pilot had given a two-blast signal when the *Mont Blanc* was on the port side. One blast would have taken the *Imo* away from the *Mont Blanc,* and that did seem more sensible. Demers wanted to know how a man on the forecastle of a light ship could not feel the vibration of an engine moving astern. "He did not notice," the interpreter said after a few words with B'Jonnas. Demers was losing his patience. He looked at the interpreter. "He did not take much notice of anything?" he asked wryly.

On December 17 Pilot Mackey took the stand. Although he had already given newspaper interviews, people eagerly awaited his testimony. He was, after all, from Halifax and did not have to speak through an interpreter.

His evidence turned out to be more or less the same as that of Le Medec. He, too, said that there had been no problem of communication or understanding. Anyway, he maintained, he always used hand signals, as well as words, to indicate directions. Charles Burchell later asked Mackey to say in French the terms used on the bridge of a ship. The pilot did fairly well until he was asked to spell out the words written on the telegraph of a French vessel. He said *half-speed* was *demi-mitesse,* probably comprehensible to a French seaman, but he spelled it *demi-tasse,* meaning "small cup."

There was no doubt that Burchell was going to try to establish Mackey's guilt. A native of Cape Breton who had been living in Halifax for twelve years, Burchell had already been involved in harrowing rescue and relief work, and it had affected him deeply. He had a strong personality, and his adversarial approach, that of a prosecutor before a jury, had come to dominate the entire proceedings. At the beginning of the inquiry he had made his position clear. "It is a question of two pilots," he announced, "whether both or one … are at fault—they are responsible for the whole accident…. Pilot Mackey is really on trial in this court; but the other pilot [Hayes] unfortunately is dead, and cannot be put on trial." He had also emphasized that the witnesses most important to his case, the men on the bridge of the *Imo,* were dead.

Burchell pointed out that there had been enough time between the collision and the explosion for the men on the *Mont Blanc* to have warned people about the danger. Many lives could have been saved. Paying little attention to Mackey's claims that the men had yelled warnings, the lawyer then got specific. Did Mackey know Pilot Hayes? Mackey said he had known him for many years and had a high respect for his ability.

Charles Burchell's strong personality came to dominate the entire proceedings.
(COURTESY CHARLES W. BURCHELL, QC)

Burchell spoke of the dock workers that had been killed on the wharves and named various ships that had been damaged or destroyed. "Did you know the captain of the *Stella Maris?*"

"Yes."

"What is his name?"

"Brannan [*sic*]."

"Do you know he was killed?" Burchell pressed.

"I heard he was killed."

"Do you know there were 24 men killed on the ship?"

"I heard that," Mackey said quietly.

"Do you know as a matter of fact that the *Stella Maris* did go alongside [the *Mont Blanc*] and that the captain and the officers performed a great deed of heroism in trying to put this fire out?"

"I heard that," Mackey repeated.

The inquisition continued relentlessly. It was the afternoon of the funeral service for the ninety-five unidentified dead. "Do you know the bells are ringing now for this funeral?" Burchell asked.

"I have not heard them," Mackey replied.

Softly, almost pleadingly, Burchell said, "I want to ask you now, knowing that this is the hour for the funeral, if you are willing to admit frankly that you have been deliberately perjuring yourself for the last two days?"

"No."

"You say that everything you told us is absolutely true?"

"To the best of my knowledge; to the best of my ability."

Twice Burchell asked, "You say that at this hour?"

Twice Mackey replied, "Yes."

Finally Burchell changed his tack. The next questions concerned Mackey's drinking habits. Was he a man that frequently got drunk? Mackey said he might have been a long time ago but not any more. Then the lawyer asked about his salary. Was it one thousand dollars a month? The pilot said it was not that much but was vague about the actual amount.

During questioning by Crown Prosecutor Andrew Cluney, it emerged that Mackey had piloted the *Imo* twice during the previous summer and that Captain From had been in command. Cluney wanted to know whether From had seemed competent and capable of navigating a ship. "Not in the mood that I found him," Mackey answered.

Mackey was alluding to a newspaper story that had appeared on December 15. (A Boston correspondent had sent it to counsel associated with the inquiry.) In Philadelphia, about a month earlier, From had refused to pay bills for some repair work on the *Imo*. He left port but was intercepted and served with a warrant by a United States marshall who forced From to go to Wilmington, Delaware, the nearest port. Gustav Schmall, president of the firm that had carried out the repairs, accompanied by his lawyer, visited the ship. When the lawyer left to make a telephone call, From savagely beat up Schmall. "He was like a maniac," Schmall reported. The attorney who represented From in the ensuing court case claimed that the captain was intensely anti-German and resented Schmall's name.

Twenty-two witnesses were heard and four statements taken from crew members of the *Highflyer* before the inquiry adjourned on December 21. Some had even been brought from their hospital beds. On December 19 one newspaper observed that few spectators had stayed more than a little while each day. No wonder. The testimony was technical, much of it involving numerical estimates: the speeds, the distances, the whistle signals, the exact point of collision, and how much the course of the *Mont Blanc* had changed because of the accident. The evidence also became more and more inconsistent. A few witnesses even contradicted their own previous statements concerning the sequence of signal blasts. One man said simply, "There was an awful lot of whistling." It had all happened so quickly. Only seven or eight minutes had elapsed between the first whistle and the collision. The legalities, the nautical terms, the numbers, much of it through an interpreter, were wearisome.

Only one revelation caused considerable interest and speculation. On

December 21 newspaper headlines reported the testimony of two seamen from the British *Calonne*. Both had said they had seen two sailors, probably British, on board the *Mont Blanc* before she exploded. It has been written that sailors from the HMCS *Niobe*'s boat had gone aboard, but both crew members of the *Stella Maris*, who testified at the inquiry, said they had seen no one on board. Contemporary newspapers delved no further.

After all the rumours there was no real evidence of German treachery or intrigue. It seemed instead that someone had simply blundered. For most people it was a real muddle, and they found it difficult to blame one ship or the other. But one thing was certain. They bitterly resented the harm done by the *Mont Blanc*'s cargo.

*　　*　　*　　*　　*

The inquiry reconvened on January 21. The only survivor from the bridge of the *Imo*, John Johansen, took the stand. He had not appeared earlier because he had been at Bellevue Hospital and then detained. At Bellevue he had acted in an excited manner, tried to leave, and offered a large sum of money to anyone who would buy him a newspaper. The military then placed the sailor under arrest as a suspicious character. Charles Burchell intervened, and Johansen was moved to a military hospital. Later it was discovered that it had been a case of mistaken identity. Johansen, however, was still in solitary confinement and under armed guard. As a result, he was fast becoming sullen and morose. After his release his spirits improved, and with proper treatment, he was fit to testify.

As Johansen had lived in the United States for five years and had spent time in the United States Navy, he spoke fluent English and did not require the use of an interpreter. On December 6 he had been at the wheel of the *Imo*. But he could not see the telegraph and did not know what orders were being sent to the engine room. He heard some signal blasts being exchanged with an American steamer (the one piloted by Edward Renner), but he was not paying much attention. When they passed, the American ship was between the *Imo* and the Halifax shore. He also heard Renner shout that another ship was coming behind and that they should keep a sharp lookout. The *Imo* moved up the middle of the Narrows, and then Johansen noticed the tugboat towing two scows heading out from shore, almost in mid-channel. His ship issued a whistle signal, but he was not sure what it was or even to which ship it was directed. When pressed to estimate how far they had been from the tug, he would not even hazard a guess. Just after the *Imo* passed the tug, Johansen saw the *Mont Blanc*, nearly opposite the HMS *Highflyer.* About that time he was given the order "Steady on, a little port." Dominion counsel Henry asked what that meant on a Norwegian ship. Johansen explained that it caused the vessel to move to starboard, the same system as on British ships. (The French had simplified their commands, so that the order and the direction the ship turned were the same. "*A gauche*" meant turn the wheel to the left, and the ship also moved to the left. Pilots must have been accustomed to the difference, but was Mackey? He had said in his evidence that the French system was the same as the British and the Norwegian, but this point was never fully resolved, perhaps because he had said he had supplemented his commands with hand signals.)

The first signal Johansen said he had heard was two blasts from the *Mont Blanc.* She was on the Dartmouth side but had already changed course and was heading towards the *Imo.* It looked, he said, as if the *Mont Blanc* was going to run right into the *Imo.* Then he remembered that his ship had blown a single blast immediately before and that he had turned the ship slightly towards the Halifax shore. The next thing he heard, just a second before the collision, was a three-blast signal from his own ship, but he did not know whether the engines had been reversed. The *Imo* struck the *Mont Blanc* on the starboard side, but Johansen did not feel the shock of the blow.

He did see the lifeboats leave the *Mont Blanc,* as one moved right by the *Imo.* "Did they call out to you or say anything as they passed?" Henry asked.

"No sir," Johansen said confidently.

"At the time of collision the *Mont Blanc* must have been heading toward the Halifax shore?"

"She was."

"Did she continue to move through the water after the collision?"

"Yes sir."

"Which way?"

"Right into the pier." Johansen was sure that her propeller was turning and her engines going ahead until she struck the pier.

Imo counsel Burchell elicited from Johansen that Pilot Hayes had seen the accident coming. When the *Mont Blanc* turned across the *Imo*'s bow, the helmsman said, Hayes "hollered out to the captain" that there was going to be a collision.

Humphrey Mellish, for the owners of the *Mont Blanc,* and Captain Demers both questioned Johansen further on the series of signal whistles and on distances, but the sailor refused to be definite. After hearing the answer "I could not say" to most of his questions, Demers once more lost his temper. He had established that Johansen had ten years' experience as a seaman and wished to further his career. "For a man with an ambition to become an officer, you seem to take little note of what goes on around you," he remarked caustically.

"A man at the wheel does not pay attention to whistles," Johansen replied. "He watches the helm only." When pressed by Demers, Johansen said that signals were the pilot's responsibility, not his.

Demers moved on to the *Mont Blanc*'s engines. Johansen still maintained they had kept going after she had been abandoned. But he now said he had not seen the propeller. Johansen even claimed at one point that the *Mont Blanc* had hit the *Imo*, not the other way around. Demers had been persistent, and perhaps the sailor had been confused. In any event, Johansen's testimony had been disappointing. As he was the only man alive from the bridge of the *Imo*, the court had hoped he would clear up many points, but he was inconsistent and indecisive.

Walter Brannen and William Nickerson, first and second mates of the *Stella Maris*, could not shed any light on the sequence of whistle signals, either. Both heard a signal from the *Imo* as she was near their tug, but their captain said that it could not have been for them. Brannen thought that it had been one blast, but Nickerson was not sure.

Captain Le Medec was recalled, as one part of Mackey's evidence had contradicted his. Mackey had said that after the collision he had given an order that the engines be put at full speed ahead to force water through the holds. There had been no response, and the order had not been carried out. Both Le Medec and the engineer testified that no command other than "stop engines" had been made or carried out.

This discrepancy caused little comment or excitement. But the fact that Le Medec was suddenly testifying in English certainly did. Henry established that in France captains had to take examinations in English. Although Le Medec was not fluent, his understanding and his ability to express himself were at least adequate, and he knew all the nautical terms. When questioned, he maintained he had been nervous about using the language in court. Perhaps his stay in Halifax had refreshed his skills.

The following day, January 22, saw the beginning of testimony from those in charge of Halifax Harbour. It also saw an end to the apathy. This was more comprehensible than whistles and other nautical details. Large headlines now reported the proceedings.

Under questioning by William Henry, Captain Frederick Pasco, acting superintendent of the dockyard, outlined the new regulations that had been introduced in the Port of Halifax since the explosion. His evidence was startling in its revelations of previous conditions: the scarcity of pilots, the neglect of rules, the dangerous cargoes treated with scant respect. The new regulations made Haligonians feel somewhat safer, though they were of little comfort to those with nothing more to lose.

There was not much need to press Pasco for information. He talked freely and eloquently. He reported that munitions ships were now held at the examination anchorage on arrival and were not allowed to move until all large ships had been stopped. They could then proceed to an anchorage at the most remote part of Bedford Basin. Movement in the harbour was resumed only when the munitions ship was anchored. When convoys left the basin, all incoming traffic was stopped, and no movement of seagoing vessels was allowed. In addition, a signal station was being erected at the entrance to the Narrows, and no vessels would be permitted to pass in the Narrows, no matter whether they were carrying munitions. Contact between the various control ships had been increased, and permission to sail or change anchorage or to enter the harbour was now being obtained without exception. Pilots were co-operating, and their system, too, would soon be overhauled.

Pasco was then questioned about the events leading up to the explosion. He maintained he had no notice that the *Mont Blanc* was coming through the harbour. In his opinion, the ship's cargo had been exceptionally dangerous. But when asked about the advisability of carrying a red flag in war conditions, he said bluntly, "It would be suicidal—giving information to enemy agents."

Cargoes of munitions, he continued, had been coming in and out of Canadian ports for three years without mishap; for example, one out of every three or five ships leaving Montreal carried munitions. Henry pointed out that special regulations might be necessary to prevent other ships from violating the rules of the road. But Pasco did not agree. "It certainly did not occur to me that a ship would be coming up a harbour like a piece of fireworks ready to be exploded," he retorted, adding, "I don't expect a ship to blow up because she has had a collision." In his opinion, the improper stowing of munitions had caused the explosion. The drums of benzol, broken during the collision, should never have been placed on deck. "I am surprised any ship would allow it to be loaded," he said. "I am surprised the people on the ship didn't leave in a body." As Pasco was a man of forty years' experience, his words carried weight.

Late in his evidence, under examination by Charles Burchell, Pasco divulged an astounding piece of information. "I didn't want to bring that in my evidence at all but the CXO told me the *Imo* did not get permission from him to leave." He added that the chief commanding officer (CXO) was the only man who had the authority to stop her.

Commander Frederick Wyatt, CXO, then took the stand. He testified that he had been informed of the arrival of the *Mont Blanc* and that he had been notified of her cargo. But he knew nothing of the benzol. He did not pass on the information, and he did not give any instructions to the examining officer, who also knew about the explosives. It was dark, and the ship would not be allowed to enter the harbour until morning, anyway.

Pilots, Wyatt said, had orders to report to the CXO on landing a ship at anchorage and to ask his permission before moving a ship to another berth or taking one out to sea. He insisted he had given absolutely no permission for any ship to leave on the morning of December 6. The *Mont Blanc* should have had a clear passage.

Because of the difficulties in communicating with neutral vessels, Wyatt had placed the onus of notifying his office entirely on the pilots. He had sent a memo to this effect to the pilotage commission on May 4, 1917. He admitted that pilots had sometimes disobeyed the order but said that there was no way he could reprimand them, as they came under a different authority.

The examining officer on duty on December 5 and 6, Terence Freeman, a mate in the Royal Canadian Naval Volunteer Reserve, confirmed he had gone aboard the *Mont Blanc* on December 5 and had told the captain and the pilot they could proceed to the basin as soon as the gate opened in the morning unless they received further word. Usually, if there were "any ships coming out of the harbour worthwhile," the CXO's office on the *Niobe* notified him to hold everything. He had no direct communication with the guard ship, in the basin. He knew that the *Mont Blanc* was carrying explosives, but he did not realize how dangerous they were, and he had never heard of benzol.

James Hall, sheriff of Halifax County, was chairman of the pilotage commission, the voluntary board that oversaw the conduct of pilots. He testified to the good character, sobriety, and industriousness of pilots Mackey and Hayes. He admitted that there might have been some complaints about certain pilots doing their work too hastily and one or two cases where the CXO criticized them for not reporting to him. But he could not give specific instances.

Crown Prosecutor Cluney asked him whether there was a shortage of pilots. He stated that there had been fourteen in 1917 and nineteen the previous year; there were also eight apprentices. The commission had passed a bylaw asking Ottawa for permission to employ ships' masters to help manage the increase in shipping caused by the war but was still waiting for confirmation.

Hall said that all requests for pilots went through the office on Bedford Row, in downtown Halifax, where there was a secretary and a clerk who took the messages. Notices for the pilots were pinned to a wall in the office, where the pilots were bound to see them.

Wyatt was recalled, and Burchell began the examination. Burchell was outraged that Wyatt had said that Pilot Hayes had taken the *Imo* out of the basin without permission. "For a man to make a charge against a dead man which is unfair and unwarranted would be very much against British fair play?"

"Neither unfair or unwarranted, seeing it is an absolute fact," Wyatt insisted.

Although other lawyers occasionally objected when Burchell used such tactics with witnesses, the judge did little to curb him. He continued in the same manner, hinting that Wyatt's relations with Pasco were poor, as he had taken so long to inform him about the *Imo*'s infringement. But Wyatt denied it. He was also adamant that the easiest, quickest, and most accurate way of keeping track of ships was by means of pilots' reports. His office on the *Niobe* was manned day and night; he was on duty fourteen hours a day and available by telephone at most other times. He admitted that there had been other instances of ships leaving without permission but gave the impression that it was not common. Occasionally they were stopped, but it was too dangerous to fire at all of them with so many other ships around.

Then, quite gently, Burchell began, "I have talked with four pilots—"

"I gather that. Yesterday afternoon," Wyatt interjected.

Burchell ignored the interruption. "Four or five pilots since you were on the stand yesterday and these pilots tell me that for several months prior to December 6 they had not reported to you."

"I have that letter in my pocket here in which I reported it to the Captain Superintendent."

"Then that statement is correct that a number of the pilots never reported to you at all?"

"Have not been doing so."

"Prior to the 6th December?"

"Yes."

"Didn't you intend to give us the impression yesterday that all pilots had been reporting to you and that this case of Pilot Hayes was something extraordinary?"

"I didn't."

Burchell continued inexorably. He had been interviewing everyone connected with the pilotage office, and they had maintained they had had trouble finding Wyatt. All along, without much success, he had been trying to establish Wyatt's inefficiency and negligence. Finally he was triumphant. Pilots had become tired of wasting their time trying to get in touch with Wyatt, and so the clerk in the pilotage office had been asked to phone in lists of departing ships. Wyatt said he usually received them himself, and he thought it was always a pilot on the telephone. Sometimes ships' names, fourteen or fifteen at a time, were called in.

Now came the bombshell. The clerk had told Burchell that he had stopped telephoning after six or seven weeks because he thought they just laughed at him in the CXO's office. This meant that no reports had been called in since July 1, 1917. Wyatt conceded only that it had been some time. He had complained several times to his superior officer, Captain Martin, who was responsible for approaching the pilotage commission. (Martin had been in England since before the explosion and therefore was unable to testify.)

Burchell asked Wyatt whether he could repeat the new regulations regarding munitions ships. Wyatt did. Did he know, however, that the day before, an oil tanker, the *Appalache,* met a munitions ship, the *Galileo,* at almost the same place as the collision between the *Imo* and the *Mont Blanc?*

No, Wyatt had been in court at the time. "Is it up to me when anything goes wrong wherever I am?" he asked bitterly. But he promised to investigate. (*The Morning Chronicle* had exaggerated the incident into a probable repetition of the explosion, causing considerable alarm. Mr Justice Drysdale, the following day, issued a reprimand in court, warning he would take steps to prevent the public from being excited by inaccurate reporting.)

Wyatt left the stand, but he must have known he would come under further scrutiny. The secretary of the pilotage commission, James W. Creighton, testified that when he was notified that not all pilots were reporting to the CXO, he told the clerk to undertake the task as much as possible. He had, however, often heard pilots telephone the CXO. Information for the pilots—what ship was sailing or entering, who should take it in or out, and so on—was written on a large slate on the office wall. The only complaints he had heard recently were of ships being taken to the wrong berth.

On Saturday, January 26, the clerk, Edward Beazley, took the stand. His youthful appearance caused surprise. Could this boy really have been responsible for receiving and communicating pilots' reports to naval authorities?

"How old are you?" William Henry asked.

"16 years on last Saturday," Edward answered proudly.

Edward had been employed by the commission since March 12, 1917. When first told to take over reporting, he carried out the order faithfully. Usually he rang once a day, sometimes twice if there were a large number of ships. A ship's agent would telephone that a certain vessel was cleared to sail. He would then tell the CXO the time the agent wanted a pilot. Soon, however, he discovered that if he gave the names of several ships very fast, he was seldom asked to repeat them, except by Wyatt and then only sometimes. He felt that the others were not taking down any names; once in a while they even laughed. So he stopped telephoning. Henry asked whether anyone had told him not to telephone any more. He said no, he had just decided not to do it.

"Did you tell Mr Creighton of your decision?"

"No, sir," Edward answered briefly.

Next Edward recounted the events of the day before the explosion. On December 5 he had phoned Pilot Hayes at home to tell him to be at the wharf of the *Imo*'s agent, Pickford & Black, at 2:00 p.m., to take the ship out to sea. Hayes came to the office, and the order was posted, as usual, on the slate. The boy saw Hayes again about five, just when he was closing up, and learned of the delay. He did not rub the original order off the blackboard at that time but waited until morning.

Meanwhile local newspapers were mounting an attack on Wyatt. Burchell had tried to undermine Wyatt's credibility further by suggesting that it had been the CXO, an hour after the explosion, who had given the original order for the evacuation to open fields, which had caused so much needless suffering. Wyatt was enraged and demanded to know who had made the accusation. Burchell, however, could only produce one name, and he eventually backed down. Nonetheless, the exchange left a bad impression. This, coupled with the evidence that Wyatt had known about the *Mont Blanc*'s cargo and the failure of pilots to report to the CXO's office, caused tremendous outrage. *The Halifax Herald*, for one, demanded that Wyatt not be allowed to continue another hour in charge of Halifax Harbour.

Wyatt was recalled yet again. He reiterated he had complained about the situation to his superior officer, who had merely insisted that the navy had no control over pilots. Wyatt said he had put in writing that he would not be responsible for any accident. "For months and months I saw an accident or collision was coming," he testified, "and I could see there was somebody going to be made the goat for this, and I did not wish to be made the goat— you can call it intuition if you like, but that was my idea." He had said earlier that the December 6 collision was totally unnecessary. The great liners the *Olympic* and the *Mauretania*, far bigger than the *Imo* or the *Mont Blanc*, had passed perfectly safely in the Narrows, where there was less room than where the collision had occurred.

When Captain Martin, Wyatt's superior officer, returned, he said he had no recollection of receiving Wyatt's letters. Wyatt had produced carbon copies, and Martin's secretary had searched his files, but no trace of the originals was found. Because the material was confidential, Wyatt insisted he had typed them himself. He had taken the carbon copies from the pigeonhole in his office at the beginning of the inquiry, as he had suspected he might be blamed. Henry pleaded that some explanation be found for this direct conflict in testimony, but surprisingly it was not pursued.

The British navy did not wait for Mr Justice Drysdale to hand down his findings before acting on the evidence. On January 26 newspapers announced that Wyatt had been superseded by a temporary replacement. As well, Vice Admiral C. W. Story had succeeded Martin as chief naval authority in Halifax. "An Englishman by birth," the *Herald* reported, "he joined the Royal Navy in 1871, and, in the course of a career unmarred by a single mishap, he had command of some of the finest and most powerful ships of the navy." Story was given full authority to reorganize the Halifax administration. Captain Pasco, meanwhile, returned to his previous post, St John's, Newfoundland. Pilot Mackey, however, had remained at work. A rumour that he had piloted a ship involved in a near collision caused him to be brought back to court, but the allegation was disproved.

On February 4, after hearing evidence from more than fifty witnesses, Drysdale read his conclusions. It took no more than fifteen minutes.

1. The explosion on the steamship *Mont Blanc* on December 6 was undoubtedly the result of a collision in the harbour of Halifax between the steamship *Mont Blanc* and the steamship *Imo*.

2. Such a collision was caused by violation of the rules of navigation.

3. That the pilot and master of the steamship *Mont Blanc* were wholly responsible for violating the rules of the road.

4. That Pilot Mackey, by reason of his gross negligence, should be forthwith dismissed by the pilotage authorities and his licence cancelled.

5. In view of the gross neglect of the rules of navigation by Pilot Mackey the attention of law officers of the Crown should be called to the evidence taken on this investigation with a view to a criminal prosecution of such pilot.

6. We recommend to the French authorities such evidence with a view to having Captain Le Medec's licence cancelled, and such captain dealt with according to the law of his country.

7. That it appearing that pilotage authorities in Halifax have been permitting Pilot Mackey to pilot ships since the investigation commenced and

since the collision above referred to, we think the authorities deserving of censure. In our opinion the authorities should have promptly suspended such pilot.

8. The master and pilot of the *Mont Blanc* are guilty of neglect of public safety in not taking proper steps to warn the inhabitants of the city of a probable explosion.

9. Commander Wyatt is guilty of neglect in performing his duty as C.X.O. in not taking proper steps to ensure the regulations being carried out and especially in not keeping himself fully acquainted with the movements and intended movements of vessels in the harbour.

10. In dealing with the C.X.O.'s negligence in not ensuring the efficient carrying out of traffic regulations by pilots, we have to report that the evidence is far from satisfactory that he ever took any efficient steps to bring to the notice of the superintendent neglect on the part of the pilots.

11. In view of the allegations of disobedience of the C.X.O.'s orders by the pilots, we do not consider such disobedience was the proximate cause of the collision.

12. It would seem that the pilots of Halifax attempt to vary the rules of the road and in this connection we think Pilot Renner, in charge of an American tramp steamer on the morning of the collision, deserving of censure.

13. That the regulations governing the traffic in Halifax Harbour in force since the war were prepared by the competent Naval Authorities; that such traffic regulations do not satisfactorily deal with the handling of such ships laden with explosives and we have to recommend that such competent Authority forthwith take up and make satisfactory regulations dealing with such subject; we realize that while war goes on under present conditions explosives must move but, in view of what has happened, we strongly recommend that the subject be dealt with satisfactorily by the proper authorities.

Most Haligonians heartily agreed with Drysdale's findings, though many in legal and naval circles were less certain. That the *Mont Blanc*'s crew had made little effort to render the ship less dangerous after the collision or to issue widespread warnings strongly influenced public opinion. So did the fact that many men on the *Imo* had died, while those on the French ship had escaped almost scot-free. The public also blamed naval authorities for their apparent negligence and ineptitude. If there were culprits in this tragedy, they should be punished.

The public soon got its way. Mackey was arrested as he left court, and Le Medec was apprehended after he had walked a block. They were arraigned that day and released on bail. The next morning, on February 5, the headlines in the *Herald* read, "Failing action by the Federal Authorities, Attorney-General Daniels promptly causes the Arrest of Mont Blanc's Pilot and Captain: The Herald demands that Commander Wyatt be Immediately Arrested and Also 'Subjected to the Tender Mercies of a Criminal Court.'"

Wyatt was arrested. The preliminary hearing in the case against Mackey and Le Medec was being heard that morning, and Wyatt was asked to remain. The three men huddled in their overcoats in the same battered courtroom. The charge against them was manslaughter; the pilot of the *Imo,* William Hayes, was the only named victim; John Johansen, the helmsman of the *Imo,* was the only witness. He restated most of what he had said at the inquiry. Bail for Mackey and Wyatt was set at six thousand dollars; for Le Medec, ten thousand. All three were released.

Meanwhile a government-appointed commission of independent experts, only one of whom was from Halifax, began meeting on February 8 to investigate pilotage conditions. The headline "ILLEGAL EXTORTIONS OF $8,000-A-YEAR HALIFAX PILOTS EXPOSED" greeted amazed *Herald* readers on February 12. Control exercised by the pilotage commission, it seemed, had been minimal, and pilots had been "sticking" ships for illegal extras. They made few reports, not even of accidents, and they came and went to suit themselves. One reporter, in *The Evening Mail,* compared pilots' earnings with those of other professions: "Some of them earned 100% MORE than the Prime Minister of Nova Scotia; 40% more than the Chief Justice and fully 300% more than any Arch Bishop, Bishop, College President, Educationalist or Clergyman." It was later revealed that ships' masters were being paid "gratuities" of five to twenty dollars to bring their vessels into the harbour without a pilot, while their companies were being charged pilotage fees of up to sixty dollars. The pilots were pocketing the difference.

The commission next came under review. It owned no boat, and if ships' agents did not supply one to take a pilot to an outward-bound ship, he had to hire one himself. The training of apprentices was also a haphazard affair, as was the selection. The commission filed complaints of its own. On more than one occasion naval authorities had shifted buoys without giving notice, and the Canadian department of Marine and Fisheries had ignored new bylaws recommended six or seven years earlier to improve efficiency.

The findings of the inquiry into the pilotage system brought about significant improvements, making Halifax Harbour one of the best-run and safest ports in North America. The effects were far reaching. The Port of New York tightened up its regulations. With the number of ships carrying explosives leaving its harbour, it could well have suffered a fate similar to that of Halifax. Closer to home, Montreal and Saint John also benefited from the conclusions of the inquiry.

*   *   *   *   *

For weeks it seemed as if the court cases and the inquiries would never end. On January 10 the owners of the *Mont Blanc* had filed an action against the owners of the *Imo* for $2 million in damages and costs. The owners of the *Imo* had counterclaimed on February 6 for the same amount.

The proceedings began on March 7, 1918, in the Nova Scotia district of the Exchequer Court of Canada, and surprisingly they were heard by the same judge that had presided over the inquiry into the collision: Mr Justice Arthur Drysdale. For the most part the evidence given at the inquiry was presented, with one further witness. On April 27 Drysdale handed down his decision: the *Mont Blanc* was solely to blame because the ship had been in the wrong channel and had cut in front of the *Imo*. The story told by the crew of the *Mont Blanc,* he said, was "absurd and impossible."

In the meantime the manslaughter charges against Commander Wyatt, Captain Le Medec, and Pilot Mackey were dismissed because there was insufficient evidence to prove "gross negligence imputing criminal culpability." The case never made it to trial.

After Drysdale announced his judgment, the owners of the *Mont Blanc* quickly filed an appeal to the Supreme Court of Canada. It was just as promptly followed by a cross-appeal from the owners of the *Imo*. On May 19, 1919, the five judges announced their decision. Chief Justice Davis and Mr Justice Idington agreed with Drysdale. "Once you reach the conclusion that the collision happened on the Halifax side of the channel," they held, "that crucial fact settled the issue." Mr Justice Brodeur and Mr Justice Mignault decided that the *Imo* alone was to blame, as she had been the cause of placing the ships on a collision course in the first place. The fifth judge, Mr Justice Anglin, believed that the two vessels had not been in such danger of collision to justify the *Mont Blanc*'s turn to port. The *Imo* had inexcusably maintained her wrong course, and even though the *Mont Blanc* had made the mistaken decision to come to port, the ships were on a parallel course and could probably have passed safely if the *Imo* had not reversed her engines, thus swinging around. In his opinion, both ships were equally at fault. Drysdale's finding was reversed.

The ships' owners were still not satisfied. The ultimate judicial authority at the time, the Privy Council in London, England, was then called on to hear appeals. The Privy Council, agreeing with Anglin, decreed that each ship had acted in an imprudent manner and therefore shared responsibility for the collision.

By this time Francis Mackey had been exonerated and reinstated as a pilot. He and his family had remained in Halifax, though at times their situation was difficult.

Captain Aimé Le Medec received no censure from the French government and continued his career.

Commander Frederick Wyatt was posted away from Halifax.

The *Imo* was refloated and repaired. With a change in name, she was used again as a whaler. On December 3, 1921, three days before the fourth anniversary of the explosion, however, she struck a rock off the Falkland Islands. Her crew was rescued, but she was not. To this day she remains in that frigid sea.

SABOTAGE?

ALTHOUGH THE WISDOM of the judges of the Supreme Court of Canada and of the Privy Council in London were never seriously questioned, many people remained of the opinion that, somehow, the Germans had been at the bottom of everything. *The Halifax Herald,* on December 8, 1917, had expressed that opinion. "Behind all, as responsible for the disaster, is that arch criminal, the Kaiser of Germany, who forced our Empire and her allies into the fearful war."

The same day, the first reports of the explosion appeared in German newspapers. *Die Neue Preussische Zeitung* quoted Reuter, the London-based international news agency. The report was reasonably accurate and contained no propaganda. The only reference to the war was that there were no troops waiting in Halifax for transport to Europe at the time. That piece of information, though inconsequential, was interesting. What source had it come from? The account in another Berlin newspaper contained more errors and had reached it via Holland. Later, in early January, German newspapers took a different tone. An editorial in the *Kölnische Zeitung,* a paper that heavily supported the Kaiser's government, was quoted in the *Herald:*

> Not without emotion can one note the news of the devastation of the hard hit Canadian town. And yet is it not better that these munitions should not have reached the theatre of war and the trenches, there to be used against our people in its hard struggle for freedom and independence, our people which did not seek war, and also did not produce these munitions which have now struck those who wanted to trouble us with them?
>
> Canada is getting war experience at the front and also at Halifax. We hope that its lesson may open the eyes of the warlike section of the people to the fact that humanity has higher ideals to defend than those represented by Wilson, Lloyd George and other business politicians.

There had been a lot of speculation about spying and sabotage. One widespread rumour, for example, suggested that William Hayes, the pilot of the *Imo,* and possibly Haakon From, the captain, had been murdered by a crew member before the collision. This could have allowed someone on the bridge of the ship to engineer an accident in the harbour. At the inquiry Pilot Francis Mackey stated that when he saw the erratic behaviour of the *Imo,* it had struck him forcibly that she was not acting under Hayes's orders. He had not known that Hayes was on board until he heard of his death. John Johansen, the helmsman, the only witness from the bridge of the *Imo,* said that Hayes had given all commands and signals. News items also led readers to believe that sabotage was certainly a possibility. January 24, 1918, saw the headline "HUN PLOT TO DESTROY STEAMERS, TRANSPORTS, PIERS, FACTORIES and FOOD and OTHER SUPPLIES in NEW YORK HARBOUR."

In addition, during the inquiry two witnesses had made revelations about breaches in security that were never adequately explained. On January 24 George Smith, the Pickford & Black agent who looked after neutral ships, was examined. He recalled a December 5 telephone call from a man purporting to be the examining officer on the HMCS *Niobe.* The caller asked for the destination of the Danish ship the *Kentucky* and also asked whether the *Imo* had sailed. Smith gave him the information he wanted, telling him about the *Imo*'s delay. He had received calls like that before and had always answered the questions if he could. Callers always specified they were from the chief commanding officer's office. In this instance the man spoke with an English accent that Smith did not recognize. He knew Commander Frederick Wyatt's voice but none of the others'. Roland Iceton, the commander's assistant, had been on duty on December 5, and he maintained he had not placed the call. As he was a Nova Scotian, born in Cow Bay, his accent was certainly not English. Lawyers at the inquiry questioned Smith closely about these incidents, but he said he just took the man's word that he was from the *Niobe.* Counsel then asked whether Smith took special precautions before giving out information about ships. Smith said he was more careful about British ships, but he did not seem to think it mattered so much about neutral ones. The matter was dropped.

When Edward Beazley, the clerk at the pilotage office, was on the witness stand, he innocently revealed that he, too, received calls from someone who said he was from the CXO's office and that he, too, always gave the person information on the sailing times of individual ships. Edward added that he phoned pilots at home to make arrangements if they were not in the office, and some pilots had party lines. Newspaper headlines at the end of January reflected the general shock and anger caused by these revelations. "SECRET NEWS SENT BY PUBLIC PHONE" was one. The fact that a blackboard in an easily entered office displayed information that could help the enemy also came in for censure.

Two weeks later a paragraph in the *Herald* may not have attracted too much attention, as the front page featured the manslaughter case against Wyatt. It read, "New York, February 5. Frank Kintellen, German agent, and ten co-defendants, all Germans, were today found guilty by a federal jury of conspiring to destroy munition and food ships of the entente allies."

Further mention of sabotage did not emerge for more than a decade. In December 1931 Dr Samuel Prince read a paper to the Nova Scotia Historical Society entitled "The Halifax Explosion, Fourteen Years After." A professor at the University of King's College and author of *Catastrophe and Social Change,* a sociological study of the explosion, he suggested that sabotage was a real possibility. "A large number believed and some still believe that Hunnish propaganda was at least the disaster's secondary cause," he wrote. "The suspicion which attached to certain members of the *Imo*'s crew has more method than madness in it. The helmsman of the *Imo* was arrested, and later on released, and the release was regretted."

Belgian ports were infested with German spies, Dr Prince maintained, and crews of Belgian relief ships were known to mingle with them. "It is not beyond the range of possibility that aboard the *Imo* might have been the murderous agents of William Hohenzollern." He mentioned as well that in June 1922, in Seattle, a man named Johnson confessed to having caused the explosion before committing suicide. Johansen, anglicized as Johnson, was the name of the helmsman of the *Imo,* the one who had been arrested and later released.

The story made front-page headlines in the *Herald* on June 15, 1922. Johnson, the paper reported, had supposedly been a Finnish chemist known to have strong German sympathies. He had lived in a remote cabin in the state of Washington and had been experimenting with explosive formulae. He had confessed his sins to a watchman, J. R. Cox, employed at a mine in the area. Cox thought that fear of disclosure had caused the suicide. It was established, the *Herald* maintained, that Johnson had been in Halifax in December 1917 and that government agents from both Canada and the United States were investigating.

The Evening Echo (Halifax), also of June 15, contained an article saying that William Johnson was not the helmsman. It quoted an earlier story that had appeared in a Seattle newspaper: "It has already been established that Johnson was in Halifax in the British transport service. An address at which he later resided in Halifax is known to agents." As well, the man had at least two aliases. Obviously further investigation had taken place. To have caused the explosion, the *Echo* argued, he or an accomplice would have had to be on one of the two ships. "As far as can be ascertained," the newspaper concluded, "there was no man by the name of Johnson in the transport branch of the local naval department."

Was he John Johansen, the helmsman of the *Imo*? After Johansen's arrest and detention in Halifax in 1917, Charles Burchell, lawyer for the owners of the *Imo*, requested that Major General Benson, commander of Military District 6 in Halifax, provide papers clearing the seaman of any charges. Johansen was going back to the United States, and Burchell said he needed something to show people who might have read incriminating newspaper reports to make it clear that the arrest at Bellevue Hospital had been a mistake. At the preliminary hearing in the case against Wyatt, Captain Aimé Le Medec, and Mackey in early February, in fact, Johansen said he had been so adamant about getting a newspaper at Bellevue because he wanted to read what was being said about him. He was afraid that he was being branded a German spy and that he would have difficulty finding a new job.

Premeditated sabotage seems unlikely when the complex circumstances of the collision are considered. No clear picture ever emerged of what had happened on the bridge of the *Imo*. The collision was unnecessary, but the results of the inquiry were inconclusive and unsatisfactory.

In July 1918 a hospital ship, the *Landovery Castle*, with all lights aglow, was torpedoed by a German submarine a few days out of Halifax, and there was heavy loss of life. It seemed that the enemy had thought that the ship was carrying eight flying officers, and it was believed in responsible naval circles that the submarine captain had acted on information received from German agents in Halifax. Eight medical officers were on board the *Landovery Castle*. Halifax City Council unanimously endorsed a motion calling for immediate action to prevent further leaks of this kind.

Dr Prince briefly mentioned this episode in his paper. "If spy activity abounded in July, 1918," he said, "is it not conceivable that sabotage was possible seven months earlier?" It was probable that history would accept the verdict of the Privy Council in London, he concluded. "Yet there are … many who held and still hold to the theory of an engineered crime."

Much later, in 1939, a survivor from the *Imo*, Gustav Astrom, told his story to a Swedish newspaper. He said that the entire crew of the *Imo* had been suspected of sabotage and had even been interned on the HMS *Highflyer* for a few days. Suggesting that someone had thought that Johansen had been responsible for the collision, Astrom noted that the helmsman's food had been poisoned and his life saved by a doctor. As far as Astrom was concerned, however, the *Imo* had accidentally collided with the hold of the French ship, and if it were not for the testimony of Johansen at the inquiry, the *Imo*, not the *Mont Blanc*, might have been blamed.

THE RETURN
TO NORMAL

"RELIEF, NOT COMPENSATION"

BY APRIL 1918 Halifax was beginning to return to normal. With the recovery of the city under way and the cause of the explosion explained, people were feeling more optimistic.

Much had been accomplished, but emergency relief, claims, and temporary housing were all costing a considerable sum. The *Canadian Annual Review* for 1918 reported that expenditures totalled $18.5 million. Material losses were $35 million, including Dominion government and shipping losses of about $10 million; railway, about $1.2 million; dwellings, about $6.5 million; churches, $1 million; personal belongings, about $3.3 million; merchandise, about $1 million; and manufacturing plants, about $3.5 million. The staggering amount of donations, totalling $23,153,792.78 by the spring, lessened the financial blow. Insurance payments later reduced the debt even more.

The Halifax Relief Commission's work was really just beginning. In April the commission, its offices in a temporary two-storey structure on Sackville Street, was incorporated, giving it complete discretion over the allocation of relief funds. It was now a permanent fixture—much to the chagrin of some Haligonians. In 1918 a woman leaning on crutches sold a pamphlet at a street corner in the South End. A few sentences summed up the tone of the booklet: "My main object in writing this is to bring before the public how the Halifax Relief Commission have dealt with the sufferers…. Are not the sufferers testifying to the fact that the suffering entailed upon them by the explosion is only a drop in the bucket, compared to that which they have suffered and are suffering by the cruel hand of the commissioners and their co-workers." The money, she said, was going towards the likes of medical boards and social workers, not the needy. Others shared her dissatisfaction.

One of the primary functions of the commission was to set up and pay out pensions to surviving dependants of wage earners who had been killed in the explosion. It studied different schemes for some time before deciding to base its scale on the military one, which prorated payments according to rank. There was one significant difference: military pensions were set regardless of family circumstances; the commission's, on the other hand, went down or stopped altogether if the late breadwinner had left enough property or savings to support his dependants. Time and again the commission reiterated its philosophy "relief, not compensation."

The first pensions were issued in May, and the commission assumed responsibility for Workmen's Compensation Board payments in June. Industry, it was believed, should not be penalized for an accident of the war. Generally, the scale was graduated according to previous household income:

Monthly Income	Widow's Monthly Pension
$110 or less	$40
$111–$125	$42.50
$125–$150	$50
$150–$190	$60
$190 or more	$65

In addition, widows, no matter which category they were in, received eight dollars a month for each dependent child. (Most people fell into the lowest income bracket.) If, however, a widow's total payments exceeded household income before the explosion, the commission reduced the amount. Pensions were also lowered if dependants owned property worth more than three thousand dollars:

Property Value	Percentage Reduction
$3,000–$5,000	20%
$6,000–$10,000	40%
$11,000–$15,000	50%
$16,000–$20,000	60%
$21,000 or more	100%

Few fell into the last category.

The commission, not wanting to discourage "thrift and labour," did not reduce payments to a widow who went to work. If she remarried, she was given a year's pension as a dowry, usually $480. But if a woman's morality came into question, she could lose her pension temporarily or permanently.

(This restriction also applied to military pensions.) The commission placed the woman on probation for six months and, if she behaved, resumed the payments. Two cancellations for immorality, however, meant the end of the pension. If a pensioner moved to another country, usually the United States, occasionally Britain, the pension would be paid in the funds of that country.

Those blinded in the explosion also received compensation. A blind man got fifty dollars a month; a blind woman, thirty dollars. Adult survivors who had lost one eye received thirty dollars a year.

Blinded or seriously sight-impaired children did not qualify directly for pensions. Instead, the commission covered their board at the School for the Blind or paid teachers for special classes and arranged holidays in the country in summer. When they completed their schooling, or at age seventeen, these children went before a medical board to determine the percentage of disability, and pensions were paid accordingly. On their twenty-first birthday they were given a gift of one hundred dollars. A medical board decided the scale for other disabilities. Similar to that of the blind, the scale was based on the effect the disability had on former occupation.

The commission offered a choice between pensions and lump-sum payments. Because thirty dollars a year was not much, even in those days, the majority of the partially disabled opted for a lump-sum payment. Most of the amputees took this course after artificial limbs had been fitted and seemed relatively trouble free. Those who had lost one eye were advised not to settle, as additional problems might arise, and the accepting of a lump sum absolved the commission, which hardly ever reversed a decision, of any further responsibility. In later years some disabled, especially amputees, suffered complications, and they applied for pensions, even though they had earlier taken a cash settlement. In some cases medical bills were paid. People on pensions had medical expenses connected with their injury paid for the rest of their lives.

The commission computed lump sums according to age and to extent of disability. A twenty-five-year-old with a pension of $30 a year was offered $500; a sixty-two-year-old receiving the same amount got $275. Those eligible for the monthly rate were paid higher amounts, tempting at the time: in 1918, $3,000 bought a small farm. Lump-sum awards to children were meant for the benefit of the child, for education for the future, not for the support of the family. One, for an injured child whose parents decided to take a lump sum, was $500, but it was paid in Victory Bonds, not cash, so that it could be held in trust for the child.

Many disabled were not swayed by the appeal of a large payment. Mrs Crowdis, wife of the Reverend Charles Crowdis, celebrated the arrival of her pension, fifteen dollars every six months, by buying peppermint candies. Millicent Upham, receiving the same amount after she left the School for the Blind, initially used hers to pay the premiums on a small insurance policy. One woman, so badly injured that she was a complete invalid, sent two wreaths every year on the anniversary of the explosion, even after she moved away from Halifax. One was in memory of her children who had been killed; the other, in honour of the unidentified dead. When she died, her daughter continued the custom. An official of the commission placed the wreaths on the grave and by the memorial to the unidentified dead at Fairview Cemetery.

Orphans were included in the pension scheme. A "full orphan" got sixteen dollars a month; a "half-orphan"—which really meant that the father had been killed—received the same as a dependent child: eight dollars. Orphans' pensions ended at age seventeen, when the child was expected to finish school. If a child attended school irregularly for any reason except for poor health, the commission withheld payment. Orphans who wanted to continue their education after high school could apply for an extension. The commission did not grant extensions freely, and only after an investigation, though it did seem more generous where disabled young pensioners were concerned. Sometimes it issued a loan for further education. Children who left school before age seventeen lost their pension altogether. The payments enabled some orphans to complete high school. Under normal circumstances they might have dropped out, as it was common in those days for children to go to work as young as age fourteen.

In adoptions that did not work out, it often seemed that the child had been taken in mainly because of the pension. Many years later a woman who had not been happy with her relatives wrote, "That sixteen dollars certainly didn't go on my back." Usually, however, people regarded the pension as too little for the child's keep. A few others, who were better off, refused the payments or put them in the bank for the child's future.

The pension receipt forms had to be signed and sent back regularly. If not, the commission sent a letter of reproof. One boy went to live with his grandfather in the country. The grandfather, however, was not in favour of "those claim forms," which, he believed, took a lot of time and trouble for little in return. "You know as well as I do that those children has to be pervided for," he wrote.

The commission was not responsible for pensions to servicemen or their families, paid by the Dominion government, or to seamen from foreign ships or their families, covered by their native country's war insurance. It did make the odd exception. Sigurd Olsen, a sailor on the *Imo,* had lost an arm

The Reverend Charles Crowdis witnessed hundreds of claim forms after the explosion; Mrs Crowdis celebrated the arrival of her pension by buying peppermints. (COURTESY HELEN CROWDIS FAWCETT)

Millicent (Upham) Swindells, shown here with her husband, Wilbert, initially bought a small insurance policy with her pension. Later in life she came to regard it as "mad money." (RON E. MERRICK)

A pensioner annually sent two wreaths to the Halifax Relief Commission, which dutifully placed one on the memorial for the unidentified dead at Fairview Cemetery. (PANS)

Matteo Cicione, age twenty-four, was a recent immigrant to Halifax. He had regularly mailed money to his father in Italy, in the form of drafts from the Canadian Imperial Bank of Commerce. (MARITIME MUSEUM)

in the explosion and had been taken to Hantsport for treatment. An unexpected romantic note crept into the report: "It seems that we have inadvertently provided Mr Olsen with a wife. He wished to become the husband of a young lady to whose charms he has fallen a slave." The sailor received a monetary wedding gift.

The commission did issue pensions to the dependants of Canadians killed on merchant ships not owned by the navy. In Montreal the widow of the foreman on the *Calonne*, for example, received forty dollars a month.

Not all cases were clear-cut. Dilemmas arose when a person had given money to parents or other relatives, not necessarily a regular sum but one that the recipients had relied on. It was usually hard to prove, and the commission had to question other family members, workmates, or employers, which was often resented. Claims such as "he always sent ten dollars whenever he could" might mean one hundred or twenty dollars a year. Local clergymen were once again called on to testify to integrity and financial status. The commission rarely complied and certainly gave no more than ten dollars a month in such cases. Usually it gave a lump sum: for the death of a son who had helped support a widowed mother, five hundred dollars was the norm, though the amount decreased according to the support previously received and to the family's means.

One claim came from a man who lived in a hill town in Italy. Twenty-four-year-old Matteo Cicione had been a recent immigrant to Halifax, working as a stevedore and earning about $90 a month. His father stated that Matteo had sent, every month, the equivalent of half his father's earnings. The letter was in Italian and was hard to make out, even for the Italian consul in Montreal, to whom it had to be sent. Letters went back and forth via the consulate in an attempt to sort out the claim. The man could not write, and some of the letters were in beautiful copperplate, probably the script of the village priest. Matteo had been the oldest of seven children. One brother was a shepherd like his father; another was "under the colours." A friend of Matteo's had identified his body and was able to confirm that he had indeed sent money to his father, in the form of drafts from the Canadian Imperial Bank of Commerce. After some negotiation the father received $350. (In Italy, it was reported, the compensation for a similar situation would have been $2,000.) Among Matteo's effects, left unclaimed in his mortuary bag, were two copies of these bank drafts. If they had been seen at the time, they would have saved a great deal of correspondence.

*   *   *   *   *

Social workers from the medical–social service visited pensioners to check up on their welfare, usually once every six months if all was well, more often if there were difficulties. The inspections annoyed many people, but good things came out of them. Social workers discovered tuberculosis cases, and they made sure that children received medical attention for physical ailments that might have gone untreated. If a family seemed in dire need, the social worker could usually find the means from special funds to tide them over.

Commission workers also made sure that pensioners who left Halifax were monitored. They contacted the Red Cross or a charitable organization and asked it to keep in touch with the person. If an orphan was not being treated well, for example, something could be done. Some widows moved frequently, often between Boston, where sons and daughters were living, and Canada, where they had other relatives. Their pensions followed them. So did the annual attestation form, which had to be signed to confirm that payment was still justified.

In the first four years after the explosion the commission disbursed $1 million in pensions and lump-sum payments. In 1920 there were 1,028 pensioners: 198 were widows, down from the 1918 figure of 239. Remarriage was the main cause of the decrease. Orphans and half-orphans accounted for 481; dependants, 62; and disabled, 287, including the 23 blind adults.

From October 1919 to June 1921, in response to the soaring cost of living, the commission paid a bonus of 20 percent on all pensions. But it withdrew the bonus just as quickly when the cost of living went down. This caused tremendous outrage, but the commission pointed out that there might not be enough money in the fund to pay pensions for life. Beginning in 1920 orphans enjoyed an increase. The oldest child in a family now received thirty dollars a month; the second oldest, twenty; and all others, sixteen. That, too, was later revoked, and there was another outcry. But the commission stood firm.

BREAKING
NEW GROUND

O N FRIDAY, APRIL 12, 1918, *The Halifax Herald* printed its reconstruction number. Beneath the city coat of arms was written in large letters, "CONFIDENCE AND PROGRESS," and, below that, "THE NEW AND GREATER HALIFAX OF OUR NOBLEST DREAMS." Farther down on the same page a citizen might read, with satisfaction or surprise, that this new and greater Halifax was even then springing to birth. "Halifax is prosperous" was the claim. The agony, the newspaper said, had fallen on the far north, not on the business section.

The Halifax Relief Commission's goal was to spread that prosperity by creating good-quality permanent housing. The first consideration had been the salvage of inhabitable houses to provide permanent accommodation as fast as possible for a large number of refugees. Some 750 houses had been destroyed, and 750 more needed extensive repairs; 9,000 needed repairs of some sort. (The commission arrived at these statistics after appraisals had been made. It had been found that some properties previously thought unsalvageable could be used again if extensive repairs were carried out.) The five thousand people in temporary structures and many more living outside the city needed homes. About two hundred families had been so decimated that rehousing would not be necessary.

At first the commission intended to rebuild houses for individuals, but negotiations proved too difficult. Consequently it bought sites and put up single-frame houses containing five or six rooms. The rents ranged from twenty to twenty-five dollars a month; they dropped to twelve dollars for former homeowners waiting for their houses to be rebuilt.

The most imaginative and controversial scheme was the creation of a new town in the North End. Thomas Adams, a British urban planner famous for his garden cities, provided the design, and a Montreal architectural firm, Ross & Macdonald, was engaged to carry it out.

Richmond residents were not so excited about the idea. In April 1918 a public meeting was held to discuss the bill to incorporate the relief commission, which gave it broad powers in expropriation and town planning. At the meeting the plans for the new community were also presented. For many in attendance the scheme was much too grand and much too impractical. Some were outspoken in their opposition. "While it might be ideal for a new town, on the prairie, and quite idealistic," one man said, "it is not suitable for conditions as they exist in the North End." People also objected to the fact that the commission had contracted out work without putting it up for tender. Another man grumbled that plumbing fit for a mansion had already been put into temporary dwellings, so what further extravagance would be committed for permanent ones? Dr Arthur Hawkins then rose to his feet. A man much respected in the North End—he had treated many explosion victims and had stood up for the rights of others—he became mayor later that year. He eloquently summarized the overall opinion at the meeting: "It is unjust that this government should attempt to take money which has been contributed to those people who have lost their all, and expend it for a fanciful town planning scheme. It is a blow to democracy. The people should have a chance to build the homes they want."

The plan also included building new roads, some with less-steep gradients, and this seemed like a further waste. The Reverend William Swetnam, who had lost his home, wife, and son made an impassioned plea punctuated by a tremendous ovation. "What would the boys overseas think if they could know that the legislature was considering a measure of how to make roads instead of houses?" he asked. "The people are more concerned with getting back to where they had been than in walking on new pavements. We walked the rough roads and climbed the hills in the past without any sympathy." It was clear that North Enders wanted to turn back the clock: they wanted the old Richmond resurrected.

The provincial legislature, however, was not swayed. The bill incorporating the commission and confirming its powers passed with only minor amendments and was approved by the Dominion government.

Construction on the site, bordered by Young, Agricola, Duffus, and Gottingen streets, with Fort Needham behind, began in September 1918. The commission had expropriated more than one hundred parcels of land, comprising an area of twenty-three and a quarter acres. Hydrostone, a type of cement block moulded under pressure and developed in Chicago, was the chosen material for the new dwellings. It was strong—and fireproof. A specially constructed narrow-gauge railway transported about three thousand blocks, made in the Eastern Passage, beyond Dartmouth, to the site every day.

Cavicchi & Pagano workers were still clearing the devastated area in June 1918. It is hard to believe that this was once a thriving community.

The Hydrostone development, encompassing ten parallel blocks, was under construction for about two years. (MARITIME MUSEUM/VAUGHAN)

In ten parallel blocks 328 dwellings were constructed: 96 houses of four and a half rooms, 96 of five and a half, and 64 of six, in addition to 32 flats of four rooms, 22 of five and a half, and 14 of six to seven. Design varied, and so did the type of building, with single houses, duplexes, and larger units. Lots ranged from twenty feet by one hundred feet to sixty feet by one hundred feet. Fifteen stores and 3 offices were also built. Each house had a front porch, a pantry or a storeroom, and every bedroom a clothes closet. Features included full plumbing, electric lights, and basements with laundry trays. The roofs were sloping, better for snowy conditions than the flat ones more common before. Behind each row of houses ran a service lane, where all utility poles were placed and, in front, an open space with grass and trees, where children could play. Street names for the development gave some feeling of breaking new ground: Livingstone, Stanley, Columbus, Cabot, Sebastian. Different names were proposed for the community, but the building material supplied the name generally used, and it stuck: the Hydrostone.

The first twenty-four dwellings were ready for occupation at the end of March 1919, with twenty more to be finished every fortnight. Dame Nellie Melba, who had earlier sung at a benefit concert for Halifax, visited the area at that time and complimented the design. The next month the Prince of Wales toured the Hydrostone and spoke to the new residents.

It was mid-1921, however, before the project was actually finished. Labour disputes had slowed progress. Although there was no longer a shortage of union men, the commission had used non-union labour in the summer of 1919, causing some discontent among workers. The commission, however, disclaimed responsibility, maintaining that it did not employ men directly but used contractors. If a strike occurred, it announced publicly the reasons for the delay in construction. Public opinion had played a large part in the settlement of previous strikes, and the commission did not hesitate to appeal to sentiment.

Finally all was completed, and before long, about two thousand people people were living in the Hydrostone. Monthly rents varied, from $25.00 for a four-room flat to $50.00 for a seven-room house. The row of stores and the bank stood on Young Street. The bank's rental was $134.16 per month; each store's, from $55.00 to $100.00.

Evelyn Johnson's family had been among the first to move in. They lived in a corner house, with only three other homes on the block. Life was not always easy for the Johnsons. Initially they relied solely on their monthly pension from the commission, but then both boys found work, and that helped. Mrs Johnson did her best to make her children happy. Evelyn recalled one incident vividly. She was in a school play, and all the girls were going to wear silk stockings. She knew that her mother had to be careful with money, to have enough for food and rent, but Evelyn could not help mentioning those stockings. Her mother looked worried but said, "If all the others have them, you will too." She sent Evelyn to a little store nearby where the owner, an old lady, sold real bargains. "Tell her I can't pay today," Mrs Johnson said, "but she will have the money the moment the pension cheque comes." Evelyn got her stockings, but the feeling that she had been selfish and had caused her mother worry spoiled much of her pleasure in them. The happiness in the Johnson home did not last long. Mrs Johnson died in 1923, probably from untreated explosion injuries that had left her in a weakened condition. Evelyn then went to live with an aunt.

The Driscolls lived on Duffus Street, in one of the larger-sized houses at the northern end, for more than ten years. Then Mrs Driscoll died, and family members gradually married and moved away. "It was very comfortable," Noble said. "The settlement was well designed, with plenty of room around the buildings." The Davidsons settled in the Hydrostone, too. "When we dug in the garden," Eric recalled, "we often found bits of metal. We thought they must have come from the *Mont Blanc*."

By 1921 there were eleven businesses and offices in the Hydrostone, leaving only one vacant store. The Halifax City Directory listed the Royal Bank of Canada; the North End Pharmacy; Wallace Bros, Boots and Shoes; Cushen and Demoine, Barbers; *The Halifax Herald* and *The Evening Mail* branch offices; Nielson and Mills, Ladieswear, Millinery, Custom Tailoring and Dry Goods; Colwell Bros, Hatters and Men's Furnishers; Beckford's Furniture; the Economy Grocery; the Halifax Relief Commission's headquarters; Glube Bros, Tobacconist and Stationer.

Joe Glube was part owner of Glube Bros. To begin with, like the other stores, it did well. With people still spending money from claims and with the activity of rebuilding, the usual postwar decline, when the port lost much of its importance, had been delayed. By the mid-twenties, however, it had set in, and Halifax was suffering a deep economic depression before the rest of the country. Local trade declined, and Joe and many others closed down their shops.

*   *   *   *   *

Elsewhere in the North End in 1918 shattered businesses were rebuilding, though not necessarily in the same location. Hillis & Sons Foundry, where young Frank Burford had worked, opened in a temporary location and planned expansion at a new site. Already the firm had purchased fine new equipment, and it would soon be in a position to start manufacturing its line of stoves again.

Reconstruction and modernization were taking place throughout the area but less by the harbour and more westward. Up-to-date labour-saving machinery replaced equipment that had been destroyed, often enhancing the efficiency of the firm. Once again trains were chugging regularly into the city. The tracks had been cleared quickly, and normal service had resumed within a week after the explosion. The new south-end terminals had been nearly completed in December and came into use sooner than intended. The impressive station at the foot of South Street eventually replaced the badly damaged North Street Station. New docks, wharves, and shipyards were being built but no longer entirely in the North End.

The damage done to store fronts led to ideas in renovation. Interest shown by the outside world made people more conscious of the city's appearance, and the constant newspaper and magazine articles about reconstruction and town planning increased awareness of possibilities for improvement. Housing in the North End had improved. New sewer and water pipes, better roads, and new schools all contributed. Most buildings throughout the city had needed refurbishment, and so much fresh paint gave a brighter appearance.

In 1919 the future looked promising. New businesses were investing, and real-estate prices had increased. The number of building permits had leaped to unprecedented highs, extending city boundaries to the west and the northwest. The population, though down about 4 percent because of the explosion, increased by five thousand in 1919. Part of the prosperity undoubtedly resulted from the influx of people directly or indirectly involved in reconstruction work. Some of the larger projects, such as the Halifax shipyards, cost in the neighbourhood of $10 million to complete.

The explosion brought about radical social changes as well. Women were filling traditionally male occupations because so many men found they could earn more in reconstruction work. Early in 1918, for the first time in Halifax, there were female streetcar conductors. Although rather self-conscious and the butt of some humour in the beginning, they took the money and gave out the tickets in certain cars, and were soon accepted without comment.

Relief commission social workers visited less often as conditions improved but continued to supervise all who were on pension. Doctors regularly saw those with physical disabilities, leading to the discovery of other health concerns. The explosion had brought to light many long-existing problems, as so many experts in different fields had been in the city.

In July 1918 the Massachusetts–Halifax relief committee, which no longer needed to supply furniture, prepared a "constructive health program for the city." Ten months later it became the Massachusetts–Halifax Health Commission, devoting its remaining $250,000 to public health. With an additional $15,000 a year from the relief commission and financial aid from the three levels of government, it helped improve sanitary conditions and health in Halifax and Dartmouth by setting up a completely equipped medical centre at Admiralty House, in the North End. The clinic catered to all ages and offered classes in pre-natal care and infant welfare. The local medical profession heartily supported the project, giving their services free. At the peak of its existence the clinic employed seventeen nurses, who made home visits when necessary. In this way, it filled the void left after the closing of the temporary hospitals, the YMCA clinics, and the TB. sanatorium— and for a much wider spectrum of the population. Dalhousie University also began courses in public health, probably inspired by the new interest.

When the health commission ceased to function on May 30, 1928, it donated the remainder of its funds, $13,589.51, to Dalhousie for the purchase of vaccines and sera and for the prevention and treatment of communicable diseases. In the meantime Halifax's health system had graduated from being one of the worst in the country to being one of the best.

Religious tolerance was another by-product of the explosion, bringing people of different faiths together in the temporary communities on the Commons, the Garrison Grounds, and the Exhibition Grounds. Parishioners from the four Richmond churches had been widely dispersed. Some members never returned to the area, but as repairs were done and as housing became available, people gradually came back. Even if they had to come from a distance, most preferred their old friends and their old minister.

For one hundred days the dispossessed accepted the hospitality of other churches. Then, on March 17, 1918, the first service was held in the "tarpaper" church, a temporary building at the corner of Young and Gottingen streets. Built with Methodist and Presbyterian funds, it was the first place of worship put up in the devastated area. For nearly three years, it was home to what was left of Kaye Street Methodist and Grove Presbyterian congregations; for a short time Anglicans and Catholics attended service there, waiting for their own churches to be rebuilt. A somewhat motley collection of people attended that first service. Many wore the black of bereavement, and some, blinded, were led by a relative;

serious injuries were evident in others, and scarred faces commonplace. Archie Upham, and his father, Charles, were there, but Millicent was not yet able to go out. Reg Rasley and his now-depleted family attended. One of Reg's younger sisters had died of injuries received in the explosion. The service was not, as might have been expected, one of mourning. Instead, it was a celebration of being together again. Although there were some tears as missing faces were recalled, people looked to the future rather than the past. Indeed, the anniversary of this service is still celebrated.

The diminished Methodist and Presbyterian congregations fitted well together, and they decided to form the Kaye–Grove Church. To begin with, each group had its own minister and its own service. Both ministers had worked tirelessly for their troubled flocks. Eventually the Reverend William Swetnam left Halifax for Bridgewater, and the Reverend Charles Crowdis became the sole pastor. In June 1920 the union was officially recognized, and the name changed to the United Memorial Church, preceding the establishment of the United Church of Canada by more than four years.

Fund raising for a permanent building had been going on steadily since March 1918. Mr Crowdis wrote a booklet that was sold to raise money, and it was called *A Common Sorrow and a Common Concern,* a short history of Kaye Methodist and Grove Presbyterian that contained photographs from before and after the explosion. Sales of every kind were held, and money from flower shows, races, garden parties, and the sale of individual bricks all swelled the funds. By April 1921 the new building was ready for occupation, and the tarpaper church closed down forever.

The dedication ceremony for United Memorial took place on September 18, 1921. Barbara Orr, now living with her aunt Edna and uncle William, presented a chime of bronze bells to the church. Her uncle had purchased them from a firm in New York, and her aunt had furnished funds to complete the tower to hold the bells. Barbara, a little nervous of making a mistake that would be heard over the entire area, played the carillon at the dedication. The inscription on the largest bell read, "In Memoriam. Samuel Orr and his wife Annie S. Orr, and their children, Ian, Mary, Archie, Isabel and James, who departed this life December 6th, 1917. Presented by their daughter Barbara, 1920."

Today various memorials in the church testify to its heritage. One stained-glass window, given by his wife, Catherine, remembers Constant Upham; others, from Dorothy (Swetnam) Hare, recall her mother, Lizzie Louise, and her father, William; another, donated by Charles Upham, commemorates his children Charles, Ellen, and Jennie and his wife, Annie. The organ, donated by William MacTaggart Orr, honours his brother David, killed at the Richmond Printing Company. The pulpit, chairs, and communion table, given by Bertha (Bond) Wournell and Ethel (Bond) Hockin, are in memory of their father, Alexander. The baptismal font, given by their mother, Annie, and their aunt, commemorates Catherine and Alan Pattison. In addition to these and other memorials, a plaque records the names of the 239 parishioners of Grove Presbyterian and Kaye Street Methodist who died on December 6, 1917.

*   *   *   *   *

It took five months for education to return to some semblance of normal after the explosion. Even then, classes were not full time for all children. In the devastated area, Richmond and St Joseph's schools had had to be rebuilt, and the others, Alexander McKay and Bloomfield, had needed extensive repairs. Several schools in other areas of Halifax had been used for relief purposes, and teachers had been involved in organization. Most of them needed repairs and refurbishing before being put back into use. Children had also been scattered. Those whose homes had been destroyed or badly damaged often no longer lived in the same school district. For some time after the schools reopened, classes doubled up, and part-time education was the norm for many a child.

After education returned to some semblance of normality, Richmond children, including Noble Driscoll (front row, centre), attended Alexander McKay School on a part-time basis. (MARITIME MUSEUM/COURTESY NOBLE DRISCOLL)

At first Richmond and St Joseph's pupils attended Alexander McKay, the new boys' school on Russell Street. After his family returned from South Uniacke, Noble Driscoll went there. His teacher was the former principal of Richmond School: George M. Huggins. Despite the half-day schedule, Mr Huggins was trying hard to provide a decent education for his sadly reduced number of pupils. Eventually he told Noble, age fifteen by then, "You would be much better out at work. I do not have the time to teach you properly, and it is just a waste of your time." So Noble, like many others, left school and found a job.

The new Richmond School, where Devonshire Drive and Dartmouth Avenue (streets that did not exist before the explosion) join, was completed in 1921, and Mr Huggins was its first principal. A spacious, well-designed building, it stood out among its still-empty surroundings, Fort Needham rising beside it.

On February 1, 1924, a dedication ceremony was held in the school assembly hall. With money raised by the children and by others, Mr Huggins had purchased a bronze plaque recording the names of the eighty-eight pupils who had lost their lives in the explosion, his own daughter, Merle, among them. It was his last day at school, as he had never fully recovered from his injuries. A special section of the hall was reserved for relatives of the children who had been killed, and many still bore the scars inflicted on December 6. Friends had tried to dissuade Mr Huggins from holding this service, maintaining that it would bring back unwanted memories, but he persisted. A number of the children had not been found, and so the uncertainty surrounding their loss had never cleared.

For some the ceremony served as an antidote to their grief. One mother said the service, with its prayer, hymns, and sounding of "The Last Post," was the funeral her boy and girl had never had. "For the first time since I lost my children I was able to find relief in tears and it did me all the good in the world," she said.

In his address Dr A. H. MacKay, superintendent of education, talked about the two companies of school cadets that had been Mr Huggins's pride. They had won honours, taking fourteenth place nationally. The morning of the explosion the principal, on his way to school, had been talking to a friend about his boys' success. Before he was in the building, however, all but one of the thirty-four bright, keen lads had been killed, and he lay gravely injured. Tom Burford had been a company leader, Ian Orr a corporal, and Archie Orr and Alan Pattison privates.

Three hundred out of the five hundred pupils in the school had lost close relatives, and their quiet attentiveness during the service was noticeable, especially during the roll call of the names on the plaque. "One could not but think that the names on the bronze tablet represented just such a ... group of children as these," a reporter from *The Evening Mail* wrote, "yet they had been blotted out, almost in an instant."

Hazel Moore's name was on the plaque. Her mother had still not given up hope that, somewhere, she and her other two children, Gerald and Hilda, might be alive. Many of the surnames were repeated more than once: Orr, Pattison, Burford, Upham.

GUARDIANS
OF THE PENSION

THROUGHOUT THE 1920s pension and property administration were the major preoccupation of the Halifax Relief Commission. The commissioners not only concerned themselves with the financial side of their duties but also with the human side. They made decisions about giving extra money in times of need—money for education, for funeral expenses, for medical care—and they sent letters of every kind—letters of condolence, of encouragement, of stricture. Payment, for the most part, was routine, but some pensioners needed additional support.

The commission during this time consisted of two of the original appointees: Chairman T. Sherman Rogers, now a Supreme Court judge, and county court judge William Wallace. Businessman Frederick Fowke had gone back to Oshawa in early 1919 and had not been replaced. However, William E. Tibbs, a returned army officer with part of an arm amputated, was appointed secretary–comptroller in 1919. As their work-load had lessened, the two commissioners' stipends had decreased from $7,500 to $1,875. Tibbs's annual salary was $5,000, and he was in charge of the day-to-day running of the commission; the commissioners now attended only to overall management, not details.

In 1928 Rogers and Wallace both died. By the following year there were once again three commissioners: Major H. B. Stairs, chairman, Richard Beazley, a former member of the legislative council who had served on the original fuel committee and the Massachusetts–Halifax relief committee, and Tibbs, secretary–comptroller as well. Stipends remained about the same, and there were now seven staff: a works superintendent, an accountant, a clerk–cashier, a rent collector, a caretaker, and two stenographers.

The medical–social service was still functioning, but by 1929 the number of social workers had dwindled to one. Jane Lockward had carried out her duties with enthusiasm and compassion. The last of her reports to the commission is dated August 1929, more than thirteen and a half years after the blast. During the month of July she had made 250 calls. She had brought the more serious problems of survivors to the attention of the commissioners, who, in turn, discussed her reports at their meetings. All the ups and downs were considered and, if necessary, acted on.

But the commission was flexible only to a point. Throughout the Depression pensioners often pleaded for an increase or an advance in payments: forty dollars a month had been adequate in 1918, but by 1929 it was considered insufficient. The commission, however, did not concede an increase. Although unemployment was high and some families were totally dependent on their pensions, few exceptions were made. The fear that the pension fund might run out always loomed large in the foreground.

Apart from the occasional bonus payment, the commission did not increase pension amounts until 1950, when it raised them by 87.5 per cent. Its fear of running out of money had abated to a great extent. Halifax had not slid into an economic slump after World War II, the commission's investments had continued to prosper, and the number of pensioners had decreased. Thereafter the amounts increased periodically, mostly for those under seventy years of age, a distinction that could be made for fewer and fewer pensioners as time wore on. In 1946 Tibbs explained the commission's philosophy in a report. "Pensions were not granted solely for the damage to the Human Machine," he wrote, "but on the extent to which injuries were disability as regards former occupation." He added that it was a fairly well-established fact that those in receipt of regular allowances had a higher life expectancy. As completed reports on pensioners usually had an obituary attached, he must have made a thorough perusal of such columns.

* * * * *

The Depression hit the Hydrostone hard. Houses and shops did not come close to full occupancy, numerous buildings were boarded up, and many businesses folded. A widow on a pension of forty dollars a month, with two children still receiving eight dollars a month each, and an older child earning ten dollars a week, paid out nearly half their income on rent. She certainly could not afford a fine wool coat or any other luxuries. Annie Liggins had moved into one of the houses when she was ten. Her father had remarried a widow with children of her own, and now they were a family of nine. The surrounding houses were empty, and with windows smashed, they looked derelict. Her father boarded up the downstairs windows of their house, and they lived upstairs most of the time because it was warmer. They stayed only about a year.

In 1939 the Halifax City Directory showed fewer stores, and nine were vacant. The only two left, a drugstore and a market, sold necessities; one other building still housed the relief commission offices. When conditions were at their worst, in the mid-thirties, 152 houses were empty, almost half of the total number. House and store tenants appealed to the commission to lower rents in the Hydrostone but to no avail.

With the outbreak of World War II in 1939, circumstances changed dramatically. Halifax was yet again a war base seething with uniforms and ships. Housing was at a premium, including the Hydrostone and other relief commission properties.

In July 1947 the commission increased its rents by 10 percent and gave tenants two-year leases. Nevertheless, Hydrostone rents were among the cheapest in the city. In 1948 such a waiting list had built up that the commission was forced to issue a special form for applicants in dire need of inexpensive accommodation so that they could be given higher priority. By that time some people had been on the list for seven years.

The same year, the commission decided to relinquish its landlord status. Beginning on January 1, 1949, it offered to sell its properties to tenants, announcing its new policy "to encourage home ownership, release capital for the pension fund, place properties on the city tax roll and to conform to the general policy of the Federal Government." There had always been disagreement between the City and the commission, and it increased after properties went up in value. Although it had given grants to the City, the commission had never had to pay property taxes. City council had made several unsuccessful appeals to Ottawa, not only for tax payments but also for the release of surplus relief funds. The commission's argument, however, was always more persuasive: "When our last pensioner dies, he or she will be paid from the Commission's last resource."

Many tenants objected to the proposed sales, especially returned service-men who had recently settled back into civilian life and were reluctant to seek a mortgage. Prices started at twenty-five hundred dollars for a four-and-a-half-room apartment, three thousand for a five-and-a-half-room house, and thirty-five hundred for six rooms—low compared with similar properties at the time. But many of the buyers had paid rents for years, often with hardship, and were not prepared to purchase a house immediately. Annie Liggins, now Annie Welsh, moved back to the Hydrostone with her husband and family. They bought their house on Kane Place and still live there. (At present the semi-detached houses sell for more than ninety thousand dollars.)

In 1955 the commission reported that the sales to tenants had been

During the Depression Annie Liggins lived in the Hydrostone. About twenty years later she moved back, this time as Annie Welsh, with her own husband and family. All along she cherished the photograph taken of her in hospital in December 1917. (RON E. MERRICK)

completed, but it had kept several units, including its offices, to "offset any decline in value affecting other resources, or counterbalance any increase in liabilities not presently discernible." The pension fund had to be kept secure.

Soon after the commission started to put properties on the market, it began to discuss plans to turn Fort Needham into a memorial park including playing fields and picnic areas. The initial cost was estimated at about $110,000, but by the end of 1957, just before handing the park over to the City, the commission had spent about $165,000. Meanwhile, in 1951, it contributed $7,500 towards sidewalk improvements in the Hydrostone.

The City, along with the Province, again tried to secure relief funds in the summer of 1958. The commission, in turn, presented its case in a report to the federal government, rejecting any notion of handing over its monies. The funds were already lessened by a third, owing to increased pensions and higher medical costs. The cost of living was rising, and the commission would need fifteen more years to fulfil its duties to pensioners.

The commission, however, continued to spend money on the betterment of the North End. In the mid-1960s it donated $100,000 to the building of the North End Memorial Library, on Gottingen Street, a monument to the victims of the explosion. Again the commission came under fire. People objected to funds being used to refurbish parks or build libraries, rather than to help those who had suffered. It was pointed out, though, that the library would certainly benefit the North End and, presumably, explosion survivors.

Charges of misplaced priorities were levelled against the commission until its dissolution in the mid-seventies. In 1971 a radio program discussed the use of relief funds and caused a spate of letters from survivors who felt they had been poorly treated or who thought they had a right to a pension for complaints that were probably explosion related. One woman wrote that her facial scars had ruined her life. "My beauty was gone," she said. Few of these appeals were successful, though a small number of medical bills were paid.

*   *   *   *   *

The bill to repeal the act that incorporated the Halifax Relief Commission had its first reading in the House of Commons on December 4, 1975, two days before the fifty-eighth anniversary of the explosion. Under the proposed legislation all assets of the commission would be transferred to the Canada Pensions Commission, where they would be kept in a special fund, the Halifax Explosion Pension Account. The bill stipulated that after all pensioners had died, the balance would be handed over to a Nova Scotia or Halifax government body for further rehabilitation of the area damaged by the blast.

December 31, 1975, had been the original date for the disbanding of the commission, but it was postponed until June 11, 1976. The commission had spent more than $30 million on the relief and reconstruction of Halifax. More than $27 million had been amassed for the purpose, and through its investments and real-estate income it had been able to add to its funds. In all, it had disbursed $3,970,808.76 on emergency relief, $20,231,727.45 on claims, construction, and temporary housing, and $6,420,000 on pensions and medical care. It had also been able to cover all other expenses, including salaries for staff and stipends for commissioners and to hand over $1.5 million to the federal finance minister to defray the costs of pensions to explosion victims for the rest of their lives. The necessary reserve had been calculated at $1,126,950.

The commission had been in operation for nearly six decades and had seen a small turnover in commissioners. Only nine men had served, and four had died in office. The two commissioners at the time of dissolution (William Tibbs had retired and had not been replaced), A. M. Butler, chairman, and F. H. Flinn, served twenty-nine and twenty-six years respectively. Tibbs, however, had had the longest connection. He was secretary–comptroller from 1919 to 1951 and a commissioner from 1929 to 1973, making a total of fifty-four years. Two clerical staff remained. One had worked as cashier–typist for fifty-one years; the other, twenty-four and a half.

The commission's offices at 139 Young Street were sold to the federal government for seventy-five thousand dollars. Some of its voluminous records remained in the basement vault; others were entrusted to the Canada Pensions Commission and the Public Archives of Nova Scotia.

On January 1, 1976, six months before it met for the last time, the commission introduced one final pension increase, 11.3 percent for all. Sixty-six pensioners remained. Five widows were now receiving $199.44 a month; one dependant, $119.66; nine disabled, from $40.00 to $290.00; four blind men, from $372.28 to $422.28; seven blind women, from $265.00 to $319.10; and forty partially blind men and women, $99.72. Three pensioners died before the dissolution in June.

In January 1989, according to the Department of Veterans Affairs, which now handles the pension fund, there were thirty survivors still receiving pensions: five blind men and women (now on the same amount), two widows, twenty-one partially blind, and two suffering from general disability. The rates average $362.08, and they are indexed according to the cost of living and adjusted each January. Seventy-two years after the explosion, nearly $800,000 remains. The Halifax Relief Commission, it seems, succeeded in its oft-repeated goal of making sure that the fund would endure as long as the last pensioner.

EPILOGUE

AS TIME WENT ON, some survivors were able to forget the awful events of 1917, but others could never let it go. There were many families whose circumstances had changed so drastically that life rarely approached a return to normal.

The lives of many children took a completely different direction. Barbara Orr grew up in the family of her aunt and uncle, and her two cousins helped make up for her lost brothers and sisters. After initial difficulties with her injured leg, she became adept at sports. Also musical and artistic, she received her teacher's certificate in art from the Halifax Ladies College, where she met Frances MacLennan, who later taught there. Barbara eventually married T. W. Thompson. She spent her last years in their home, overlooking not Halifax Harbour, but St Margaret's Bay, in French Village, Nova Scotia. She died at the end of November 1987, just before the seventieth anniversary of the explosion.

Jean Crowdis, daughter of the Reverend Charles Crowdis, taught at Richmond School from 1935 to 1939, when the school was so crowded that her classroom was half of the hall. Marjorie Davidson, Eric's sister, taught in the other half. Jean continued the family tradition by marrying a minister, the Reverend Lewis Murray. Music features prominently in their lives. Her brother, Don, also taught for a time and then became involved in museum work. He was director of the Nova Scotia Museum and is now with the Alexander Graham Bell Museum, in Baddeck. Their father received an honorary doctorate from Pinehill Divinity College in 1956.

George Mitchell left the Royal Naval College of Canada in 1920 and attended McGill University in Montreal. After that, he went into the family firm, G. P. Mitchell & Sons Ltd, West India and General Commission Merchants, on Mitchell's Wharf, Lower Water Street. He later continued his naval career, serving in World War II. The scar on his upper lip is a legacy of the explosion.

Ethel Mitchell, in 1922, married Edwin Morash, who had come in his car to take her to his parents' home on the day of the explosion. Now a widow, she resides in Dartmouth, and her daughter has come home to be with her. They have a black-and-white cat much larger than Buttons.

Leighton Dillman, another Dartmouth survivor, did not return to the ropeworks but went to work in the Rosedale Nursery just across the road. Asthma, however, forced him to leave the nursery after eighteen years. Then he and his brother became land developers. A good proportion of their profits went towards maintaining a park Leighton created on the Dartmouth Common, to preserve it for the future. At the time of his death in 1988 the fund amounted to seventy thousand dollars, as well as two thousand for waterfowl feeding. The park now carries his name. His widow, Alma, lives in Dartmouth.

Jack Tappen continued to work for Burns & Kelleher until the firm went out of business. He took courses in machine design, plumbing, and heating at the Nova Scotia Technical College. In 1929 he was interviewed for a position at the firm Stairs, William, Son and Morrow. He was asked how long he would he stay. "For the rest of my working life, I hope," he replied. And so he did. In 1973 he retired from his position as manager of the plumbing and heating department. He and Amelia, his wife of fifty-seven years, have remained in Halifax.

The depleted Pattison family stayed in Dartmouth with Mrs Pattison's father and mother. For the rest of her life—she died at age ninety-nine—Mrs Pattison refused to talk about the explosion. When James left high school, he became an apprentice with the Imperial Oil Company and took courses in drafting and mechanics at the technical college. Imperial Oil later sent him to Peru for three years, and when he returned, he became foreman of the mechanical department at the Dartmouth refinery. After forty-six years with the company, he retired. He and his wife, Catherine, now have an attractive home in Kentville, Nova Scotia.

The Driscolls returned to the North End. With a close-knit family of fourteen—eight boys (Gordon had been the ninth) and five girls—the Driscoll household was never dull. Cliff, Al, and Noble stayed close friends all their lives. Cliff and Al, like their father, worked on the railway; Noble drove a team for the new Creighton's store that opened after the explosion. The store never reached its previous size or stocked the variety of goods that it had before the explosion. Eventually Noble worked for the Nova Scotia Liquor Commission and was in charge of the large outlet on Agricola Street. Cliff died in 1989. His oldest daughter, born less than a month after the explosion, still has the little coral brooch her mother was wearing when she escaped from the home on Duffus Street, the only thing she saved. Al and Noble, both widowers now, are energetic and busy. In 1986 the Driscolls had a family reunion, and about 150 relatives attended.

Frank Burford, while with his aunt in Liscombe, on the Eastern Shore, received a letter from a firm on Water Street saying he had been accepted as an apprentice to learn the plumbing trade. "I loved sheet metal work. I loved the plumbing business," he said much later. Now a widower, he lives in Halifax, his sister, Winnie, not far away.

Archie Upham followed in his father's footsteps and worked on the railway for most of his life. He died in 1987. His sister, Millicent, mar-

James Pattison's schoolbag probably saved him from serious injuries. He has kept it, along with the pocketwatch recovered in the spring of 1918.
(RON E. MERRICK)

Reg Rasley had his piece of the *Mont Blanc* silvered. The chunk of metal smashed a chair beside his grandfather's coffin, in the parlour. (RON E. MERRICK)

Maxwell Barnes, another explosion survivor, also has a memento from the *Mont Blanc*. It, too, came crashing through the roof of his family's home.

ried Wilbert Swindells, who had also lost his home in the explosion and had suffered facial injuries. All her life Millicent kept the nightshirt her father had been wearing when the house collapsed and burned. No matter how often she washed it, the soot and oil from the explosion would not come out, and it remains a dull grey. Until her death in 1988 a small, red, uncomfortable spot would appear from time to time, usually on her face or neck, as another sliver of glass worked its way out. This was common among many survivors who had stood in the path of splintering windows.

Dorothy Swetnam, now Dorothy Hare, lives in Calgary with her husband, Clayton. She, like her mother before her, is a pianist, and trained as a music teacher. Her father, the Reverend William Swetnam, remarried, and Dorothy acquired a new family.

The three pupils who escaped from St Joseph's School all reside in Halifax. Helena Duggan, now Helena Wheeler, treasures pre-explosion keepsakes from her aunt's house; nothing was left from her own. Evelyn Johnson, now Evelyn Lawrence, is a widow, and her health no longer enables her to maintain a household. Eileen Ryan, after working in an office for several years, decided to become a nun. Sister Eileen now lives in the Mother House at Mount Saint Vincent University.

After the war Garnet Colwell returned to work in the family business, Colwell Bros Ltd, Hatters and Men's Furnishers, Wholesale and Retail, established in 1905. In 1922 he met Linda Colquhoun, who had been at the Maritime Business College at the time of the explosion and who had helped with relief work at Camp Hill Hospital. They were married in 1924. Lieutenant Colonel Colwell, as he became, continued to pursue his military interests with the Princess Louise Fusiliers. He died in 1986.

Joe Glube, unsuccessful in his venture to establish a shop in the Hydrostone, went on to be much more successful in another type of business, selling furniture. Glube's large store on Gottingen Street, and its several branches, became well known. Joe still goes to the office every day, but now the large firm has been sold.

Dr Percy McGrath later established a practice in Kentville. In the early days he travelled over the hills by horse and buggy, performing operations on the most suitable table, boiling instruments in a copper. He practised for sixty-three years but stopped operating when he reached age eighty-three. When he was ninety-one, he told me, "I could still operate. My hands are steady, and my eyesight good." He died in 1988, at age ninety-five.

Some survivors own homes in the Hydrostone. Annie (Liggins) Welsh still lives in the house she and her husband bought from the Halifax Relief Commission. Jean Hunter moved to the Hydrostone in 1988, leaving the

Al (rear), Noble (front), and Cliff Driscoll remained close friends all their lives.
(RON E. MERRICK; COURTESY DORIS DRISCOLL DUNSWORTH)

family house on Agricola Street. She spent her working life at the firm Jas. Simmonds Ltd, when it was run by Colonel Ralph Simmonds, in charge of rescue work in Richmond in 1917, and later by his son, Leo. Eventually becoming the book-keeper, Miss Hunter was with the firm from December 16, 1925, until June 30, 1980, after it became Mills Simmonds.

Eric Davidson made a remarkable adjustment to his blindness. He left the School for the Blind in 1932, during the Depression, when jobs were scarce. For a time he worked at home and then for the Canadian National Institute for the Blind. In 1944 he began an apprenticeship with a car-repair company and got his mechanic's papers. He moved to Ottawa and then Toronto, and as he did when he was a boy, he soon managed to find his way around, by public transport and on foot. Eventually he returned to Halifax and continued his career. Antique cars became his specialty, and he has owned some beauties himself, including a vintage Rolls Royce. Eric also pursued his interest in music. At least twice a week he plays the banjo in a band and entertains senior citizens. He is married and has three children and seven grandchildren.

The present mayor of Halifax, Ronald Wallace, still has the large chunk of metal that fell into the garden when he was a baby.

*   *   *   *   *

Many of these survivors have been members of the United Memorial Church. Since 1921 the church has stood as a symbol of the cohesion and strength of a community. For nearly fifty of those years the bells in its tower marked occasions in the reconstructed area, announcing when it was time to leave for church, playing joyful hymns for weddings and sad ones for funerals and carols at Christmas. Eric Davidson and William Orr, Barbara's cousin, each pulled the great levers and loved to listen to the melodies they sent ringing over the harbour.

By the mid-1960s, however, the future of the bells looked uncertain. Because of a structural weakness in the tower, exacerbated by the vibration and the weight of the bells, it was no longer safe to play them. In 1975 the congregation reluctantly decided to remove them from the tower, and they lay, covered in tarpaulins, on the lawn in front of the church. Elders tried to solve the problem by approaching the City and by exploring many other avenues to find the means to build a new tower.

Finally, on Monday, July 3, 1983, Edmund Morris, MLA for Needham, announced a provincial government grant to build a new tower as a home for the bells and as an explosion memorial. The Halifax Explosion Memorial Bells Committee was formed the same day, with Reginald. E. Prest as chairman and four others, including explosion survivors Roy Wilson and Bruce Nickerson, as members. Morris and Judge Robert Inglis, a spry ninety-six-year-old active in the affairs of the church for more than sixty years, became honorary chairmen. Unfortunately Judge Inglis died in September 1984, before the completion of the project so dear to his heart. At least he had helped choose the plans. Thirteen other individuals with special skills and interests later joined the committee.

As so often in Halifax's history, the Canadian navy was called in to help, to move the bells to the naval armament property, where they could be examined and refurbished. During a ceremony on July 26 a crane raised the heavy frame into the clear morning sky. More than one person's eyes were damp as the carillon of bells left on the first stage of its journey.

Fund raising and ironing out of difficulties over the proposed site on Fort Needham then occupied the committee. Private donations arrived from as far afield as Scotland and California, and many came from survivors. Some were in memory of relatives who had been killed. The Stockall family, for example, gave twenty-five thousand dollars in honour of seven of their close relatives who had lost their lives. Letters recounting explosion experiences accompanied many donations, and some were very moving.

On June 1, 1984, Barbara (Orr) Thompson, with many other survivors present, turned the first sod on Fort Needham. It was close to the spot where she had landed in the explosion, and she wondered what might be found during the excavations. Maybe her boot?

The bell tower reminds some survivors of the silhouettes of the broken buildings left standing after the explosion. (CHRISTINE CALLAGHAN)

Then, on the warm, sunny afternoon of June 9, 1985, the dedication ceremony took place. The bell tower, its ten bronze bells gleaming like new, stood majestically above the large crowd. With its strong, upthrust shape, the architect, Keith Graham of the Core Design Group, envisaged it as emblematic of the rebirth of the city. The structure reminded some of the silhouettes of the broken buildings left standing after the explosion; it gave others a feeling of optimism. Some spectators had travelled a considerable distance to be there. Dr Percy McGrath, now more than ninety years old, came from Kentville just as he had in 1917, but in much more clement weather. Millicent Upham, now Millicent Swindells, and her husband, Wilbert, also attended. So did Archie Upham, Cliff, Al, and Noble Driscoll, Eric Davidson, Jean Hunter, Reg Rasley, Gordon Brannen, grandson of the captain of the *Stella Maris,* Roy Campbell, and many other explosion survivors or their descendants. A common bond linked everyone on the hill.

The highlight, of course, was hearing the sound of the bells once more peal out over the area that was formerly Richmond. It was heard across the harbour in Tufts Cove, where the Micmac settlement had been destroyed by the explosion, and in north Dartmouth. Once again, as in 1921, Barbara Orr played the carillon, with the help of her cousin William. This time there was no need to pull down large levers: the bells are electrically operated and can now be played from a small keyboard in a chamber in the tower or with a cassette, and they can be programmed to ring at certain times.

On December 6, 1985, just before 9:05 a.m., a time capsule containing explosion-related artefacts was placed in a cavity in the bell tower. It is a fifteen-inch cube made of acid-free plastic and filled in conditions of minimum humidity. The contents, wrapped in acid-free bags supplied by the Maritime Museum of the Atlantic, encompass the history of the explosion and its aftermath: Halifax Relief Commission forms and reports, 1917 menus from the Halifax Hotel and the Green Lantern Restaurant, a 1917 grocery bill from Constant Upham's grocery store, the list of the dead from the 1918 Halifax City Directory, descriptions of the unidentified dead, reproductions of explosion photographs, Richmond School class portraits, the booklet *A Common Sorrow and a Common Concern,* by the Reverend Charles Crowdis, a 1917 coin, the story of the bells, the Orr family, and the bell tower, along with other present-day artefacts.

Millicent (Upham) Swindells placed the time capsule in its niche, helped by her granddaughter Anne Louise Ihasz, a twenty-year-old student at Dalhousie University. It is hoped that Anne will be present when the capsule is opened on December 6, 2017, exactly a hundred years after one of the worst manmade disasters in history.

Every year on December 6, at 9 a.m., a memorial service is held at the bell tower. The same hymns sung at the funeral service for the unidentified dead on December 17, 1917, and in the churches on New Year's Day, 1918, when every church in Halifax and Dartmouth held a special ceremony, are played on the carillon. "O God, Our Help in Ages Past" and "Abide with Me" ring throughout the North End.

The tower and its bells are a permanent memorial not only to the Orr family but also to the men, women, and children who were killed, to the identified and the unidentified, to those who were never found, to the maimed, the blinded, the orphaned, to the thousands who lost loved ones, homes, and possessions in the Halifax Explosion of December 6, 1917.

INDEX